A guide
to teaching practice

SECOND EDITION

Louis Cohen
and
Lawrence Manion

Methuen

LONDON and NEW YORK

First published in 1977 by
Methuen & Co. Ltd
11 New Fetter Lane, London EC4P 4EE
Second edition 1983
Reprinted three times
Reprinted 1987

Published in the USA by
Methuen & Co.
in association with Methuen, Inc.
29 West 35th Street, New York, NY 10001

Printed in Great Britain by
Richard Clay Ltd, Bungay, Suffolk

British Library Cataloguing in Publication Data
Cohen, Louis
A guide to teaching practice.—2nd ed.
1. Student teaching
I. Title   II. Manion, Lawrence
370'.7'33   LB2157.A3
ISBN 0-416-34090-3
ISBN 0-416-34100-4 Pbk

Library of Congress Cataloging in Publication Data
Cohen, Louis, 1928–
A guide to teaching practice.

Bibliography: p.
Includes index.
1. Student teaching—Great Britain.   2. Teachers—
Training of—Great Britain.   I. Manion, Lawrence.
II. Title.
LB2157.G7C64 1983   370'.7'33   83-13190
ISBN 0-416-34090-3
ISBN 0-416-34100-4 (pbk.)

To
all student teachers
on teaching practice

Contents

A guide to teaching practice

Gabrielle McCann.

28/11/88

Acknowledgements

In preparing this second edition of *A Guide to Teaching Practice* we wish to express our thanks to Ian Kane and colleagues on the PGCE course at Didsbury School of Education, Manchester Polytechnic, for their help.

We would also like to thank the following for their permission to reproduce copyright material: E.J. Arnold for the figures from the Schools Council Project on Teaching English to West Indian Children, and from the Schools Council Project on English for Immigrant Children; George Allen & Unwin for the diagrams from *Learning in the Primary School* by K. Haslam and from *Classroom Language: What Sort* by J.W. Richards; Heinemann Educational for the extracts from *The Language of Teaching* by A.D. Edwards and V.J. Furlong; Kogan Page for the diagram from *The Selection and Use of Instructional Media* by A.J. Romiszowski; McGraw-Hill for the extracts from *Class Control and Behaviour* by M. Saunders; Macmillan for the extracts from *Class Management and Control* by E.C. Wragg, and the table from *Teaching and Training* by H.R. Mills; Ward Lock for the diagram from *Educating Pupils with Special Needs in the Ordinary School* by S. Hegarty, K. Pocklington and D. Lucas.

List of boxes

List of figures

Preface

In our conversations with students it is apparent that many feel both ill-prepared for the situations that face them in the classroom and not a little exasperated with what they see as the irrelevance of much of the course work that constitutes the so-called 'disciplines' of education (philosophy, history, sociology and psychology) to the challenges of teaching practice.

While no teacher can expect to be fully prepared to meet the demands of the classroom before teaching practice, he may reasonably anticipate that the assistance he receives prior to his school experience is *directly relevant* to the teaching tasks he will face. We believe that there is substance in student complaints about the relevance of some of the work they are required to undertake and that there is legitimacy in student demands for the practical applicability of their studies. It should be the case that the philosophical, psychological and sociological aspects of the education course in which student teachers are required to engage *do* illuminate the classroom situations in which they are required to practise; in many cases, they plainly do not.

In this text it is our concern to use aspects of the psychology, sociology and philosophy of education in ways which are directly relevant to the student teacher in his preparation for teaching practice and his actual classroom teaching.

A Guide to Teaching Practice develops *one* approach to teaching and learning which we believe can be of help to students in the preparation of their work and the management of their classes. Our contacts with student teachers, college tutors and external examiners have persuaded us that an 'objectives' approach to teaching practice preparation is widely used and commands considerable support in colleges of higher education and in teacher education departments in universities and polytechnics. An objectives approach involves first, the specification of behavioural and non-behavioural objectives in advance of any teaching activity. Second, the development of teaching strategies and classroom management techniques in the light of the specified objectives. Finally, the selection and use of appropriate evaluative techniques by way of identifying the extent to which the objectives have been attained. We hasten to stress that an objectives approach to the organization of teaching and learning is *one* approach, not *the* approach. Nor is the

method which we outline and develop here without its shortcomings
and its critics. This is not the place, however, to rehearse its limitations —
indeed, the onus is upon the critics of an objectives approach to produce
an *alternative* guide which students will find useful in their preparation to
teach.

In developing our particular view of the planning and the practice of
teaching we have drawn upon theories and concepts from psychology
and, to a lesser degree, from sociology and philosophy. These are used to
illustrate and illuminate a model of the teaching-learning process
outlined in Box 2, page 16. Whether our choice of concepts or, indeed,
our objectives approach is relevant to the tasks facing the student
teacher, you, the reader, must judge. The selection of materials has not
been without difficulty. What may be relevant, for example, to one
student practising in some delightful suburban first school may sound
like so much educational claptrap to another engaged in a struggle for
survival in some inner urban secondary school.

A Guide to Teaching Practice is organized into four parts.

In Part I, which we call *Some perspectives on teaching and learning*, we start
out with a brief look at a number of changes taking place in the planning
and provision of primary and secondary education, and suggest how
they impinge upon the work of those entering teaching during the 1980s.
We say something too about the school as an organization, the teacher's
way of life in school and children as learners.

Part II is concerned with *Preparation and planning* to teach. Here, we
discuss the nature of teaching and present a basic model of the
teaching–learning process which guides much of our subsequent
discussions in Parts II, III and IV. Included in Part II, and
fundamental to our objectives approach, is a discussion of aims and
objectives. This is followed by an outline of ways in which student
teachers can develop aims and objectives appropriate to their classroom
activities during teaching practice. The development of schemes of work
and lesson notes which comprises the latter section follows logically from
the central theme of Part II of the text.

Part III, entitled *Practising teaching*, deals directly with the tasks that
face the beginning teacher in managing the classroom, in developing
appropriate teaching strategies, in exercising control and discipline, and
in organizing both the in-school and out-of-school activities of the
children for whom he is responsible.

Part IV, which we call *Evaluation, assessment and record-keeping*, discusses
the tasks of evaluation and assessment during teaching practice. It
suggests a number of techniques which student teachers might find
useful in judging the extent to which their teaching objectives have been
realized.

The book contains five appendices dealing, respectively, with re-source materials and technical aids; useful information and sources; lists of addresses in connection with audio-visual aids; addresses of publishers of children's literature; and a section dealing with questions and questioning.

Throughout *A Guide to Teaching Practice* we have attempted to 'scale down' the complexity of the total teaching situation by means of the teaching–learning model presented in Part II. That model has been broken down into its component parts so that students might, with guidance, examine each part separately in order to better grasp the whole. This is not, however, something to be done or to be 'gone through' prior to teaching practice. Rather it is our hope that the text will prove as useful to students, supervising teachers and college tutors in their discussions after the event as, we trust, it is *before*.

PART I
Some perspectives
on teaching and learning

TEACHING IN THE 1980s

Our task in this first part of the book is to identify changes taking place in the planning and provision of primary and secondary schooling in Britain, to discuss the reasons for these changes and to suggest how they impinge upon the work of those entering teaching during the 1980s.

Perhaps the best description of the underlying trend that is currently emerging in education is that there is a *shift to the centre*. The origins and ramifications of this move towards greater centralization of control form the substance of this section.

Primary education

The 1970s saw a revival of political interest in primary education, particularly in respect of the content and control of primary schools. Interest, according to Blyth and Clayfield,[1] centred on three issues.

The first had to do with compensatory education, the objective of which was to develop positive relationships between schools and communities in order to make up for supposed deficits in the early childhood experiences of 'disadvantaged' pupils.

The second concerned the series of events at the William Tyndale Junior School, London. Mr Robin Auld QC, who conducted a lengthy inquiry into its teaching, organization and management, had a good deal to say about the way in which the William Tyndale school functioned. He went on to relate the behaviour of those involved in the conflict to the practices and attitudes that determine the control of primary schools generally. Just one year later, in 1976, Neville Bennett's book, *Teaching Styles and Pupils' Progress*,[2] suggested that children taught by informal methods made less 'progress' than those taught by formal methods, an interpretation, incidentally, that has been drastically altered in light of re-working of the original data.

The third event, which it is believed[1] may have gained impetus from the second, was the Ruskin College Speech of the then Prime Minister,

James Callaghan, which signalled the beginning of the Great Debate,[3] placing primary education, *inter alia*, on the national political agenda. Callaghan criticized education for failing to provide children with the basic skills necessary for industry. The schools, he asserted, were failing to prepare pupils for their future roles in the economy.

The Great Debate took place in 1977 in the form of a series of regional conferences focusing on four topics: (1) the school curriculum, (2) the assessment of standards, (3) the education and training of teachers, and (4) school and working life.

Two reports, published within a year of each other, suggest[1] that the autonomy of individual schools may henceforth be somewhat curtailed in light of the requirements of national policy and the wishes of parents and of the community. One was the national survey of junior schools by Her Majesty's Inspectorate entitled *Primary Education in England* and published by the Department of Education and Science in 1978. Among its recommendations is a call for the strengthening of curriculum structure, sequence and content. The second was the Taylor Report (1977) with its suggestions of ways in which the wider community might be given greater representation of school governing bodies. We take up the question of school curriculum in more detail later in this section.

Secondary education

Dancy[4] identifies two major themes in recent developments in secondary education in Britain. First, the move towards comprehensivization and its consequences; second, the growth of public criticism, especially of the secondary system, and the response of the educational service to that discontent.

Whereas 30 per cent of children received their secondary education in comprehensive schools at the beginning of 1970, by the end of the decade 83 per cent of boys and girls attended comprehensive schools in England and Wales. While the campaign for secondary reorganization, according to Dancy, is now effectively over, the war is by no means won, for supporters of the *comprehensive principle* continue to work for the removal or at least the weakening of Direct Grant and Independent schools which lie outside the maintained sector. An on-going contention, too, is ability grouping in comprehensive schools. Streaming, it is argued, is a negation of the comprehensive principle. Most schools, however, seem to have adopted a compromise position; certainly there is no massive move to mixed ability grouping at present.

What of life and work in secondary schools in the 1970s and early 1980s? In respect of *school work*, Dancy notes the spreading influence of curriculum innovation in such areas as mathematics, science, history, geography, and moral and religious education. So, too, the emergence of the pastoral or guidance curriculum with its particular concerns for careers and health education. Recent changes in the secondary examination system are, in part, a consequence of these innovations and developments in the secondary school curriculum. In connection with *school life*, Dancy identifies changing styles of school leadership in which traditional headmastering is giving way to corporate planning by the school management team, and in parallel, prefect systems are being replaced by more representative school councils, the common philosophical trend pervading both these moves being one of *liberalization*. At the national level, however, an opposite trend is discernible – a consequence of public disquiet and loss of confidence in the education system. It is to this that we now turn.

Dancy traces the loss of public confidence and the reassertion of central control over education services currently taking place as reactions to what have, in retrospect, turned out to be excessively high hopes and claims for the power of education to transform and enrich society and, to no small extent, to a scapegoating of education as 'the god that failed' in a period of lasting recession exacerbated by increasing levels of youth unemployment. Since the beginning of the 1970s there has been increasing public concern at falling educational standards, school discipline, the neglect of the 3Rs, the introduction of new-fangled ideas such as integrated studies, poor spelling, 'modern' mathematics, and general neglect by schools of the world of work, some of these complaints, Dancy notes, being better founded than others.*

Explicit moves towards the reassertion of greater central control over educational services can be identified from 1973 onwards. In that year Her Majesty's Inspectorate instituted the Curriculum Publications Group and announced plans to conduct systematic surveys of various areas of the school curriculum from 1975 onwards. In 1974, the Department of Education and Science set up the Assessment of Performance Unit, the intention of which was to devise methods of national monitoring of standards of achievement in basic areas of the curriculum. At the same time, the DES increased its control of the Schools Council, an organization largely concerned with encouraging new approaches in curriculum development. Following the Great Debate of 1977 the time was opportune for the DES to exercise increasing control over educational provision, particularly in matters of

---

* Anxieties about mixed ability teaching (see page 89) were shared by HMI and many educationalists. So too, the economic arguments favouring a common core in the school curriculum in light of notoriously uneconomical 'options' offered in many secondary schools.

finance and in the form and conduct of national examinations. Circular 14/77 *required* Local Education Authorities to report on the curricula in their schools by January 1978, and a DES Consultative paper, *A Framework for the Curriculum* (1980), went so far as to suggest minimum time allocations for various school subjects.

Much the most effective channel of influence, however, according to Dancy, was through Her Majesty's Inspectorate whose reputation rose considerably in light of the *Matters For Discussion* series which touched upon such emotive topics as mixed ability teaching and gifted children, and various aspects of both primary and secondary education.

And what of the schools' reaction to the furore of the 1970s and early 1980s? Dancy concludes that, by and large, schools are showing themselves to be reasonably responsive to the criticisms levelled against them. This is not to say, of course, that the issues raised in the Great Debate are now resolved, or that the cries for greater accountability on that part of the education services are necessarily less intense. It is, perhaps, more a realization that 'nobody can easily control from outside what lies at . . . [the school's centre]. That is the teacher's relationship with those he teaches and the influence he thereby exerts over them by the interpretation he puts on the subject matter he teaches, the values and attitudes he transmits, the skills he helps them develop, and the standards he sets by example and precept.'[5]

Our account to this point has touched upon events, such as the William Tyndale School inquiry, and trends, such as the loss of public confidence in education, both of which are directly concerned with the school curriculum.

We have shown that two general issues began to emerge in the 1970s which will continue to engage public attentic.1 as we move further into the present decade. They have to do with the *content* of the curriculum and the *control* of the curriculum.

The curriculum and curriculum change

Two quite different approaches to the curriculum are contained in questions to do with its *content* and its *control*. The first ('content'), according to Lawton,[6] represents a *behavioural objectives* model and focuses on the *efficiency* of the curriculum; the second ('control'), to do with the *justification* of the curriculum, may be conceived of as a *cultural analysis* model.

Let us see how Lawton's account of these two contrasting models relates to some of the issues that have already been raised.

The *behavioural objectives* model takes existing curriculum patterns more or less for granted. It is a conservative model, finding support among those concerned with standards, measurement and minimal competency. By contrast, the *cultural analysis* model is radical in its orientation, asking fundamental questions about the purpose of schools, the nature of knowledge and the types of experiences in which children should engage in order to participate in society now and in the future.

It is clear that the DES consultative document *A Framework for the School Curriculum* (1980), with its idea of a core curriculum and the testing of standards of competency in various areas of the school curriculum, was very much cast in the mould of a behavioural objectives model. So too must the intentions of the Assessment of Performance Unit be judged in respect of monitoring standards. On the other hand, the *Curriculum 11–16* document of Her Majesty's Inspectorate propounding the idea of access to a common culture by means of a common curriculum is firmly anchored in a cultural analysis approach, though it is doubtful, says Lawton, that the Inspectors realized this. The 'areas of experience' approach of *Curriculum 11–16*, together with the tone of various primary and secondary surveys by HMI, must be seen as fundamentally different from the assumptions that underpin the Assessment of Performance Unit. Lawton's cogent analysis seems to imply that we are at somewhat of a crossroads:

> Curriculum planning by behavioural objectives will take us in the direction of a core of subjects (narrowly based) backed by powerful testing: a common curriculum based on cultural analysis . . . would take us in the direction of an improved version of the Inspectors' document *Curriculum 11–16*.

Whichever road is chosen has enormous implications for the work of those entering teaching in the 1980s.

The social and economic context

It is time now to place the trends in provision and control of education that we have been discussing within a wider context of social and economic change in order that we might better grasp the consequences for teachers and schools that arise from the continuing contraction of the education system and the growing problems of unemployment and leisure.

The growth of new industries, the development of new technologies and the spread of large bureaucratic corporations have featured large in the industrial and commercial face of Britain since the end of the Second World War. Developments such as these foretell even greater changes in the years ahead as new technologies based on micro-processors and robots effect rapid decline in employment opportunities

in manufacturing, commerce, banking, insurance and communication
organizations. Problems attendant upon such changes and their
implications for schools have been identified by Lacey and Lawton.[7]

Box 1

Problems for British society in the 1980s

1 Many jobs in traditional industries have disappeared and with them
  many skills and traditional methods of entry into industry. Although
  schools have not been closely geared to the needs of industry, the
  uncertainty and the feeling of being out of touch with recent events have
  made it difficult for schools to prepare pupils for their first employment
  and enable them to make sensible choices.
2 Many new jobs have been created in the tertiary sector calling for
  linguistic/literary, numerical and social skills at the same time as many
  other occupations have been de-skilled. Once again schools have found it
  difficult to keep up with these trends despite greater efforts put into the
  growing careers advisory service.
3 Regional imbalance has been caused by large losses of jobs occurring in
  'traditional industrial areas' while new jobs were being created around
  London and in the Midlands and south-east.
4 Local imbalance has occurred as city centres declined with respect to the
  suburbs, a problem contributed to by both the affluence (which
  increased emigration) and the subsequent stagnation and decline of the
  economy (which slowed down redevelopment and renovation). Both
  regional and local imbalance have given rise to overcrowding in some
  schools and falling rolls in others. Recent decreases in the birth rate have
  combined with migration to produce acute problems of falling rolls in
  some inner city schools. Selective migration has produced concent-
  rations of acute educational and social problems for some schools.
5 Immigration from the old colonial territories, encouraged during the
  1950s and 1960s because of labour shortages in some industries, has
  given rise to communities in inner city areas which have to overcome
  cultural and language barriers in order to compete with the native
  population. Once again inner city schools are most affected.
6 After a period of relative decline Britain's economy went into a period of
  absolute decline during the 1970s and unemployment grew to $1\frac{1}{2}$ million.
  Unemployment has become a permanent feature of the economy and
  poses a particular problem for young school leavers trying to get jobs.
  Once again inner city schools have been hit hardest and at a time of
  shrinking resources made available to education.

Source: adapted from Lacey and Lawton[7]

The contraction of the system

In the twenty-five or so years after 1950 there was a substantial growth in the school population which peaked at some 9 million pupils in 1977. Greater numbers of children in schools required greater provision in terms of buildings, teachers, ancillary helpers, books and equipment. It was widely accepted that the increasing demands on the public purse made by an expanding education service would continue into the future.

Those halcyon days of expansion are now over. Projected school enrolment for 1990 in England and Wales is put at 7 million. By 1987, primary totals[8] which reached 6.3 million in 1973 may be as low as 4.5 million, and whereas secondary numbers were 3.6 million in 1978, the forecast for 1990 is 2.5 million.

What are the consequences of this substantial contraction in the number of children attending schools? Clearly, many institutions will close and staff will lose jobs. Increasingly, according to Taylor,[8] the effect of closures will be felt by three types of educational establishment – primary schools, particularly in rural areas, colleges of higher education, and secondary schools, especially those situated in urban areas. Institutions will merge; secondary schools with non-viable sixth forms will have their older, academic students relocated on a single site. There are further implications of falling rolls for school organization and staff deployment.

Research[9] on the specific effects of declining numbers shows the increasing difficulty of some secondary schools in teaching the sciences as separate subjects, in offering more than one foreign language and in retaining music on the timetable. In junior and middle schools, too, shortages of specialist teachers present particular difficulties in areas such as craft, music, French and home economics. Taylor[8] suggests that the problem of deploying staff efficiently among individual schools will lead to a slowing down in the trend towards decentralizing timetabling and curriculum decision-making. There will be less incentive for 'block' timetabling. In this sense, he observes, falling rolls are likely to compound the effects of the back-to-basics movement about which we spoke earlier.

Unemployment and leisure

It was twenty years ago that members of the Newsom Committee declared education for leisure as one of the school's most important tasks. Their proposal did not arise from the fear that future school leavers were destined to join dole queues;[10] on the contrary, the Committee envisaged a time when technological innovation would generate demands for an even larger pool of youthful talent. That time is here and now but the picture, alas, is very different from the one forecast by Newsom in 1963. Unemployment in the early 1980s is running at 3 million. As we approach the middle of the decade unemployment figures are expected to reach 4 million and, perhaps, 5 million by 1990.

The Newsom Report got it wrong about employment but right about the increase in leisure and the prediction that education would be seen as a crucial element in solving the so-called problem of work and leisure. According to Hargreaves,[10] solutions to that problem generally appear in two forms: *education-as-leisure* and *education-for-leisure*. The former covers a wide spectrum ranging from simply using schools and further education centres as cheap and convenient sponges for soaking up unemployed youth to proposals for life-long or recurrent education for all. The second solution (*education-for-leisure*) calls for far-reaching changes in secondary school curricula, involving the construction of specific syllabuses designed to introduce leisure skills to children.

The problem of leisure raises important questions for teachers and schools in the 1980s. Should schools be wholly responsive to the 'message of the markets'[8] or is there room for autonomy and initiative on their part? Should 'leisure studies' be separated from the rest of the curriculum and the whole range of skills that schools seek to develop in their pupils? Should we not be looking for solutions to the problems of unemployment and leisure at a more fundamental level? Hargreaves, for example, suggests that only by contemplating how we can radically restructure society can we transcend the conventional distinction between work and leisure and the mischief it works on our search for alternatives.

The question of the degree of autonomy and initiative that schools should enjoy leads directly to the last issue that we wish to raise in this introductory section, namely *accountability*.

Accountability[11]

Accountability refers to the obligation on the part of persons or institutions to *deliver an account of what they do*. In the case of teachers and schools, delivering an account of what they do presupposes that answers can be found to two key questions:

To *whom* should teachers or schools be accountable?
For *what* are teachers or schools accountable?

Sockett's[11] discussion of these key issues shows the difficulties that arise in arriving at adequate conceptions of *school accountability* and *teacher accountability*. There are good grounds, he shows, for arguing that teachers ought to be accountable to a broad spectrum of interests ranging from individual pupils and parents to LEAs, the Government and industry at large and that each of these 'constituencies', as he calls them, may expect different things from teachers. Precisely *what* teachers ought to be accountable for is more problematic, for to say that teachers ought to be required to state their objectives precisely in terms of what children should learn and that they should then be held accountable for producing results runs counter to the suggestion that teachers, above all else, should *educate* their pupils, a point of view that leads to the position that teachers ought to be accountable not just for the *outcomes* of learning but also for *the principles embedded in the procedures they employ*. Thus a *professional* model of teacher accountability cannot solely be equated with a *results-based* criterion. As Sockett observes, accountability should be for adherence to principles of practice rather than for results embodied in pupil performances, all of which leads to the proposition that a system of teacher accountability must rest upon the following considerations:

> First, while a teacher certainly has influence over children and must take a measure of responsibility for their achievements and failures, the mere testing of results assumes that a teacher has greater control than is possible. Second, by shifting the focus of accountability on to results only, we fail to consider the quality of the conditions and opportunities for learning – the schooling process, if you like – within which much more sophisticated judgments may be made about a teacher's effectiveness.

In the sections that follow, student teachers will recognize that while we are anxious that they derive maximum benefit from a results-based (i.e. an objectives) approach to the planning, execution and evaluation of their individual lessons during teaching practice, essentially we are concerned with the *schooling process as a whole*, with student teachers' personal development as professional educators – persons whose actions and behaviours in classroom settings rest upon their being informed and guided by a body of appropriate theory upon which they can draw intelligently and judiciously as situations require.

THE SCHOOL AS AN ORGANIZATION

The school is an organization with identifiable boundaries. It has a recognizable structure consisting of positions which are related one to another yet are differentiated in terms of the duties required of their various occupants. French teachers are expected to teach French; caretakers are expected to clean. In other words, rules and expectations define the interdependent behaviour of members of the school be they the headteacher, senior masters, teachers or ancillary staff. This network of school positions and their accompanying role requirements is often referred to as the school's *formal* organizational structure. Student teachers visiting a school should familiarize themselves with its formal organizational structure as soon as possible. It is clearly advantageous to know how the school is organized, who is responsible for specific aspects of its routine and what the rules are governing such and such a situation.

As well as the formal structuring of relationships among members of the school there is generally an *informal* organizational structure, that is a system of social relationships developed by members of staff outside any formalized requirements for their professional behaviour. The informal structure can often be seen operating in the staffroom friendship groups which cut across subject area, age or seniority. It is through the informal organizational structure that communications about important decisions often become known to members of staff long before official pronouncements from the head. For the visiting student teacher an appreciation of the informal structuring of relationships within a school is equally as important to his understanding of that organization as is his knowledge of its formal structure.

So far no mention has been made of pupils as members of the school organization. Although in one sense children occupy the lowest rung of the hierarchical ladder that represents the formal organizational structure of the school, they are by no means lacking in their ability to exert influence upon its adult members. Most pupils have clear expectations about what a teacher should do and how he should behave towards them. To no small extent success in working with children is dependent upon an awareness of their expectations of teacher behaviour.

The teacher's way of life in school

In their attachments to schools, student teachers encounter a wide variety of ways of organizing the teaching day. In most secondary schools, for example, fixed timetables still generally regulate the arrangements throughout the teaching day, and children are brought together into smaller, more manageable teaching groups by some method of *streaming* – by ability or age or by *setting* in certain subject areas. In other schools, particularly those catering for younger children, fixed timetabling has often been discarded or drastically modified so as to permit the teacher maximum autonomy in planning the learning experiences of his pupils. In first schools, for example, *vertical* grouping (or *family grouping*, as it is sometimes called) is often employed in order to bring together different age-groups, enabling the younger to learn from the older and individuals in both age-groups to progress at their own speeds.

Common to all the ways of organizing the teaching day that have been mentioned so far is the fact that, for most of the time, teaching is what one adult does with a group of some twenty to thirty children assigned to his care. What is done and how it is done depends, as we have seen, upon a number of factors – the particular subject area, topic or skill under consideration, the age and the capabilities of the pupils, the range of equipment and materials available and so on.

What is particularly important for the beginning teacher is the amount of time devoted to preparation for lesson instruction. It is no mere accident when a class of children is happily engaged in a variety of rewarding activities. That 'busy classroom hum' which to the experienced ear signals purposeful work and sustained interest is the result of careful, systematic and intelligent planning;

> What is the most effective way of organizing activity A for such-and-such a group of children?
> How much time will they need? What equipment and materials will be required and what is the most efficient way of organizing its distribution, utilization and eventual collection and re-storing?
> What will groups B, C, D and E be engaged in in the meanwhile? How best can their work be organized and sequenced so as to fit in with activity A? Where, in all of this activity, can help be given to individuals F, G and H?

Questions such as these are part and parcel of the teacher's way of life in school.

Children as learners

For most children, the transition from home to school is marked by important changes in what is required of them both by adults and by their peers. In the first place, they are formally required to attend school whether they wish to or not; they are also required to submit to the authority of an adult other than a parent.

The multiplicity of new roles demanded of pupils within the classroom group has been outlined by Jackson[12] in a provocative book entitled *Life in Classrooms*. Children must accustom themselves to the continuous distractions and interruptions going on about them; they must learn to take their turn, to be patient, to control their impulsiveness, to work harmoniously with others. Above all, they must accommodate to the *constant evaluation* of themselves and their school performance by their teachers and fellow pupils.

Discussing evaluation, Jackson suggests that the pupil has three tasks. First, he must learn to behave so as to reduce the probability of punishment and maximize the likelihood of praise; that is, he must learn how the classroom reward structure operates. Second, he must learn how to publicize any praise that accrues to him and conceal any negative evaluations he incurs. Third, he must find ways of earning at one and the same time the approval of his teacher and his fellow pupils.

Living with others, under conditions of power and authority and under constant evaluation, constitutes the *hidden curriculum* with which every pupil must come to terms if he is to succeed in school. By coming to terms with the demands of the school, the child develops a conception of himself as a learner. Through innumerable classroom interactions and exchanges with his teacher and fellow pupils, he learns to take-the-role-of-the-other, constructing through the eyes of others a picture of himself. It is this self-picture which serves to direct much of the child's on-going behaviour.

Teachers' perceptions of children and their expectations for their achievement serve as important stimuli to pupils' developing self-images. In a study of junior school classrooms, for example, Nash[13] observed that essential *cultural messages* were being conveyed to the children, messages that were only marginally concerned with school learning in the conventional sense of the term, but which had everything to do with the children's self-images, their status within the classroom and their aspirations for the future. Likewise, in a study of secondary school pupils, Hargreaves[14] showed how inextricably interwoven were the self-images, attitudes and aspirations of the pupils and the expectations of their teachers for the boys' behaviour and attainment.

The importance of these findings for the student teacher is clear. There can be little doubt that some teachers hold expectations for children's achievement that are often based upon little or no evidence. Where expectations are based upon factors that have genuine predictive value for the attainment of individual children, they assist the teacher in his planning and provision to meet their individual needs. Where expectations are based upon hearsay or unquestioned assumptions and prejudices, they can all too readily lead to a chain of teacher–pupil interactions that make for unwarranted failure on the part of the child.

Notes and references

1 Blyth, A. and Clayfield, R. (1983) Primary education. In Cohen, L., Thomas, J.B. and Manion, L. (eds) *Educational Research and Development in Britain, 1970–80*. Windsor: NFER-Nelson.

2 Bennett, N. (1976) *Teaching Styles and Pupils' Progress*. London: Open Books.

3 For one account of events leading up to the Great Debate see Sarup, M. (1982) *Education, State and Crisis: A Marxist Perspective.* London: Routledge and Kegan Paul.

4 Dancy, J. (1983) Secondary education. In Cohen, L., Thomas, J.B. and Manion, L. (eds) *Educational Research and Development in Britain, 1970–80.* Windsor: NFER-Nelson.

5 Sir Toby Weaver, quoted by Dancy, from Open University (1979) Course E222, Unit 2, *The DES and Central Control of Education.* Milton Keynes: Open University Press.

6 Lawton, D. (1981) The curriculum and curriculum change. In Simon, B. and Taylor, W. (eds) *Education in the Eighties: The Central Issues.* London: Batsford.

7 Lacey, C. and Lawton, D. (eds) (1981) *Issues in Evaluation and Accountability.* London: Methuen.

8 Taylor, W. (1981) Contraction in context. In Simon, B. and Taylor, W. (eds) *Education in the Eighties: The Central Issues.* London: Batsford.

9 Briault, E. and Smith, F. (1980) *Falling Rolls in Secondary Schools.* Windsor: NFER.

10 Hargreaves, D.H. (1981) Unemployment, leisure and education. *Oxford Review of Education,* 7 (3), 197–210.

11 Sockett, H., Bailey, C., Bridges, D., Elliott, J., Gibson, R., Scrimshaw, P. and White, J. (1980) *Accountability in the English Educational System.* London: Hodder and Stoughton.

12 Jackson, P.W. (1968) *Life in Classrooms.* New York: Holt, Rinehart and Winston.

13 Nash, R. (1973) *Classrooms Observed.* London: Routledge and Kegan Paul.

14 Hargreaves, D.H. (1967) *Social Relations in a Secondary School.* London: Routledge and Kegan Paul.

PART II
Preparation and planning

INTRODUCTION

One of the most crucial factors in the teaching practice situation for the student teacher is preparation – finding out as much as possible about the school beforehand, formulating aims and objectives purposefully, selecting appropriate content, deciding the best methods of presentation and writing the actual lesson notes. A study undertaken by Leeds Institute of Education[1] indicated that among the sample of practising teachers interviewed, the majority felt that student teachers set about their block practices inadequately prepared. It is our purpose in this section, therefore, to examine in some detail the components listed above so that the reader's preparation may be more thorough and meaningful in these respects, thereby meeting his or her needs, together with those of school and college, more satisfactorily.

The student teacher can adopt a variety of roles on teaching practice. Some of these arise from his status *qua* student teacher. One such role is that of *experimenter*. The theory and training he has received in college prior to his first practice and subsequently cannot possibly provide him with answers for all the problems and contingencies he is likely to encounter in the school and the classroom. At best, they will provide general principles and guidelines as a basis for action. For this reason, he must be prepared to interpret and apply these principles and guidelines in specific situations and it is here that he can don his experimenter role. Inevitably, some of his endeavours will not work out, but such occasions can be just as educative as the successful ones. It is in the preparation and planning stages, therefore, that we recommend the student to see himself or herself from time to time in this particular role, for it is in this capacity that he will be able to think out imaginative and innovatory approaches to traditional problems and to decide in what ways the theory can inform the practice. Naturally, to follow up such recommendations will involve a certain amount of risk-taking. Providing such risks are carefully calculated the advantages will outweigh the disadvantages.

As we intimated in the introduction, we shall be adopting the *objectives model* as a basis for our discussions on preparation and planning. Briefly, this involves specifying the desired outcomes of the learning situation in advance so that the means to achieving them can be ordered in a logical and systematic way. The objectives model itself is associated with the rational approach to curriculum planning and as such has its critics. Those holding progressive views on education, for example, would argue that such an approach, in which the teacher pre-specifies the learning outcomes, ignores objectives the children may have and tends to discount the value of unintended outcomes. As one writer[2] puts it:

> The teacher's task is not to prespecify outcomes, rather to place children in learning situations which stimulate them in a host of ways but whose outcomes will emerge gradually from the constant interaction and negotiation between teacher and pupil.

Other critics point to the mismatch between the cold rationality of the objectives model and the constantly changing realities of school life. Shipman,[3] for instance, writes:

> Curriculum development does not proceed through a clear cycle from a statement of objectives to an evaluation of the learning strategies used. It consists of interaction, accommodation and compromise. Horse trading and horse sense are the concrete curriculum scene, not the clinical alignment of means with ends that is the official version.

While conceding that such criticisms are perfectly valid, we for our part share the belief of the objectives school that the purpose of formal education is to bring about desired changes in children.[2] Thus, if we want them to acquire certain kinds of knowledge and skills and to develop particular attitudes, we must identify them at the outset and formulate them in terms of aims and objectives. At the same time, we do not necessarily see them as fixed and unchanging: all kinds of chance factors are operating in the classroom which will affect our planning willy nilly. There is, moreover, room for accommodation and modification. Indeed, we would agree with Jeffcoate[2] when he said:

> Prespecified objectives should not acquire the status of sacrosanct unalterable absolutes. Instead they should be open to constant review, adaptation and revision. . . . Hilda Taba[4] best conveys this notion of flexibility in the definition and use of objectives when she suggests they should be seen as 'developmental', representing 'roads to travel rather than terminal points'.

In Box 2 we illustrate the objectives model modified for the teaching practice situation: from it you will see how the more important and tangible components of the teaching–learning process fit together. We

A guide to teaching practice

draw the reader's attention to the process's most important feature – its cyclical nature. This means that the teaching–learning process is completed by (1) informing the children of the outcomes of their efforts; and (2) checking these same outcomes against the original aims and objectives to assess the extent to which they have been achieved. These two important aspects affecting the pupil and teacher respectively are indicated appropriately in the model.

Box 2

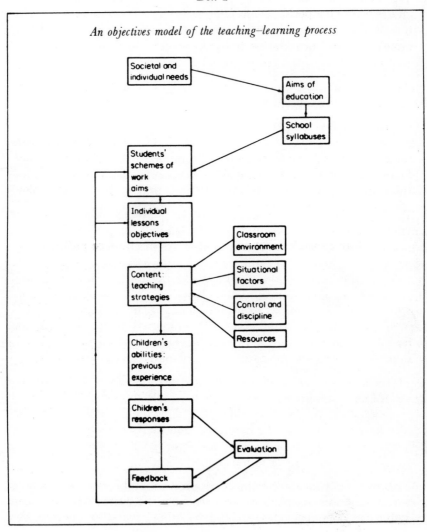

An objectives model of the teaching–learning process

Preparation and planning

It must be emphasized that the separation of the teaching–le
process into stages is necessary for the purposes of analys
subsequent discussion. In practice, however, some stages may in
with others and occur at the same time. Objectives, for example, c
really be separated from the means of achieving them, nor the content of
a lesson from the methods of teaching and learning being used.

THE PRELIMINARY VISIT

Student teachers are normally given the opportunity to visit their
schools before the period of teaching practice formally begins. This may
take the form of an observation week or a system of school attachments
in the period leading up to the block practice. The following points will
be of interest to students offered such facilities.

The purpose of the preliminary visit

The preliminary visit enables the student teacher to meet the headteacher, the teacher in charge of students (where such an office exists),
and the rest of the staff; to become acquainted with his class or subject
teacher; to see the children he will be teaching; to get to know the nature,
layout and resources of the school; and to gather specific information
relevant to the work he will undertake during the practice.

What to look for and what information to collect

It follows from what we said in the preceding paragraph that to make
the most of the preliminary visit, the student must systematically take
note of and, where he feels it helpful, record those aspects of the school's
organization, policy and methods in so far as they will relate to his own
work in the school. To help him in these respects, we offer the following
guidelines which arise from *the physical features, the school in general, the
classroom* and *particular information to record*. We stress that some of the
points raised, e.g. in the physical features, will be more pertinent to the
work of the primary teacher than the secondary specialist.

The physical features

We suggest you begin by investigating features and resources of the
neighbourhood in which the school is situated. Some of these may prove
to be relevant to the lessons you will be teaching and organizing, e.g. the
social nature of the area – is it urban, suburban or rural, for instance?
You could then build up a basic topography of the locality to include the

pattern of the main roads; churches and other buildings of significance; places of historical, geographical or social interest; recent developments; means of transport; details of houses, shops, businesses and industries; parks and beauty spots; museums; canals, rivers and bridges; docks; reservoirs; and markets. If there is a library near by, the librarian may be able to supply information on local history, or even arrange a special display for your class.

The *layout of the school* should next engage your attention. Observe the general architectural style. Is the school's design conventional, or open plan, for example? Approximately how old is the building? When might it have been built – in the late Victorian period or between the wars, for instance? Has the school an annexe or other buildings on another site? The latter is quite common where previously separate schools have merged as a result of reorganization. Find out where the head's room, the staffroom, the general office and assembly hall are to be found (if these are not immediately apparent). Are any rooms used for specialization? Where are these located? Is there an audio-visual centre? Or a resources centre? How are the rooms numbered? If the school is a single-storey construction and extensive in its layout, you may find it useful initially to draw a rough plan of the building.

The school in general

Find out how many pupils there are in the school, the size of its annual intake and the approximate location of its catchment area or areas. The school's recent history may prove interesting, especially if it includes reorganization.

The school's ethos has an important bearing on the work of both teachers and pupils. Check nerve points in the school's life to ascertain what the prevailing atmosphere is like in this respect, e.g. the staffroom, or morning assembly, for instance. Make provisional assessments of the quality of the relationships between the head and his staff, between staff and pupils, and among the staff themselves. If the school has a healthy atmosphere, you should have little difficulty fitting in and helping to maintain it. Where the atmosphere is less than wholesome, however, then you must decide what personal and professional qualities you can display that will improve it.

The prevailing system of *control and discipline* operating in the school is of very great importance and you should find out how it works. What are the school rules, for example? Are they do's or don'ts? Who decides the rules? How explicit are they? Do all members of staff enforce them? What rewards and punishments are used? Who determines them? Who administers punishment? How effective is it? Which rules are broken?

And how often? How are the more extreme forms of misbehaviour like classroom violence handled? (See Box 3 for the kinds of behaviour governed by rules.)

Box 3

Classroom rules

In their study of classroom rules, Hargreaves, Hestor and Mellor[5] began by grouping rules into five themes as set out below with brief explanatory comment. We suggest you use these five themes as a starting point to determine the rules operating in the class, or classes, you will eventually be teaching. Begin by asking the teacher what rules are embraced by a particular theme, then use your powers of observation to see whether these actually conform to what is practised.

1   *The talk theme.* Many of the rules related to the area of pupil talk. One of the most frequent teacher statements was 'stop talking'. We included in this theme all talk-related conduct, such as noise and laughter.
2   *The movement theme.* The many rules about standing and sitting, entering and leaving the room, moving around the classroom, seemed to bear a common movement theme.
3   *The time theme.* This theme included the rules about arriving late, about 'wasting time' and about the time taken by pupils to complete tasks assigned to them.
4   *The teacher–pupil relationship theme.* The ways in which pupils were expected to treat the teachers were a common focus for a variety of rules. The most obvious rules covered obedience, manners and insolence.
5   *The pupil–pupil relationship theme.* This theme included all the rules about how the pupils were expected to treat one another. Examples would be rules about fighting, name-calling and the various forms of interfering with another pupil and his work.

Source: Hargreaves, Hestor and Mellor[5]

Alternatively, how do individual teachers cope where there is no such clearly defined framework of rules? Or where an ineffectual one exists? Or where chaos reigns? Which teachers appear to be most effective in such circumstances? And why? How will *you* relate to one or other of these situations when you have to work in the school?

It can also be of value to find out what the school's *philosophy of education* is. Naturally, it will not be voiced explicitly, and there may even be a clash of philosophies in some schools. However, one can get some idea of the way in which teachers think in these respects by studying the organization of the school and the lessons. Some schools, for example, foster and encourage competition; others, co-operative behaviour. Some are restrictive and authoritarian; others, by contrast, encourage autonomy and freedom of expression. Teaching methods are another obvious indication of a school's philosophy or philosophies. Are they mainly traditional or progressive? An important question arises for the student teacher in this connection: given an established system of teaching in the school, how does he or she fit in? The answer is that whereas the student teacher will generally adopt whatever method or methods are already in use, especially if they are well-tried and effective, there is no reason why he or she should not introduce alternative ones. One could, for instance, employ group methods with a class that had only experienced the traditional or teacher-centred approach. As a matter of courtesy, however, the class teacher should be consulted before introducing such a change, not the least reason being that rearrangements of the room may be required. Box 4 summarizes three contrasting perspectives on educational thought this century that may help the reader decide on his school's philosophy.

It is particularly important to discover what forms of grouping are employed in the school – horizontal, vertical or transitional, for instance. Likewise, where integrated days and integrated curricula operate, how are they organized? Where other features such as mixed ability grouping and team-teaching obtain they too should be investigated. A student teacher placed in a school where one or more of these approaches are used should make a special effort to find out how work and routines are organized.

It can also be helpful to get to know something of *the school's expectations of him* with respect to time of arrival, attendance at morning assembly, involvement with extra-curricular activities, free periods, leaving the school premises, dress, general appearance, preparation of lessons and behaviour *vis-à-vis* the rest of the staff. Box 5 provides a list of basic points one should try to keep in mind on teaching practice.

There will be a number of *significant people* in the school whom you should at least meet and, better still, become acquainted with. These will include the head (or heads, if there is an upper and lower school), his or her deputy, the teacher in charge of students and the class teacher(s) with whom you will be working. It can also be useful to introduce yourself to the school secretary, technicians or laboratory assistants (where relevant), and the caretaker.

Finally, if the school has its own librarian, find out what the procedures are (1) for borrowing books for yourself, and (2) for utilizing the library's resources with the children you will be teaching, e.g. in topic or project work, for example. You can save yourself a lot of time

Box 4

Contrasting value systems behind classical, romantic and modern perspectives towards the curriculum

Davis[6] distinguishes three perspectives that reflect developing educational thought in this century. Each perspective rests upon different assumptions and reflects different value structures. Using the characteristics identified below, decide what kind of perspective your school adopts towards the curriculum.

Classical perspective	*Romantic perspective*	*Modern perspective*
class teaching	individualized learning	flexible grouping
autocratic	*laissez-faire*	participative
conservative	abdication	liberal
subject emphasis	method emphasis	process emphasis
teacher dominated	child centred	inquiry centred
teaching aids	audio-visual	learning resources
discipline	freedom	experience
skills	discovery	creativity
active	reactive	transactive
certainty	confusion	probability
competitive	co-operative	growth
other directed	inner directed	self-fulfilling
discipline	freedom	responsibility
doing things to	doing things for	doing things with

Source: Davis[6]

Box 5

Professional courtesy on teaching practice

1 If you are absent, let the school know promptly.
2 On return from an absence, let the headteacher know you're back. Do not let him find out from hearsay.
3 Lateness calls at least for an apology and possibly an explanation.
4 Be respectful to senior colleagues, e.g. concerning chairs in the staffroom.
5 Be prompt, tidy and accurate in whatever administrative work you have to do, e.g. registers.
6 Maintain adequate standards of dress and appearance.
7 Leave a classroom tidy and the blackboard clean at the end of a lesson.

and trouble by preliminary enquiries of this kind before your block practice begins.

The classroom

We have already stressed the importance of finding out what system of *control and discipline* operates in the school. It is even more important to ascertain what management and control systems are used in the class(es) you yourself will be teaching. Where the class is taught chiefly by one teacher, make a note of established rules, especially those relating to day-to-day matters such as speaking to the teacher, moving about the room, asking and answering questions, talking, finishing early and so on. (To help you make a start in these respects, we have listed guidelines in Boxes 3 and 6.)

Observe what sanctions the teacher employs with his class in order to enforce the rules. Are individuals kept in after school, for instance, or are they asked to stay behind at the end of a lesson, or reprimanded in front of the other children? Does isolation of deviant pupils figure in a teacher's tactics? On a more positive note, find out what kinds of rewards the teacher uses. If the class is taught by other teachers, you can subsequently compare the different methods of control used and check how the class responds to them. The advantages of ascertaining prior knowledge on these matters is that you will then be able to relate your own control systems to the existing framework where this proves to be effective.

The reality of classroom life, unfortunately, is often very different from what one would like to see. Control systems may be either ineffective or non-existent. Where such is the case, you will have to decide what you can do to achieve some measure of control over the class when you eventually take over. In this connection, we recommend you read the section dealing with *management and control in the classroom.*

The successful class teacher's methods of organization will have evolved in the light of his experience and knowledge of the particular children he teaches. The student teacher does not have this experience or knowledge nor obviously the time to acquire them so it is advisable that he perpetuates effective routines established by the class teacher throughout the period of his practice (e.g. What is the established procedure for tidying up at the end of an art lesson? Or what is a child expected to do when he finishes his allotted task five minutes before the rest of the class?) Studying the classroom routines of an experienced and successful teacher requires close observation because the most effective methods are often the least obvious.

What should a student do, however, when he finds himself working

Box 6

Classroom routines

The following checklist was designed by Haysom and Sutton[7] for use in science lessons. Selecting whatever items you feel relevant, use them in one of your observation lessons to discover the rules and routines governing the classroom behaviour of the pupils.

Is it the standard practice for pupils to:

stand up at the beginning of a lesson?
choose where they sit?
go to allotted spaces?
work in self-selected groups?
help each other in their work?
expect not to consult each other?
put hands up before speaking to the teacher?
speak directly to the teacher, butting in at any time?
be silent when the teacher begins to speak?
carry on with what they're doing when the teacher speaks?
leave the room on own initiative?
move about freely during lessons?
compose their own notes?
copy notes from the board?
be expected to have with them pencils, rulers, rubbers, etc?
be allowed to borrow these items?
be allowed, if they finish early, to get on with homework?

You may feel it necessary to extend this list to accommodate rules and routines making up the standard practice in the particular situation you find yourself in.

Source: Haysom and Sutton[7]

with a disorganized teacher who has no routines? Having made a quick assessment of the position, he must then decide what he can do to improve the situation even though the extent of his influence is limited (he is, after all, in a position of dependence in a host school, and perhaps only teaching two or three lessons each day). Between the preliminary visit and his block practice, he should decide on a few basic classroom rules and routines that would impose some structure on the situation so that when he meets the class he can spend some time discussing them with the children so that they know where they stand with him. He can thus improve the original situation at worst marginally and at best significantly.

Particular information to record

You will need to bring back a certain amount of information from your preliminary visit chiefly for your own use. Thus it is important to find out details of the *resources and equipment* available in the school – the size and range of the library, the audio-visual equipment you may use, apparatus you may require, facilities for typing and duplicating, resources for individual and group work (topics and projects, for example). Check that the school has the resources, equipment and materials that *you* will require. Teachers of practical subjects like PE or specialist subjects like art or music need to be particularly alert in this respect. A games teacher, for instance, may want to know how many badminton rackets are available; an art specialist, whether there's a sink in the room he will be using; and a music teacher, the extent of facilities for creative music making. Teachers of science subjects, too, will need to anticipate equipment they will need for practical work, particularly whether there is sufficient equipment for class practicals.

You will need to gather details of the *schemes of work* you will be required to teach, together with any explanatory or ancillary information your class teacher may provide. These aspects are examined in more detail later in this section.

Coupled with details of schemes of work is the need for *information on the children you will be working with*, together with some indication of their previous experience and learning in the subject areas you will be teaching. This kind of information is crucial, as you need to know where to begin your work. Unwittingly going over ground already covered or beginning at a point or level beyond the class's understanding can result in a disastrous start for you. The obvious source of information of this nature is the class teacher. If he or she keeps records on each child, ask if you may have a look at them.

Difficulties sometimes arise when a teacher does not remember what his class has done previously, or is not clear, or is even reluctant to disclose such information. Where this occurs, you must consult either the teacher in charge of students in the school, or the head of department, or your supervising tutor. One or other of these will advise you.

The preliminary visit also gives you the opportunity to ascertain details of text books, workcards/sheets and other material used by the class. Where you feel it necessary, borrow copies or examples of the ones you will be using as they will help you when planning your lessons.

Details of *topic work* and related approaches, where relevant, should also be noted. These could include organizational procedures: individual or group work, for example; topics recently covered; the stage of development of the class or individuals in this kind of learning; and ways in which topics have been presented and evaluated in the past. *Specific information on the class(es)* you will be teaching should include:

The name of the class and, if relevant, the significance of the name.

The size of the class (the number of children makes a difference to the organization and presentation of the various subject areas and curricular activities).

The average age of the class, or its range if it is inter-age.

The stream of the class, or range of ability.

The names of the children and a seating plan (the latter can be particularly useful in the early stages of the practice as an aid to getting to know a class).

Details of groups (if appropriate) – their organizational basis.

Details of children with special needs (again where relevant) – ones with emotional problems, communication difficulties, physical disabilities or home background problems, for instance.

Details of particular problematic children, in terms of control and discipline, together with suggestions from the class teacher as to possible ways of handling them.

The *nature of organization of the timetable operating in the school* should be noted – whether it is fully structured, partially structured or completely unstructured, for example; or whether it is organized over a five- or six-day week.

Finally, details of *your own timetable* should be recorded. These will include:

Lesson details – their times and duration.

Class(es) and subjects or activities to be taught or organized.

Indications of rooms and locations to be used (Room 3, Main Building; Room 23, Lower School; Room 7, Annexe, for instance)

Details of other teachers' lessons you will be observing (where appropriate).

Free periods.

Extra-curricular activities (if relevant): Science Society after school Mondays, choir practice Thursday lunch-times, for example.

Indications of when the school will be closed in the course of the practice period (local elections, half-term, special holidays).

Indications of when you will be prevented from teaching your normal timetable (because of school examinations, for example, or rehearsals for a school play).

The name of the school, its address and its telephone number; and the names of the headteacher, the teacher in charge of students (if appropriate) and of the class teacher.

The range of suggestions given above on what information to collect includes little reference to the kinds of problems and pitfalls you may encounter in seeking this information. We conclude this section, therefore, by highlighting some of them and indicating possible ways of dealing with them.

First, there is the problem of time. Some students spend as much as a whole week on their preliminary visit, but others are not so fortunate. If you are only in for one day and time does therefore present a problem, decide on an order of priorities and begin by noting the most immediately important information that you need. The remainder can then be collected visit by visit, or during the first week of the practice itself. Even in the most favourable circumstances, it is going to take time to build up a total picture of the school, so do not expect to do it in half a day.

A second kind of problem may arise when you are confined to one or two rooms during your initial visit (if this only lasts one day) and cannot therefore move about the building. It has been known for a student on returning to college to say, 'But I hardly moved out of the head's room all day.' What you must do if you are in this position is to ask politely and tactfully if you may see other features of the school as you will be required to make fruitful contributions to discussions with your college tutor and perhaps other students on returning to college.

A third point concerns the more intangible and elusive aspects of school life. We mentioned above, for instance, the value of finding out something of the school's philosophy of education so that one can relate to it more effectively. This, however, can sometimes be a frustrating quest, as rarely is it voiced; nor is it likely to be the subject of staffroom conversation. We suggest you study Box 3 and use the checklists provided as a starting point. What is not immediately apparent can be discovered by asking questions.

One final point: what do you do when essential information you need is just not forthcoming? Or when the source of it is unreliable? Or when it is misleading? You cannot complain to the head, or ask the children! The best course is to ask the teacher in charge of students to help you, or possibly the college tutor who will be supervising you during the practice.

AIMS AND OBJECTIVES

Terminology

A student teacher hopefully seeking guidance from the current literature on *education intention* must feel like turning away in dismay. The whole area abounds in terminological confusion, being replete with words like aims, goals, tasks, objectives, learning outcomes, used freely and apparently indiscriminately. The word *aim*, for instance, formerly possessed a degree of specificity in the context of teacher education which it now appears to have lost; the words *aim* and *objective* are often used with an implied synonymity; and even the word *objective* connotes different things to different people. This confusion may result in part from national differences for, as Davis[6] has pointed out, British educators have been more interested in defining aims than in stating objectives, while American teachers have tended to think in terms of more concrete objectives.

Our purpose at this point, then, is to attempt to remove some of the confusion befogging these matters by defining terms as we shall use them in this book so that readers will at least have a reasonably systematic and consistent interpretation in the pages that follow.

Two key words will be used – *aim* and *objective*. Both refer to expressions of educational intention and purpose, but each will express varying degrees of generality and specificity respectively. In this latter respect, both meet the need to discuss educational ends at different levels depending on the issues at stake. An *aim* we will define as a general expression of intent, and the degree of generality contained in the statement may vary from the very general in the case of long-term aims to the much less general in the case of short-term aims. An *objective*, by contrast, is characterized by greater *precision* and *specificity*. Again, at one extreme will be objectives that are fairly specific, and at the other, objectives that are extremely so.

Long-term aims form the basis of a school's *raison d'être*, thus defining the nature and character of its overall educational programme in relation to societal and individual needs. Short-term aims will constitute the logical starting point for curricula construction and the devising of schemes of work. Objectives expressing varying degrees of specificity will be derived from such aims, especially the short-term ones, and will represent their translation into specific and tangible terms necessary for planning a course of lessons, individual lessons or units of learning on which the ultimate realization of the aims depends.

The following examples of aims and objectives will help the reader to see the distinction between them more clearly. We suggest he tries to locate the particular examples in each category along hypothetical continua of generality and specificity respectively.

Aims

1 To provide children with the opportunity to acquire a knowledge and understanding of the society in which they live.
2 To develop an understanding and tolerance of the world's major religions.
3 To enable pupils to develop an appreciation of art in the twentieth century.
4 To introduce the class to the concept of heat.
5 To educate the whole child.

Objectives

1 To introduce the class to the principal characteristics of the violin.
2 A review of the events leading up to the First World War.
3 To further the pupils' appreciation of Hardy's 'The Darkling Thrush'.
4 The children will circle ten sentences in a given passage of propaganda which are indicative of the author's bias.
5 The pupils will list and identify six different figures of speech in a set prose passage.

One final point: designers of educational programmes cannot always be too legislative on the question of what constitutes an aim and what constitutes an objective. What a teacher plans to do with a given statement of intent is the ultimate determinant of its nature. Aim (4) above, for instance, *to introduce the class to the concept of heat*, could conceivably form the basis of a lesson of one hour, in which case it would be seen as an objective. Alternatively, objective (1) listed above, *to introduce the class to the principal characteristics of the violin*, could equally form the basis of four weekly lessons, in which case it would be more appropriately labelled an aim.

Some characteristics of aims

Aims constitute the basic elements in educational planning. Although existing at different levels of generality, collectively they make up the building blocks of the total programme. The most general aims (referred to as 'ultimate goals' by Wheeler[8]), being broad and often abstract in their expression, will simply offer guidance as to the general direction of educational intention and will in no way indicate particular achievements within specified time limits (e.g. *to prepare children to meet the challenges of a technological age*). Aims of this nature, frequently social in character, express basic concepts of the purpose of the school and 'the expected end-products of an education carried out over time' (Wheeler).

At other levels, aims will express less generality (referred to as 'mediate goals' by Wheeler). Such will form the basis of curricula (e.g. *to achieve certain specified standards in the skills of reading and writing*). Unlike the more general aims noted above, they will suggest tangible achievements and imply rather more specified time limits. They are often statements of what can be expected to have been achieved at given stages over the formal educational period. Box 7 gives further examples of such aims from the primary sector.

Box 7

General aims in primary education

1 The child should know how to convey his meaning clearly and accurately through speech for a variety of purposes.
2 The child should be able to listen with concentration and understanding.
3 The child should be able to read fluently and accurately at a minimum reading age of eleven.
4 The child should be able to read with understanding material appropriate to his age-group and interests.
5 The child should know how to write English appropriate to different formal purposes.
6 The child should know how to observe carefully, accurately and with sensitivity.

Source: Ashton, Kneen and Davies[9]

By now you will have realized that there is a relationship between the degree of generality expressed in an aim and the time limit within which it can be expected to have been achieved. It may be expressed thus: the more general the aim, the more difficult to specify when it will be achieved, or, conversely, the less general the aim, the greater the likelihood of its being achieved within definable and predictable time limits. Thus, *to prepare children to meet the challenges of a technological age* could only be achieved at some time in the relatively distant future; one could not be any more specific than that. The aim *to achieve certain specified standards in the skills of reading and writing*, however, could conceivably be achieved by, at the latest, the age of sixteen.

This relationship has very real and practical implications for the student teacher on teaching practice. Since he is only in school for a comparatively short time (4, 6, 8 or 10 weeks, depending on the college and the particular block practice), the aims that will form the basis of his or her schemes of work will be even *less* general than the 'mediate' ones referred to above.

Now the relevance of aims for the student teacher is that they make up one of the major sources from which lesson objectives are derived; and it is essential that he understands the relationship between his aims and objectives, and between his schemes of work and the individual lessons he will be teaching. This set of interrelationships can be expressed in a simple diagram:

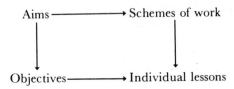

In conclusion, you may find the following checklist useful when formulating aims for schemes of work:

1 Does the aim express the appropriate level of generality?
2 Is it expressed simply, clearly and economically?
3 Does its content relate to the ability and previous experience of the class?
4 Can an appropriate number of lesson objectives be derived naturally from it?
5 Is it attainable in relation to the facilities and time available?

Two kinds of objectives: (1) behavioural and (2) non-behavioural

It has been established that *objectives* are formulations of educational intent much more specific and precise than aims. While the latter serve to indicate the overall direction and purpose of educational activities they are, by comparison with objectives, general, imprecise and lacking in specificity. They are thus of little immediate value to the teacher in planning a particular lesson or unit of learning in that they cannot inform his decisions on precise content, teaching strategy and evaluation. To meet these needs, the teacher must utilize *objectives* for

Box 8

An example of a non-behavioural and a behavioural lesson objective in poetry

Non-behavioural
To further the class's understanding of Hardy's 'The Darkling Thrush'.

Behavioural
At the end of a forty-five-minute lesson on Hardy's 'The Darkling Thrush' the class will be able:

1 To detail the images which conjure up a landscape of winter and death.
2 To compare the rhythms of the winter mood with those associated with the thrush.
3 To explain the meanings in context of, or give synonyms for: coppice, spectre, bine-stems, crypt, canopy, germ, fervourless, illimited, gaunt, carollings, terrestrial, air.
4 To account briefly for the poem's date (31.12.1900).
5 To assess whether the poem is mainly pessimistic or optimistic in meaning.
6 To describe their own emotional responses to the poem.

---

individual lessons (Wheeler[8] refers to them as 'proximate goals').

If you scrutinize the five examples of objectives given in our discussion on terminology, you will notice that numbers (4) and (5) differ from numbers (1), (2) and (3) in that they refer to overt, visible and therefore potentially quantifiable pupil behaviours which the teacher hopes to bring about (the children *will circle* ten sentences . . ., the pupils *will list and identify* six figures of speech . . .). These are examples of *behavioural objectives* and as such identify the learner's overt achievements. Examples (1), (2) and (3), however, refer to more intangible qualities and being open-ended do not explicitly state the behavioural outcomes (*To introduce* the class to . . ., *A review of* . . ., *To further* the pupils' appreciation of . . .). These may be referred to as *non-behavioural objectives* since they do not specify the precise terminal behaviour by means of which a teacher can assess whether his objectives have been achieved. They may indicate what the teacher plans to do (To introduce the class to . . .), or list the elements of content in some way or other (A review of . . .), or invoke patterns of behaviour in abstract terms (appreciation of . . .). None of these manifestations can be perceived directly or measured, however.

Behavioural objectives, if used competently, are tools which can do much to improve teaching and learning. It is important to remember, however, that they are not in and of themselves better than non-

Box 9

The Darkling Thrush
by
Thomas Hardy

I leant upon a coppice gate
  When Frost was spectre-gray,
And Winter's dregs made desolate
  The weakening eye of day.
The tangled bine-stems scored the sky
  Like strings of broken lyres,
And all mankind that haunted nigh
  Had sought their household fires.

The land's sharp features seemed to be
  The Century's corpse outleant,
His crypt the cloudy canopy,
  The wind his death-lament.
The ancient pulse of germ and birth
  Was shrunken hard and dry,
And every spirit upon earth
  Seemed fervourless as I.

At once a voice arose among
  The bleak twigs overhead
In a full-hearted evensong
  Of joy illimited;
An aged thrush, frail, gaunt, and small,
  In blast-beruffled plume,
Had chosen thus to fling his soul
  Upon the growing gloom.

So little cause for carollings
  Of such ecstatic sound
Was written on terrestrial things
  Afar or nigh around,
That I could think there trembled through
  His happy good-night air
Some blessed Hope, whereof he knew
  And I was unaware.

December 1900

---

behavioural ones. Each type has its place and contributes in its own way to the enhancement of learning. It would therefore be naïve and doctrinaire to claim that all objectives could be specified in precise behavioural terms. Some subject areas and certain kinds of learning – especially in the realms of attitudes, feelings and values – are not amenable to such specification and quantification; and 'open-endedness' is the *sine qua non* of teaching methods emphasizing creativity and discovery. We recommend therefore that you give careful thought to which of your lessons should lead towards behavioural objectives and which to non-behavioural ones. In order to help you with such decisions, a little more will now be said about behavioural and then non-behavioural objectives.

Some characteristics of behavioural objectives

A behavioural objective indicates a desired state in the learner, what a child will be able to do after a prescribed lesson, a behaviour that can be perceived by the teacher's unaided senses. When the learner can *demonstrate* that he has arrived at this state, he will then be deemed to have achieved the objective (e.g. the student teacher *will select* five behavioural objectives from a list of fifteen miscellaneous aims and objectives). Thus the behavioural objective describes the desired outcome of a lesson in such a way that most people can agree that the lesson has been a success or a failure.

Other terms used to describe behavioural objectives include *measurable objectives*, *learner objectives*, *instructional objectives*, *performance goals* and *terminal objectives*. All these terms emphasize the importance of (1) writing objectives that describe what a child should be able to do after he completes a learning experience; and (2) describing the behaviour in such a way that it can be observed and measured.

So far, so good. But what are the characteristics of meaningful behavioural objectives? And how does one write them so as to maximize the probability of achieving them?

The most important characteristic concerns the need to identify the terminal behaviour of the learner that the teacher desires. Thus a behavioural objective is useful to the extent that it indicates what the learner must be able to *do*, or *say*, or *perform* when he is demonstrating his mastery of the objective. It must describe *observable* behaviour from which the teacher can infer particular mental skills. This observable behaviour or performance may be *verbal* or *non-verbal*. Thus the learner may be asked to respond to questions orally or in writing, to demonstrate his ability to perform a certain skill or to solve a practical problem.

A second characteristic follows from the first and arises from the need for specificity and precision in phrasing the behavioural objective. There are many words which we use in everyday life that meet our need to communicate with others well enough. But for behavioural objectives they are often too general and vague. Consider the following two columns of words:

to know	to write
to understand	to explain
to be aware of	to demonstrate
to appreciate	to evaluate
to be familiar with	to list
to grasp	to construct

The words and phrases in the left-hand column are too vague and imprecise to be of use in the formulation of behavioural objectives. They are ambiguous and open to various interpretations (they are, of course, perfectly legitimate as aims and non-behavioural objectives, where their very ambiguity can be an advantage). The terms in the right-hand column, however, are more precise, open to fewer interpretations *and indicate what the learner will be doing when demonstrating that he has acquired information or skills that will contribute to, or lead to, knowing, understanding, appreciating or grasping*. Objectives using such words, then, will have been given behavioural specification. Thus if a child can *list* events in Europe leading up to the First World War and can *evaluate* their significance, his teacher can *infer* that he has some *understanding* of the subject.

A note of caution needs to be sounded here. It must not be assumed that *understand* and *list* are one and the same simply because one substitutes for the other. As Hirst[10] has pointed out, states of mind should never be confused with the evidence for them. That a child can list events in Europe leading up to the First World War merely indicates minimal mastery of the facts which, together with the achievements of related objectives on other occasions, may lead to fuller understanding subsequently. The same caution applies to similar pairings.

As suggested in parenthesis above, the kinds of words listed in the left-hand column are perfectly acceptable in the wording of *aims* and *non-behavioural* objectives. The problem for the student teacher is one of knowing *how* to translate words and phrases of this kind into observable behaviours. Perhaps the best way is to take a simple example. It begins by stating an aim of moderate generality. From this is derived a *non-behavioural* objective in which the crucial phrase is *to develop . . . awareness of*. This is then translated into a *behavioural* objective, the phrase now being replaced by the word *list*.

Aim

To further the class's understanding of the significance
of propaganda in the twentieth
century.

Non-behavioural objective	*Behavioural objective*
To develop the child's *awareness of* an author's bias in selected extracts. ⟶	The child will *list* six sentences from a passage of propaganda that reveal bias and indicate which viewpoint the author holds.

The problem is thus one of replacing open-ended infinitives such as *to appreciate, to understand, to develop an awareness of* and so on, with appropriate 'hard and clear' action verbs such as *to state, to write, to demonstrate, to identify, to distinguish, to construct, to select, to order, to make* and *to describe*. Rowntree's[11] example illustrates the point: a child would be able *to design* an experiment, *list* the precautions to be taken, *describe* his results, *evaluate* conflicting interpretations, *participate* in out-of-class discussions, etc. Gerlach and Ely[12] consider that all 'action' infinitives of this kind have their roots in five basic types of behaviour, namely, *identifying, naming, describing, ordering* and *constructing*.

Two further characteristics of behavioural objectives may be mentioned: these sharpen the focus even further. The first concerns the conditions under which the mastery will be tested. These could include such factors as time limitations, evaluative procedures or situational factors (see below for examples). The second characteristic relates to the standards by which the objective is to be judged. These may include such conditions as the percentage of problems a child must answer correctly; the number of correct answers he must obtain; or the tolerance within which he must learn.

In summary, behavioural objectives should ideally contain the following four elements:

1 An indication of *who* is to perform the desired behaviour (the child, the learner, the class).
2 A precise and succinct statement of the *specific terminal behaviour* that the learner is to perform. This will indicate what he will actually *do* and will comprise an 'action' verb and its object (list the events, identify the causes, write an essay).

3 Specifications of the *relevant conditions* under which the behaviour is to be performed. These will indicate the givens, the limitations, the restrictions imposed on the child when demonstrating the terminal behaviour (time factors, details of materials, equipment, information, sources to be used or not used).

4 Reference to the *standard* that will be used to evaluate the success of the product or performance (80 per cent correct; 7 out of 10 correct; will give 6 reasons for).

Example: given one hour and no reference materials, the pupil will write an essay synthesizing the causes and consequences of the Second World War. The essay must contain at least three of the causes and three of the consequences that were discussed in the lesson.

For further information on behavioural objectives, the reader is referred to the references[13] at the end of this section.

Box 10

An example of a non-behavioural and a behavioural lesson objective in the visual arts

Non-behavioural
To increase the class's appreciation of Roy Lichtenstein's painting 'WHAAM!'[14]

Behavioural
At the end of a forty-five-minute lesson on Roy Lichtenstein's painting 'WHAAM!' the class will be able:

1 To identify the essential visual qualities of the composition.
2 To compare the imagery with the comic strip sources and recognize the changes it has undergone.
3 To analyse the unity of the structure within the composition.
4 To explain the significance of the composition as part of the imagery of the 1960s.
5 To separate the idea of 'depiction' in the comic strip from the idea of 'unification' in the painting.
6 To describe their personal responses to the painting.

The student teacher and behavioural objectives

The example of a behavioural objective given in the preceding section, *the child will list six sentences from a passage of propaganda that reveals bias and indicate which viewpoint the author holds*, is a relatively simple one and merely illustrates the principle. It is capable of extension and may even take the form of a number of itemized sub-objectives (see Boxes 8, 10, 11 and 12 for examples). The extent of its further elaboration in this way would depend on a number of situational factors – the ability of the class or group, its previous experience in the subject area, the duration of the lesson, the teacher's knowledge of the class, his skill as a teacher, the methods he uses and so on. Simply to frame a behavioural objective *in vacuo* without reference to the kinds of factors just noted and expect it to result in favourable outcomes is seriously to violate the principle of behavioural objectives.

The practical implications of this point for the student teacher are considerable. The use of behavioural objectives in contrast to non-behavioural ones places a much greater responsibility on the user. A behavioural objective has to be tailor-made to be effective: it will therefore require more thought and preparation in relation to the situational factors than would be the case with a non-behavioural objective. The latter, being open-ended, covert and less specific, places the onus on the learner to make of it what he will, to match it up in so far as he is able with his own cognitive structures.

It follows from this that the student teacher who is only prepared to pay lip-service to behavioural objectives and go through the motions by using superficially conceived, off-the-peg ones would be better advised to eschew them altogether. For those prepared to take them seriously, the following checklist will serve as a framework, at least initially, for setting them up:

1 Decide whether a behavioural objective is appropriate to the particular learning situation you are preparing for (see *Conclusion: some suggestions*, page 44). If it is, then proceed as follows:

2 Consider the relevant situational factors the objective must relate to. These may include: the ability of the class, group, or individual; the duration of the lesson; the class's previous experience of the subject; your knowledge of the class; your skill as a teacher; and the teaching methods you intend to employ.

3 Specify who is to perform the behaviour (e.g. the child, the individual, the learner, the class, the group).

4 Specify the actual behaviour in terms of 'action' infinitives (e.g. to write, to list, to enumerate, to name, to specify, to demonstrate, to distinguish, to order, to identify, to construct, to describe, to state, to mark, to compute, to supply).

5 State the result or outcomes (the product or performance) of the behaviour which will be evaluated to determine whether the objective has been achieved (an essay, six sentences . . ., the first

four problems on page 5 . . ., or whatever). This is invariably the object or object-clause of the infinitive stated in (4).

6 Specify the relevant conditions under which the behaviour is to be performed (the information, equipment, source material, etc. that the child or class can or cannot use. Time limitations.)

7 Indicate the standard that will be used to assess the success of the product or performance. This will often take the form of an expression of the minimal level of performance (the percentage to be correct; so many out of ten correct; . . . must list all the reasons; . . . must distinguish at least *four* characteristics, etc.).

Box 11

An example of a non-behavioural and a behavioural lesson objective in music

Non-behavioural
To develop the class's appreciation of Mendelssohn's 'Hebrides' overture.

Behavioural
At the end of a forty-five-minute appreciation lesson on Mendelssohn's 'Hebrides' overture, the class will be able:

1 To summarize in one paragraph the circumstances surrounding its composition.
2 To compare the two main themes with respect to mood, shape and instruments used.
3 To describe how Mendelssohn deals with the middle section.
4 To account for the overture's description as programme music.
5 To say whether the work is 'realistic' or 'impressionistic'.
6 To comment briefly on the performance.

Non-behavioural objectives

Tyler[15] has noted that since non-behavioural objectives are obtained from a variety of sources, they are likely to be stated in a variety of ways. A desirable common characteristic, whatever their source and whatever form they take, is that they should be expressed simply and clearly so that appropriate learning experiences may follow naturally. Tyler considers that such objectives can be conveniently placed in one or other of three groups.

First, they are sometimes expressed in a manner which indicates *what the teacher does*, e.g.

To outline the theory of relativity.
To explain the principles of operant conditioning.
To introduce the work of the war poets.

To show some functions of the human ear.
To consolidate earlier work on addition and subtraction.

This is a common way of phrasing non-behavioural objectives though, as Tyler notes, because such statements tend to indicate what the teacher plans to do they are not, strictly speaking, statements of educational ends. The particular weakness of this kind of objective from the teacher's point of view is that they do not provide a satisfactory guide 'to the further steps of selecting materials and devising teaching procedures for the curriculum'.[15]

The second form often taken by non-behavioural objectives is in stating topics, concepts, generalizations or other elements of content to be covered in a lesson or course, e.g.

Transport problems in urban areas.
The concept of space. *The Perfect Cadence et.*
The air we breathe.
Trees of the neighbourhood
Castlereagh's foreign policy.

Here, the emphasis is on the content to be dealt with by the teacher and, like the preceding form, they are unsatisfactory in that they do not specify what the pupils are expected to do with the elements of content.

The third form of non-behavioural objectives identified by Tyler are those expressed in the form of generalized patterns of behaviour which usually relate to particular content areas, e.g. *the music of H + Mozart*

To *develop a fuller understanding* of Picasso's paintings.

To *develop an appreciation of* the variety of architectural styles within a five-mile radius of the school.

To *increase the pupils' sensitivity* to manifestations of beauty in art and nature.

Behaviour patterns in this context are often expressed through infinitives like *to know, to appreciate, to be aware of, to understand,* etc. Objectives of this kind can sometimes be so generalized as to be of questionable educational value. Providing, however, they possess a *behavioural aspect* and a *content aspect*, then they are the most useful of the three forms from the student teacher's point of view. Where he achieves a suitable balance between the two he will find that this will assist the structuring of his lessons and aid his decisions about teaching method, e.g.

To further the children's knowledge of the local social services.

Curriculum planners opposed to the use of behavioural objectives advocate the more general, flexible and open-ended approach of non-behavioural objectives. Class teachers, too, tend to prefer this broader interpretation and no doubt it is the one that student teachers are most familiar with. Arguments which have been advanced in favour of non-behavioural objectives include the following:

1 They permit the 'opening-up' process by means of which a child is able to match his own cognitive structures with the perceived content of the objectives. He must negotiate this match-making between his internal structures and the external world for himself.[16]
2 Human behaviour is broader in scope and purpose than the sum of specific bits of behaviour learned in isolation. Behavioural objectives fail to take account of the higher or more complex levels of functioning whereas non-behavioural objectives do not.[17]
3 Non-behavioural objectives also take account of the broad, interrelated categories of human activity and are often more in line with the long-term aims of the school.
4 They give both teacher and class greater room to manoeuvre, having an added flexibility and freedom.
5 Both teacher and class may engage in choice and decision-making and may try out alternative courses of action.
6 Non-behavioural objectives allow for the possibility of concomitant learning.

Box 12

An example of a non-behavioural and a behavioural lesson objective in the visual appreciation of architecture

Non-behavioural
To increase the class's appreciation of F.L. Wright's building, Kaufmann House, 'Falling Water', Connellsville, Pennsylvania, USA.[18]

Behavioural
At the end of a forty-five-minute lesson on F.L. Wright's building, Kaufmann House, 'Falling Water', Connellsville, Pennsylvania, USA, the class will be able:

1 To identify the essential visual and spatial qualities of the building.
2 To recognize Wright's belief in architecture's relationship to landscape and the unique suitability of a building to a site.
3 To explain what Wright meant by 'organic' architecture and 'spatial continuity' and how these relate to Kaufmann House.
4 To analyse the spatial structure of the house and recognize the unity between its parts.
5 To list the materials Wright uses and explain their integral relationship with structure, void and solid.
6 To give a brief account of their own responses to the building.

The debate surrounding the use of behavioural objectives

You will have deduced from what you have just read that the issue of behavioural objectives has incurred a degree of *odium scholasticum* in some quarters. The reasons why some are inimical to their use are numerous. Principally, they arise from a rooted hostility to *behaviourism*, a view of psychology which in its radical form rejects concepts like 'mind' and 'consciousness' and emphasizes the importance of the environment in influencing behaviour at the expense of hereditary potential. Accordingly, learning theorists adopting this extreme position, and who perceive education with similar orientations, see behavioural objectives as tools for achieving their ends. It is thus the fear that the organism will be subjected to the 'shaping' processes of this particular instructional approach without taking mental experiences into account or acknowledging the complexity of human beings that provokes reaction from its opponents. Peters,[19] for example, writes:

> If the inner life of man is banned from investigation, actions which necessarily involve intentions, emotions which necessarily involve appraisals of a situation, together with imagination, memory, perception, dreaming and pain must all be ruled out as scientifically proper objects of investigation; for none of these phenomena can be described or identified without reference to consciousness. There is precious little left of human behaviour to investigate. So the sterility of this approach to human learning is not surprising.

Advocates of behavioural objectives, on the other hand, view them from the context of a systematic approach to education. For them, behavioural objectives have been a central concept in programmed learning and educational technology, their significance having been further enhanced since they were incorporated into the theory of curriculum design. While readily conceding the weaknesses of such objectives, those promoting their cause have cogently argued a case for their limited use in some contexts. MacDonald-Ross,[20] for instance, says:

> For the present, behavioural objectives provide a well-worked-out tool for rational planning in education. They have made possible certain improvements in the technique of curriculum design; and should not be discarded in disgust just because they fail to meet more exacting standards. But the application of these objectives should be tempered by a deep understanding of their limitations.

Further accounts and summaries of the arguments for and against the use of behavioural objectives can be found in the references at the end of this section.[21]

A reappraisal

By now, you must be feeling somewhat dizzy, having been confronted with the various characteristics of the two kinds of objectives. You may even feel you have been put into a position where you have to choose between one or the other. In no circumstances must you do this. You must see the relationship between them not as an *either . . . or* one, but as complementary.

Even though the study of behavioural objectives is at a comparatively early stage of development and much has still to be learned about their application, there will be occasions when they will be useful to you, once you have acquired the skills to formulate them and have had some practice in using them. Equally, there will be frequent opportunities to utilize the more familiar non-behavioural objectives. You are reminded that teaching practice is an opportunity for experimentation and that it is therefore incumbent on you to acquire experience of, and command over, as many skills as you possibly can.

Identifying and writing objectives

You may wish at this stage to attempt to consolidate what you have read so far by trying the following examples.

(a) Distinguishing aims and objectives

In the light of what was said earlier, which of these expressions of educational intention are objectives, and which are aims? In what circumstances could some be either?

1 To encourage young people to understand the significance of maintaining good health and physical fitness.
2 To further the children's understanding of the concept of weight by giving them practice in weighing.
3 To provide opportunities to develop an appreciation of beauty in literature, art and music.
4 To introduce the world's major religions to the class.
5 To translate ten infinitives indicating various mental states into appropriate behavioural terms.
6 To demonstrate the differences between behavioural and non-behavioural objectives.
7 To give the group practice in the use of the twenty-four-hour clock.
8 To develop interests and skills so that leisure time may be used purposefully.

9 To analyse the various parts of a popular daily newspaper.
10 To enable the student to distinguish between aims and objectives.

(b) Identifying behavioural objectives

Which of the following objectives are behavioural, and which are non-behavioural?

1 The student teacher will write down four areas within the school curriculum in which there may be difficulties in expressing the outcomes of learning in behavioural terms; and he will list one reason in each case why difficulties may arise.
2 To extend the class's knowledge of the range and variety of seashore life.
3 To identify four activities in the school curriculum in which learning outcomes are behavioural, willy-nilly.
4 To develop the group's skills in the use of noun clauses.
5 To explain in one paragraph of reasonable length why it would be inappropriate to express an aesthetic response to a work of art in behavioural terms.
6 To acquire skills in writing lesson notes to meet the needs of different teaching situations.
7 To introduce the class to Elgar's 'Enigma Variations'.
8 To write a paragraph entitled 'Traffic at rush hour' which shows the difference between similes and metaphors.
9 To give the group practice in formulating behavioural objectives.
10 State four reasons for specifying learning unit objectives in behavioural terms.

(c) Using 'action' verbs

With particular reference to the age range you intend to teach (primary, junior, middle school, secondary, etc.), frame ten behavioural objectives using these 'action' verbs:

identify	distinguish
interpret	order
describe	name
evaluate	locate
apply	construct

(d) Translating non-behavioural objectives into behavioural objectives

Translate the following six non-behavioural objectives into behavioural ones. Make sure that the latter point to observable behaviours on the part of the child or student – that is, acts that can be seen or heard.

1 To develop the group's understanding of the concept of weight.
2 To further the class's knowledge of the local environment within a three-mile radius of the school.
3 To understand something of the persuasive techniques used in TV advertising.
4 To further students' appreciation of the efficacy of behavioural objectives.
5 To give practice in creative writing.
6 To stimulate an interest in the technological developments of the past thirty years.

(e) Criteria for the evaluation of behavioural objectives

Read the following behavioural objectives and assess the extent to which they meet the criteria for behavioural objectives stipulated earlier.

1 Given a list of twenty French irregular verbs and one hour, the student will conjugate at least fifteen verbs correctly (i.e. as shown in the text book) and translate them into their correct English equivalents.
2 Ten short melodies in the major and minor will be played to the class. Each child will identify a melody in the major by holding up a white card immediately after the tune is played, and a melody in the minor by holding up a black card immediately the tune has been played. The melodies will be played again in scrambled order and each child will be expected to respond correctly to at least seven out of the ten.
3 Given a forty-five-minute period and no reference books, the child will solve the first ten problems at the end of the chapter studied for homework. He will be required to get at least seven of these right before moving on to the next chapter next week.

Conclusion: some suggestions

We have been concerned here with the problems surrounding the expression of educational intention. Aims were seen as general goals formulated in clear and simple language which define the nature and direction of a school's programme or an area of work within that programme. Objectives, by contrast, were seen as more precise expressions of purpose, and of particular value in planning lessons and other units of learning. We then attempted to trace a path between the behaviourist view, advocates of which recommend the use of behavioural objectives as their principal tool of learning, and the more traditional practices in English education which employ non-behavioural objectives.

We conclude with suggestions that will guide the reader in deciding whether to use behavioural or non-behavioural objectives. A behavioural objective may be used when the desired outcome is a skill that can be performed, or when the results of instruction can be expressed or demonstrated overtly in writing or speech (language learning, native or foreign, would apply here). The acquisition of factual knowledge may likewise be formulated in behavioural terms. Where children are experiencing some difficulty in learning, the particular problem might be broken down into simpler steps or stages, each of which could then be expressed behaviourally. Individualized learning is another area where behavioural objectives would seem appropriate; and if one is producing material for programmed learning, behavioural objectives will be required.

However, when the desired outcomes of learning are more general, developmental or complex in nature and need not, or cannot, be demonstrated by acts of fragmented behaviour, then behavioural objectives are inappropriate. For example, the aesthetic and appreciative aspects of subjects like literature, art and music are better expressed in less prescriptive ways, since they involve the building up of complex, interrelated and subjective responses and the establishing of favourable attitudes. Broad, open-ended statements of intent serve teacher and pupil alike better in such contexts, though it must be remembered that some of the adjuncts to appreciation (historical, biographical or social, for instance; or technical, linguistic or stylistic) are often capable of being expressed behaviourally (see, for example, Boxes 8, 10, 11 and 12).

SCHEMES OF WORK

Having reviewed aims and objectives in the preceding part, we now consider two important tools in the preparation for teaching practice where they play a vital part – schemes of work and lesson notes. The broader aims will provide a focus for a student's schemes of work; and the more specific objectives, the starting point for individual lesson notes. By looking at the original schemata reflecting the teaching–learning process (Box 2, page 16), the reader will see how each of these tools 'fits in' to the objectives model presented there.

A scheme of work in the context of school practice may be defined as that part of a school/class syllabus that the student teacher will be required to teach during his teaching practice. In addition to its primary function in providing an outline of the subject matter and content, it may also include information on the children (age, sex, ability, number, class, groups, etc.) as well as on organizational matters, evaluative procedures and ancillary aids. As already indicated, it is also advisable for the student teacher to find out what has gone before in the particular area he will be responsible for and include some reference to this in the scheme.

The scheme will therefore indicate the amount of ground a student is likely to cover in his stay with the host school. It will be a survey of the work he will undertake and will enable him to clarify his own thinking and to plan and develop those particular curriculum experiences which he may feel will require more time and attention in preparation. Although part of a school or class syllabus, a scheme should not be seen as fixed and rigid: modifications may be made to it subsequently in the light of new ideas or further experience of the children. One knows what the broad aim is, and there is nothing to stop one taking a detour along the route – like devoting a lesson to a topic that has arisen incidentally from the children's own interests.

In situations where the student teacher is given no clear lead from the teacher as to his schemes of work (as sometimes happens), he will then have to devise ones of his own. What he must avoid in such a contingency is duplicating work already done by the class before his arrival. He must therefore tactfully ascertain from the class teacher what the position is in this respect and, where possible, discuss with him the schemes he proposes to use. When the teacher proves to be unhelpful or evasive, then the student should take the matter up with his supervising tutor.

A comparable situation may arise when a student teacher is placed in a junior school. Many schools in the primary sector have abandoned fixed timetables in which subjects are organized in isolated compartments. There may not therefore be the same need to structure the work to be covered quite so systematically. Where this is the position, the student teacher may find that he is responsible for his own schemes and for planning the timing of activities he will be organizing. This should be done in consultation with the class teacher. The criteria to bear in mind when planning one's schemes in this context are *continuity in learning and progression of experience*.

What to include in a scheme of work

The following information should generally be included in a scheme of work:

Particulars of the children in the class or group: these will cover number, age, sex, ability and stream (if appropriate).

Previous knowledge and experience of the class in respect of the subject matter.

The number and duration of the lessons.

The aim of the scheme: an outline of the subject matter and content, possibly with the objectives for each lesson or unit of learning.

Some indication of organizational factors, such as: how are the pupils to learn? What kind of work units are planned – class, group or individual? Methods of teaching and learning to be employed – formal class teaching, self-direction under guidance, etc. Sources of information – books, workcards, filmstrips, visits, etc. The manner in which the children's work will be presented – oral, written, dramatic, folders, booklets, murals, display, exhibition, etc.

Means of evaluation: how are the pupils' achievements to be assessed against the lesson objectives? What criteria will be used?

Equipment to be used: books, materials, apparatus, blackboard, learning aids, audio-visual equipment, etc.

It is usually recommended that schemes of work should be acquired or prepared before teaching practice begins. They may subsequently be included in one's lesson note file, each preceding the particular section of lesson notes to which it refers. One such arrangement is as follows:

SUBJECT: CLASS:
PARTICULARS OF CHILDREN: age, sex, ability, number, groups, etc.
SCHEME OF WORK: 1 Lessons – number and duration (where appropriate)
2 Aim of scheme
3 Previous knowledge and experience of the area(s)
4 Outline of content to be covered (possibly with lesson objectives):
  Week 1 Lesson 1, 2, etc.
  Week 2 Lesson 4, 5, etc.
5 Organizational factors
6 Evaluative procedures
7 Equipment

Sequencing

Schemes of work may be either *sequential* or *non-sequential*. A sequential scheme is one in which the components are logically related to one another and in which the achievements of the later components will depend in large measure on having mastered the earlier ones. Much successful learning in 'linear' subjects (like mathematics) depends on such organization and continuity. The components of a non-sequential scheme, however, will not necessarily be related in the same way. They will be related in that they belong to the same subject area, of course, but it is not essential that they are sequenced in one particular way; an understanding of C is not dependent on having previously mastered B, or A. Non-sequential schemes, then, are more flexible in terms of the order in which the components are presented and are thus of particular value in the various integrated approaches to learning.

Two specimen schemes

To illustrate the main points established above, two specimen conventional schemes are outlined below:

(a) An example of a sequential scheme

SUBJECT: Social Studies   CLASS: 4A
PARTICULARS OF CHILDREN: Age: 15+
                                      Sex: Mixed
                            Ability: Mixed
                          Number: 29

SCHEME OF WORK:

1 *Lessons*: One one-hour lesson per week for six weeks.
2 *Aim*: To acquaint the class with the way in which the family has changed through history, with particular reference to its structure and function.
3 *Previous knowledge*: The scheme forms part of a one-year syllabus in which the family, marriage, role and social class will be studied. The class has not previously studied the family in a formal way.
4 *Outline of content*:
   Week 1, Lesson 1:   The structure and function of the family in (a) tribal situations.
   Week 2, Lesson 2:   The structure and function of the family in (b) the Middle Ages.
   Week 3, Lesson 3:   The structure and function of the family during (c) the Industrial Revolution.
   Week 4, Lesson 4:   The structure and function of the family in (d) the earlier part of the twentieth century.
   Week 5, Lesson 5:   External and internal factors influencing changes in the family in the later twentieth century.
   Week 6, Lesson 6:   Conclusion: a review of the changes in the family as studied in the earlier lessons.
5 *Organizational factors*: Class and group learning: mainly project work supported by formal class teaching and discussion. Sources of

information: chiefly books, articles, official publications, charts, filmstrips and BBC radio and TV presentations.

6 *Evaluation*: The major categories of assessment in the project work will be: selection criteria; presentation of written and illustrative material; and attitudinal considerations, especially as manifested in enterprise and ability to work on a co-operative basis.

7 *Equipment*: Note books, pens, rulers, folders

Text books: *The Family in History*
Illustrated Social History

Official publications
Blackboard
Overhead projector
BBC radio and TV

(b) An example of a non-sequential scheme

SUBJECT: Social Studies   CLASS: 3B
PARTICULARS OF CHILDREN: Age: 13 +
                                 Sex: All boys
                                 Ability: Homogeneous
                                 Number: 34

SCHEME OF WORK:

1 *Lessons*: Two double lessons of 80 minutes each for four weeks.

2 *Aim*: To further the class's knowledge of aspects of the twentieth century, with particular reference to their social effects.

3 *Previous knowledge*: Little previous formal teaching and learning of the selected topics. Scheme designed to utilize informally acquired knowledge and to examine it in a systematic way.

4 *Outline of content*:

Week 1, Lesson 1: Communication (a) land, sea and air.

Lesson 2: Communication (b) telegraph, telephone, radio and television.

Week 2, Lesson 3: Medicine (a) the position at the beginning of the twentieth century; X-rays; drugs.

Lesson 4: Medicine (b) transplants and spare-part surgery.

Week 3, Lesson 5: Atomic energy (a) structure of matter – the atom, nucleus and electron; significant scientists.

Lesson 6: Atomic energy (b) applications of atomic and nuclear energy in peace time; advantages and disadvantages.

Week 4, Lesson 7: The space age (a) rocketry and interplanetary travel.

Lesson 8: The space age (b) satellite technology.

5 *Organizational factors*: Some formal class teaching and discussion to initiate and explore topics. The pupils will work mainly in small self-selected groups, each one having an appointed leader. Sources of information: books, booklets, charts and filmstrips. Work to be presented collectively in folders, as models, and as displays and exhibitions.

6 *Evaluation*: Assessment will be group based. The chief categories of assessment of presented work will be selection criteria, presentation criteria and attitudinal considerations.

7 *Equipment*: Note books, folders, pens, rulers, coloured paper, scissors, paste, modelling clay, wire, cardboard containers, globe and table tennis ball.

Text books: *Communication in the Twentieth Century*
Exploring the Atom
Pamphlet: 'Recent developments in medicine'
Blackboard, prepared charts and overhead projector.

Box 13 indicates the relationship between the itemized content of a scheme of work and particular lesson objectives, and how the latter may be derived from the former. The examples of objectives given are non-behavioural ones, though the reader will have little difficulty in expressing them in behavioural terms where he feels they would be warranted.

THE LESSON NOTE

Because of the complexities surrounding the teaching of children, considerable thought must be given to the *planning of instruction*. In this part, therefore, we shall make a few practical suggestions in this connection, especially with regard to individual lessons or units of learning, so that the student teacher may organize the content of his lessons or units in such a way as to bring about the best conditions for learning. There are other advantages to carefully-planned lessons – they give the student more confidence when teaching his or her class; and they help subsequently in lesson evaluations and self-appraisals.

We have shown that a scheme of work consists basically of an aim and an itemized summary of the contents to be taught. Once the contents have been placed in a suitable sequence, the student teacher can proceed with the planning and organizing of individual lessons. As a preliminary to this stage in the preparation for learning, a general orientation will be provided which will help to give the lesson contexture and direction. When planning a lesson, therefore, internal consistency among three *components of instruction* should be sought. These components are:

Box 13

How lesson objectives may be derived from the content of a scheme of work

Subject area: Social Studies   *Class*: Sixth Form
                                                      General Studies

Aim of scheme: To further the group's understanding of the function and
        meaning of sport.

Content of each of six one-hour lessons:	*Lesson objective*:
1 The appeal of sport	To investigate people's motives for taking part in sporting activities at both the amateur and professional levels.
2 Sport in Britain	To increase the group's awareness of the range of sporting activities in Britain and how they are organized.
3 The sporting personality	To study the mental, physical and charismatic factors contributing to the success of a number of prominent sporting figures.
4 Sport in school	To lead the class to a fuller appreciation of the benefits of individual and team pursuits in the realm of sport.
5 The competitive element	To explore the various manifestations of the competitive element in sport with particular reference to (a) self-competition; (b) team competition; and (c) international competitions.
6 Politics and sport	To examine the evidence for the belief that there is an inevitable connection between sport and politics.

---

1 The lesson objective.
2 The teaching methods, materials, media, aids, learning experiences and/or exercises; and their organization.
3 Evaluative procedures.

Gagné and Briggs[22] refer to these as 'anchor points' in the design of instruction, constant reference to which helps to keep the lesson 'on target'. Mager[23] expresses these same elements in terms of fundamental interrogatives, thus:

1 *Where am I going?* (Objective.)
2 *How will I get there?* (Steps by means of which the objective is achieved.)

3 *How will I know when I have arrived?* (The use of appropriate evaluative procedures.)

Evidence by Briggs[24] shows that when these 'anchor points' and corresponding questions are borne in mind in lesson planning, instruction tends to be successful. As objectives, resources and evaluative procedures are dealt with elsewhere, the remainder of this section will deal with instructional design, the planning of individual lessons and units, and ancillary matters.

The first step

We suggested in the previous section that once a scheme of work has been decided upon and its various topics and sub-topics identified and sequenced, the planning of instruction could proceed to a consideration of the individual lesson or unit of learning. The next task for the student teacher will be to express each topic or sub-topic subsumed under the aim of the scheme as a *lesson objective* (see Box 13). This should be done as far as possible with the particular children he/she will be teaching in mind; and following the guidelines laid down in the section examining objectives, it should be possible to decide whether a non-behavioural or a behavioural objective is the more appropriate. We illustrate this point with an example:

Aim of scheme: To further the class's knowledge of aspects of the twentieth century, with particular reference to their social effects.
Sub-topic: The space age: satellite technology.

From this sub-topic, we may formulate either:

(a) A *non-behavioural objective*, thus; to examine some aspects of satellite technology. Or
(b) A *behavioural objective*, thus: At the end of the lesson, the class will be able:

1 To explain what is meant by the word 'satellite' and distinguish between a natural and an artificial one.
2 To identify and name the principal external features of a satellite.
3 To explain the meanings of: gravity; orbit; eccentricity; apogee; perigee; tracking stations.
4 To name *four* uses of artificial earth satellites.
5 To comment briefly on the significance of any *four* of the following: Sputnik 1; Sputnik 2; Explorer 1; Vostok 1; Telstar 1; Molniya 1; Early Bird; ESSA 1.
6 To state *one* discovery resulting from earth satellite technology.

Having thus formulated an appropriate objective, the student may then plan a sequence of events that will result in its achievement. This sequence will then form the basis of his *lesson plan* or *unit of learning* (see below, *Two specimen lesson notes*).

We must emphasize at this point that we do not recommend a set, formalized plan for any type of lesson or unit. There is no one fixed and rigid pattern that will suit all lessons; and the student must adopt a flexible approach that will arise out of the particular objective he has in mind in relation to the various 'givens' of the classroom situation. Such flexibility will depend on the student's understanding of the psychological processes underlying an act of learning and of how these relate to the behaviour of both the teacher and learner. Given this kind of understanding, he will be in a more informed position which will enable him to tailor his plans to meet the requirements of the individual lesson or unit he is preparing, whether it be a traditional class lesson or a morning's assignments for a vertically-grouped class.

In order to give the reader some insight into these psychological processes, we will now investigate the relationship between the *learning process* through which the learner passes and the related *instructional events* to be organized and implemented by the teacher.

Learning phases and instructional events

A tiro mastering a complex skill begins as far as he is able by reducing the complexity to more manageable proportions by analysing it into its various components. It is possible to distinguish in this way the components making up the complexities of a complete learning sequence. Gagné[25] has identified *eight* such phases. These are: (1) motivation phase; (2) apprehending phase; (3) acquisition phase; (4) retention phase; (5) recall phase; (6) generalization phase; (7) performance phase; and (8) feedback phase.

Although the act of learning is continuous and seamless, an analysis of this kind does enable us to identify and examine the characteristics of each phase and reflect upon the implications for the professional educator.

(1) Motivation phase

If an individual is to learn, then he must be motivated to do so. Establishing motivation is thus the preparatory phase for an act of learning. In an educational setting, the promotion of learning is chiefly dependent upon two kinds of motivation. First, there is intrinsic motivation: this is chiefly determined by a person's own nature or internal state. In seeking a particular goal, he is in some way rewarded for achieving it. The reward is inherently connected with the activity – simple bodily pleasures (as in PE), or the mental satisfaction of feeling competent (as with any academic subject). At other times, however, the learner may not be initially motivated by the incentive of achievement. Intellectual incompetence or immaturity, the lack of sensitivity to ultimate consequences, or mere indifference, may stand in the way of intrinsic appeal. Where such is the position, a second kind of motivation is called for – that which has to be established externally, usually by a second person. Gagné suggests that established motivation of this kind can be achieved by generating within the learner *an expectancy*, or an anticipation of the reward he will obtain when achieving his goal. An example of this would be a teacher stating his objective at the beginning of a lesson and explaining the benefits that will accrue from achieving it.

(2) *Apprehending phase*

Once aroused, the learner is now confronted with the material to be learned or the skill to be acquired. These may be presented by the teacher or they may arise from the situation. Three features of the phase can be identified: *attending* to the situation in such a manner as to select those parts of the total stimulation relevant to the learner's needs; *perceiving* these same parts with the same degree of selectivity and discrimination; and *comprehending* their significance. The part played by the teacher in this phase of the learning sequence will depend upon the mental ability of the learner, his previous experience, how sophisticated a learner he is, and so on.

(3) *Acquisition phase*

The act of learning now proceeds to the acquisition phase. This includes what Gagné refers to as *the essential incident of learning*: 'the moment in time at which some newly formed entity is entered into the short-term memory, later to be further transformed into a "persisting state" in long-term memory.'

The storing of what has been acquired involves the important process of *coding*. While all efficient learners develop their own more or less successful ways of encoding data to be learned, the processes involved may be influenced externally by suggestions from the teacher (the use of mnemonic devices, for instance).

(4) Retention phase

What has been learned and encoded now enters the long-term memory. This is the phase of learning about which psychologists know least. What is known, however, is that the capacity of the long-term memory is very great and that it should not be imagined that a child's long-term memory can be overloaded.

(5) Recall phase

Where evidence is required that an act of learning has taken place, there must be a phase of recall in which the act is exhibited in some way as performance. This involves the process of retrieval. As Gagné says: 'Somehow, the memory store is searched and the learned entity revivified. What has been stored becomes accessible. The process is presumably at work even for learning which has occurred a few minutes previously.'

As with other phases and processes in the act of learning, retrieval may be influenced by external factors (a teacher's prompting and probing in a questioning session, for instance).

(6) Generalization phase

The recall of what has been learned and its application to different situations or contexts involves generalization. In school learning, this is usually referred to as transfer of learning, or simply transfer. As 'teaching for transfer' is a major aim of school learning, it is important that the process of retrieval takes place in as many varied contexts as possible.

(7) Performance phase

The performance phase is simply that part in the learning sequence where the learner is given the opportunity to show what he has learned. It is at this point, in conjunction with the ensuing 'feedback' phase, that the learner desirably experiences the inherent or established reward noted in the motivational phase. The performance phase is particularly important for the teacher, as 'the product of responding verifies that learning has taken place' (Gagné).

(8) Feedback phase

The performance phase prepares for, and leads naturally into, the feedback phase at which point the learner finds out how well or how badly he has done, whether or not he has achieved the anticipated objective.

Sometimes, the feedback is provided immediately by the learner's own performance (as when playing a game); at other times, it is supplied at a later stage by another person (written comments on an essay, for instance).

The phases described briefly above refer to the *internal* processes taking place during an act of learning. We have made the point more than once that these may be influenced by *external* factors – a teacher's comments, his questioning skill, the use of learning resources, for instance. Indeed, the whole art and science of pedagogy proceeds from the belief that one can to a considerable extent affect the other. A teacher may thus be seen as a professional instructor who facilitates, promotes, hastens or influences in some way the achievement of these internal processes. Gagné's table, illustrated in Box 14, indicates how the internal learning phases, together with their attendant processes, relate to possible instructional events deemed appropriate by the teacher.

As Gagné and Briggs[22] point out, the events of instruction are designed to make it possible for the learner to proceed from 'where he is' at the beginning of a lesson to the achievement of the capability identified as the lesson's objective. Although in some situations these events occur naturally as a result of the learner's interaction with the particular materials of the lesson, they mostly have to be deliberately arranged by the teacher for the learner's benefit.

The relationship between these three components – the learning phase, the process and the instructional event – may be briefly explained by considering each of the eight phases in turn. Thus:

(1) Motivation

Once attention has been secured, the beginning of a lesson should aim at arousing appropriate motivational states in the learner, especially where these are not strongly intrinsic. There are obviously many ways in which this may be done depending on, among other factors, the subject being taught, the nature of the class and the teacher's own insight. One way is to tell a class the objective of the lesson where this not self-evident; asking questions which tap children's interests is another; and re-channelling existing motivations yet another.

(2) Apprehending

The next instructional event in the lesson corresponding to the apprehending phase is the one which presents the appropriate stimuli – the topic or subject matter to be learned; the skill to be acquired. Success in apprehending on the part of the learner depends on the teacher's skill at timing, ordering and structuring the various stimulus events. He must draw the class's attention to significant features in the situation and explain difficulties. Varied examples will often help at this point.

(3) Acquisition

This phase concerns the beginning of the process of storing away the new learning and it is here that the teacher can facilitate the process by suggesting ways in which the data may be encoded more efficiently. The task of both teacher and learner will be greatly assisted at this stage by the way the teacher orders and structures his material in the preceding apprehending phase. But not all the work should be done by the teacher for, as Gagné notes, encouraging the learner to encode in whatever manner he chooses is often the best procedure.

(4) Retention

The consolidation of learning, the storing away of what has been learned on a more permanent basis, will take place at this phase. The teacher will provide all manner of learning guides and procedures at this point in the learning process. Verbal statements, explanations, hints, diagrams, pictures, reviews and so on, will all assist in 'stamping in' what is to be learned.

(5) Recall

The instructional event related to the recall phase of learning deals with ways of helping the learner retrieve what he has stored away. In terms of what the teacher does these may take the forms of reviews, question and answer sessions, quizzes, tests or exercises. But he is also concerned to encourage the learners to develop their own search strategies, and to introduce them to general retrieval plans.

(6) Generalization

The event corresponding to the generalization phase of learning will centre around the extent to which the teacher can provide numerous and varied contexts in which the learned material can be used and applied. It is at this point that the teacher will encourage transfer of learning.

(7) Performance

The teacher here provides opportunities for the learner to apply what he has learned. Such application may take a written, oral, creative or practical form.

(8) Feedback

Where it is not self-evident, the teacher evaluates the learner's performance and informs him of the outcomes. This is a crucial stage for the teacher too, for he finds out at this point whether the lesson objective has been achieved.

In a characteristic and orthodox class lesson, then, the external instructional events manipulated by the teacher serve the purpose of supporting, facilitating, stimulating, expediting or influencing in some way the internal processes of learning. In an ideal class lesson, the learning phases and corresponding instructional events may all occur on the one occasion, within the single lesson. This must not be taken to mean that the learning phases and their related instructional events must necessarily take place in this order; nor that all the components must be present at one and the same occasion. As Gagné and Briggs[22] record:

> The exact form of communication to the learner is not something that can or should be specified in general for all lessons, but rather it must be decided for each lesson. The particular communications chosen should fit the circumstances and be designed to have the desired effect upon the learner.

Thus, a lesson may use as its starting point the feedback phase of a previous learning occasion; and some phases and events (e.g. generalization or performance) may be omitted totally in some circumstances.

These variants point to the particular strength of this *learning phases/instructional events* model, namely, its flexibility. Because most of its components, or combinations of them, are isolatable to some extent and can therefore be omitted, elided, extended or reorganized as the occasion demands, the model may be seen as a realistic basis on which different types of lesson and units of learning may be constructed. There are two advantages to using the model in this way: first, the teacher is not committed inexorably to a rigid, unyielding pattern to which he has to accommodate his material; and second, in assembling and rearranging the various components to meet the needs of a specific lesson, he becomes very much more involved in both the planning and the content of the lesson.

We will now show how an orthodox class lesson may be derived from this model in order to meet the exigencies of the classroom situation.

Application of the learning phases/instructural events model to a class lesson

The class lesson is probably the most common form of teaching to be found in schools and although it may appear in various guises, it will be

Box 14

Learning phases, processes and instruction events		
Learning phase	Process	Instructional event
1 Motivation	Expectancy	Arousing interest; stating the lesson objective; creating rewarding learning situations.
2 Apprehending	Attention Perception Understanding	Exposition; introducing the subject; directing attention to significant features; explaining.
3 Acquisition	Coding Storage entry	Suggesting means of coding.
4 Retention	Storage	Not known.
5 Recall	Retrieval	Stimulating recall; suggesting schemes and cues for recall; providing learning guidance.
6 Generalization	Transfer	Promoting transfer by providing a variety of contexts for retrieval cueing.
7 Performance	Responding	Instances of performance.
8 Feedback	Reinforcement	Informational feedback providing verification or comparison with a standard.

Source: Gagné[25]

taken to mean all those occasions when a teacher deals with the class as a single unit. It may thus include 'chalk and talk' sessions, demonstrations, specialist and practical lessons, or any other learning situation in which work is presented to the whole class. Of course, the class lesson is not always the most fitting way of teaching, and occasions when alternative plans are to be preferred will be considered subsequently.

Using the *learning phases/instructional events* model as a starting point, it is possible to derive from it a plan for a class lesson as indicated in Figure 1 (p. 60). We stress again that this is only one of a number of ways of planning a class lesson and that all class lessons need not conform rigidly to this pattern. Because of the difficulty in distinguishing the apprehending, acquisition and retention phases in practice, these have been included in the *Presentation* stage.

Class lesson plan		Corresponding learning phases
Stage 1: Introduction	———————————	Motivation
Stage 2: Presentation	———————————	Apprehending Acquisition Retention
Stage 3: Application	———————————	Recall Generalization Performance
Stage 4: Conclusion	———————————	Feedback

Figure 1 A class lesson plan using the learning phases/instructional events model as a framework

The four stages may be briefly explained thus:

Stage 1: Introduction

This corresponds to the *motivation* phase in the model and will be the point in the lesson where instructional events designed to arouse interest are formally located. It is here that the teacher creates a desire in the children to take part in the lesson and establishes an atmosphere conductive to learning. More technically, the teacher induces a 'set', which may be defined as any means which causes a child to attend and learn. 'It directs the learner's attention to a specific task or learning sequence and there is experimental evidence which demonstrates that differences in set induction affect learning outcomes.'[26] Set induction devices may include: recall of previous knowledge of the subject; informing the pupils of the lesson objective and the ways in which they can benefit from achieving it; appealing to the basic motives and interests of the pupils; asking a provocative question; doing something unusual like lighting a candle and covering it with a bell jar as an introduction to a lesson on the composition of air; and showing the class an object and using it as a basis for a series of questions.

Stage 2: Presentation

The *presentation* stage embraces the *apprehending, acquisition* and *retention* phases in the model. Although for the purposes of analysis these have been identified as separate acts, in practice they will probably be seamless, continuous and sometimes instantaneous. It is appropriate, therefore, that they be included in the same stage of the lesson plan. This will be the point where new material to be learned or studied is introduced. This will involve presentation, exposition and explanation on the part of the teacher, and his principal functions will be to draw the class's attention to the significant features of the material, to structure it in such a way as to assist the pupils' understanding and assimilation of it, to deal with any difficulties, and to provide learning guidance to ensure a form of encoding that will enable the learner later to recover what he has learned and display it subsequently as some kind of performance. Appropriate instructional events at this stage would include: summaries, recapitulation, synthesis, revision, oral questioning, discussion and illustrations.

Depending on the nature and extent of the material, the presentation stage may be broken down into further sub-stages.

Stage 3: Application

Although the *recall* phase, together with the *generalization* and *performance* phases, has been formally included in the *application* stage, it must be remembered that it will also play a part in the preceding *presentation* stage. However, as the act of recall is an indispensable part of generalization and performance, it is perhaps more fitting to include it formally in this stage. It will be the point in the lesson where the children will have the opportunity to demonstrate what they have learned and it will therefore be incumbent on the teacher to provide opportunities for testing the newly-acquired knowledge and/or skills and for using them in novel situations. If the teacher wishes to bring about transfer of learning it is at this stage that he must consciously plan for it.

Stage 4: Conclusion

The conclusion will embrace the *feedback* stage in the model. It follows logically from the preceding application stage and will be mainly concerned with the evaluation of the children's work and informing them of the outcomes of this. The stage may also include a final summing up by the teacher, with possible suggestions for future study so that the lesson may be linked to later ones.

The body of the lesson note may be further divided vertically into *content* on the left-hand side of the page and *method* on the right-hand side. By this arrangement, the student may now state clearly and concisely in the content column just *what* he is going to do, e.g. an itemized statement of the information he is to teach, the assignments to be undertaken, etc., taking care to sequence it as logically as possible. Depending upon the amount and nature of the subject matter, it may be further subdivided within the various sections where such a procedure assists its organization (e.g. *Stage 2, Presentation*, sub-stage (i), sub-stage (ii), sub-stage (iii), etc.).

In the method column, the student will indicate *how* he intends to teach the expressed content of his lesson. In some ways, this is the most difficult part of the lesson note to write if it is to have meaning and value for the student. He should, for example, avoid writing meaningless or unhelpful statements. A remark such as 'to arouse the children's interest in the topic' does not indicate the means whereby he is going to achieve this. Similarly, instead of writing 'ask the class questions' in the method column, he should specify at least a few of the questions he intends to ask.

The method column may further state how organizational features are to be implemented (individual work, group work or free activity, for example), how the blackboard is to be used (a prepared board or one built up as the lesson unfolds), how illustrative material is to be used, how notes are to be written (independently, with guidance or from dictation), details of assignments, evaluative techniques, and so on.

It is sometimes useful to follow the main sections of the lesson note (Introduction, Presentation, Application and Conclusion) with a short 'Notes' section. This may contain information and observations not easily categorized in other parts of the lesson note (e.g. anticipation of problems or difficulties, alternative courses of action at given points in the lesson, the possible need to abbreviate or amplify the material depending on the nature of the class or the time factor, and so on). The value of having a section of this kind lies in the fact that one can, as it were, rehearse aspects of the lesson in one's mind before its implementation (timing, organization, amount of material) and have thought out alternative plans that can be introduced on the spot.

If we now take these various sections and add a *heading* and a section for *lesson criticism*, the framework for our orthodox class lesson will appear as in Figure 2.

Two specimen lesson notes

We give overleaf two specimen lesson notes based on the class lesson plan outlined below. Conceived for a double period in Social Studies, they both cover broadly the same theme (see *The first step*, p. 52). In the first, however, the objective is formulated in non-behavioural terms, whereas in the second it is expressed behaviourally.

CONTENT	METHOD
Subject: *Date:* *Class:* *Number:* *Ability:* *Duration:* *Objective:* *Equipment:*	

CONTENT	METHOD

Stage 1: Introduction
 	
 Stage 2: Presentation
   Sub-stage (i)
   Sub-stage (ii)
   Sub-stage (iii), etc.
 	
 Stage 3: Application
 	
 Stage 4: Conclusion	

Notes: (where these are felt to be helpful)

Lesson criticism:

Figure 2 Possible lesson plan

Specimen Lesson Note 1

Subject:	Social Studies	*Date:*
Class:	3B	*Number:* 30 boys
Ability:	Homogeneous	*Duration:* 80 minutes
Objective:	To examine some aspects of satellite technology.	
Equipment:	Pictures of natural and artificial satellites; globe atlas and table tennis ball; information from magazines, books and articles provided by the children; work cards.	Pens and rulers; six pairs of scissors; sellotape; cylindrical cardboard containers; cardboard; cartridge paper; wire; prepared charts and diagrams to supplement blackboard work.

CONTENT	METHOD

Stage 1: Introduction

Stimulation of interest in the subject of satellite technology.	Interest will be aroused initially because the class had been previously informed of the nature of the lesson and asked to bring along pertinent information, e.g. articles, photographs, diagrams, on both natural and artificial satellites.
The definition of a natural satellite.	Having been asked to produce whatever information they've been able to collect, the class will be led into a discussion initiated by such questions as:
Examples of natural satellites will be given from our own solar system: Moon; Phobos and Deimos; those of Jupiter; of Saturn, Uranus and Neptune.	What is a natural satellite? Which one is best known to us? Which planet in the solar system has most satellites? What are the two satellites of Mars called?
Some points of interest concerning natural satellites will be raised. The Moon's influence on the Earth. Gravity. Orbits. Apogee and perigee.	In what ways is the Earth influenced by the Moon? What keeps a satellite in position? What word is used to describe the path of a satellite? What does an astronomer mean by the words 'apogee' and 'perigee'?
	The discussion, structured by these and related questions, will be supported by prepared diagrams, blackboard illustrations and a model of the Earth and Moon using a globe and a table tennis ball.
The notion of artificial satellites in general and artificial Earth satellites in particular will be introduced.	By means of further questions, the class will be led to consider artificial satellites and the advantages of being able to place them in orbit at will. The particular value of Earth satellites will be examined. The discussion will then lead naturally into the Presentation stage.

Stage 2: Presentation

Sub-stage (i)

Some points of historical interest will be noted:

The first country to put an artificial satellite into orbit.

The name of the satellite.

The month and year of this achievement.

The rivalry between the USSR and the USA and why the Russians were the first to launch a satellite.

In order to set the subject of the lesson in historical context, the circumstances leading up to and surrounding the launching of the first satellite will be briefly described to the class.

A short summary of these facts will be built up on the blackboard in the course of the description. Sputnik I's launching in October 1957 will be noted.

Sub-stage (ii)

Technological features of artificial Earth satellites will be reviewed. These will include reference to satellite design; components and their function; identification and naming of particular features (e.g. solar paddles, horizon scanner, sun sensor, antenna, TV camera); the variations in design and function; the launch vehicle; how satellites are put into orbit; and the choice of orbit.

At this point, narrative accounts of selected aspects of the technology of Earth satellites will be given. Using simplified diagrams and prepared charts, the design of one particular satellite will be described and the more important components identified and explained. The launch vehicle will be briefly described; and the method of putting a satellite into orbit will be explained with the aid of simple diagrams.

Sub-stage (iii)

The uses of artificial Earth satellites will be noted:

Communication satellites

Meteorological satellites

Navigational satellites

Earth resources satellites

Earth resources satellites will be examined in greater detail.

The uses of artificial Earth satellites will be explored by means of narration and questioning.

The stated and elicited information will be built up in a blackboard summary.

The kinds of data provided by Earth resources satellites will be studied in more depth and a summary of selected kinds of information will again be recorded on the blackboard as indicated in the box below. This will be supported by appropriate photographs, e.g. underwater features of the Great Bahama Banks photographed from space.

Blackboard summary

---

*Earth resources satellites provide
data on the following:*

Oceans and water

the state of the oceans	world water balance
sea beds	flood forecasting
coastlines	currents and temperature
coastal erosion	marine life
sea pollution	presence of fish
hydrological cycle	movement of fish

Stage 3: Application

Groups will be allotted the following allotted tasks.

To produce:

1 A wall chart showing examples of natural satellites in our solar system.
2 A simple model of an artificial satellite.
3 A wall diagram showing the principal components of an Earth satellite.
4 A chart depicting the uses of Earth satellites.
5 A poster listing the uses of an Earth resources satellite.
6 A frieze consisting of selected photos, cuttings, articles, drawings, cartoons, supplied by the class and arranged in approximate chronological sequence.

The boys will be organized into six groups averaging approximately five boys per group. The composition of the groups will be determined partly by interest. Group leaders will be appointed and the scheme will be explained to the whole class in outline. Group assignments will then be allocated and explained to the individual groups in more detail. Each group will be given a workcard which will break down the assignment into specific tasks for its individual members. The cards will also indicate where required equipment and materials may be found.

As an aid to motivation, the criteria by which the assignments will be evaluated will be explained.

As each group finishes its assignment, it will be instructed to display it at a specified point in the room and then allowed to read until the rest of the class has finished.

The teacher will move among the groups answering questions and giving unobtrusive advice and encouragement in order to sustain interest and motivation.

Stage 4: Conclusion

When all assignments have been completed, group leaders will explain briefly to the rest of the class their respective tasks.

Each group leader will be called upon in turn to take the class through his group's assignment stressing the chief points of interest.

Oral evaluation of assignments by the teacher.

Evaluation of the completed assignments will take the form of verbal assessments with particular reference to:

The competence of each group in carrying out the tasks making up the assignment as specified by the workcard.

Presentation of the assignment – execution, neatness, effectiveness, etc.

Evidence of individual effort and group co-operation in achieving the allotted tasks.

Concluding statement which will include a brief summary of the main points of the lesson, questions to the class, and a reference to the use of artificial satellites at other planets in the solar system and the kinds of data yielded by these so far.

The main points of the lesson will be revised using existing blackboard summaries. Final questioning of the class to consolidate the material and encourage some fluency in handling it.

The class will be further stimulated to thought in this field by reference to satellites sent to Mars, Venus and Jupiter, and the kinds of information received to date.

Notes

The amount of material detailed above is rather extensive and represents the maximum one could expect to cover in a double period with a lively and interested class. Depending on the nature of the class and how it responds, however, some abbreviations may have to be made. Should these prove necessary, sub-stage (ii) of the presentation stage will be curtailed and if a further cut is required, the evaluation of finished assignments will be deferred until the next Social Studies Lesson in two days' time. The lesson is one of a series on 'Aspects of the Twentieth Century' and a selection of the boys' assignments will ultimately form part of a more comprehensive display covering this topic.

Specimen Lesson Note 2

Subject:	Social Studies	*Date:*	
Class:	3B	*Number:*	30 boys
Ability:	Homogeneous	*Duration:*	80 minutes

Objective: At the end of the lesson, the class will be able:

   1 To explain what is meant by the word 'satellite' and distinguish between a natural and an artificial one.

   2 To identify and name the principal external features of a satellite.

   3 To explain the meanings of: gravity; orbit; eccentricity; apogee; perigee; tracking stations.

   4 To name *four* uses of artificial earth satellites.

   5 To comment briefly on the significance of any *four* of the following: Sputnik 1; Sputnik 2; Explorer 1; Vostok 1; Telstar 1; Molniya 1; Early Bird; ESSA 1.

   6 To state *one* discovery resulting from earth satellite technology.

Equipment: Pictures of natural and artificial satellites; globe atlas and table tennis ball; 31 copies of school atlas. Information from magazines, books and articles; prepared charts and diagrams to supplement blackboard work; 30 copies of test sheet.

CONTENT	METHOD

Stage 1: Introduction

CONTENT	METHOD
Introduction to the topic and stimulation of interest in the subject of satellites and satellite technology.	Interest will be aroused at the outset of the lesson by (1) outlining its purpose and what it is hoped the class will be able to do at the end of it; and (2) stressing the increasing relevance of satellite technology in our everyday lives.
The definition of a natural satellite.	Drawing upon the class's general knowledge and interests, a discussion will be initiated with such questions as:
Examples of natural satellites from our own solar system will be given: Moon; Phobos and Deimos; those of Jupiter; of Saturn, Uranus and Neptune.	What is a natural satellite? Which one is best known to us? What are the two satellites of Mars called?
Explanation of what is meant by the term 'artificial satellite'.	Having established what is meant by a natural satellite, the teacher will

lead the class to consider the meaning of the term 'artificial satellite' by questioning, narration and discussion. These techniques will be supported with prepared diagrams, blackboard illustrations, and a globe and table tennis ball which will be used to show the relationship between Earth and an artificial satellite.

Some terms used by scientists and astronomers in connection with both natural and artificial satellites will be explained to the class. These will include: gravity; orbit; eccentricity; apogee; perigee; and tracking stations.

With the aid of diagrams, blackboard illustrations and, in the case of the term 'tracking stations', school atlases, the terms will be explained. Opportunities will be given for the boys to ask questions and to contribute from their own general knowledge and interests to whatever is being said.

Stage 2: Presentation

Sub-stage (i)
Some technological features of artificial Earth satellites will be reviewed. These will include components and their function – horizon scanner, sun sensor, solar paddles, infra-red scanner, TV cameras, control sections and antennae. The variety of satellite design will be noted.

Narrative accounts of selected aspects of the technology of Earth satellites will be given. Using simplified diagrams and charts based on the design of the Nimbus meteorological satellite, the teacher will identify the more important components and explain their function.

Sub-stage (ii)
The uses of Earth satellites will be briefly covered. These will include the following areas: communication, meteorology, navigation, earth resources, military and research.

These uses will be explored by means of narration and questioning, and the stated and elicited information will be built up into a blackboard summary along the lines indicated in the box below.

Blackboard summary

> *The uses of artificial Earth satellites*
>
> Communication satellites
> Meteorological satellites
> Earth resources satellites
> Navigational satellites
> Research satellites
> Military uses of satellites

Sub-stage (iii)

A brief and selective review of developments in Earth satellite technology since 1957.

The review will include detailed and passing reference to some of the more significant and well-known names such as Sputnik 1, Sputnik 2 (with dog), Explorer 1, Explorer 6, Vostok 1, Telstar 1, Early Bird, Molniya 1, ESSA 1, Cosmos 186 and Cosmos 188.

The review will be chiefly by narration, though from time to time the boys' general knowledge will be drawn upon with such questions as:
What was significant about Sputnik 2?
Were any other animals used in satellites?
How can the use of animals in this kind of work be justified?
What was unique about Telstar 1?

Sub-stage (iv)

Some of the discoveries resulting from Earth satellite technology will be presented. These will include:

1 information on the Van Allen radiation belts;
2 Vanguard 1's probe yielding data on the shape of the Earth resulting in the 'pear-shaped' concept;
3 solar winds.

Reference will be made to discoveries which probes by satellites to other planets will reveal.

The importance of satellite technology in providing hitherto unknown information will be emphasized. That yielded so far will be narrated and its importance assessed. The class will be invited to speculate on what discoveries may be made on other planets.

Stage 3: Application

The knowledge and information that the class has acquired so far will be examined at this point by means of a short test sheet.

An opportunity will be provided here for the boys to ask questions, elaborate on what has been said and to contribute to the lesson from their own experience, knowledge and interests. After this, test sheets will be distributed and the class will be given simple instructions on how to proceed. The importance of clarity of expression and correct spelling will be stressed.

The blackboard will be cleaned and other aids removed.

Stage 4: Conclusion

The boys' answers will be marked in class and difficulties or misunderstandings cleared up. Individual marks will then be recorded.

The class will be given adequate time to complete the test. They will then be asked to exchange test sheets with each other. The correct answers will be given and the markers told what mark to assign to each question. The sheets will then be returned to their owners, difficulties dealt with orally and the marks noted.

Summing up.

The main points of the lesson will be briefly summarized; and reference will be made to events currently taking place in the sphere of satellite technology and to the possibilities in the future.

Notes

In the recent past, this class has proved to be very lively and responsive. These qualities have been revealed not least in the ease with which the boys assimilate and use the information given to them. It may therefore be necessary to amplify the material at given points in the lesson. If this proves to be so, sub-stage (ii) of the presentation stage (the uses of Earth satellites) will be examined more fully.

WORKSHEET

Earth Satellite Technology

Name: .... *Form:* ....

Attempt all the questions:

(1) What is the difference between a *natural* and an *artificial* satellite?

....

....

....

....

(2) Here is a simplified diagram based on a Nimbus meteorological satellite. Name the parts indicated by numbers in the spaces provided overleaf.

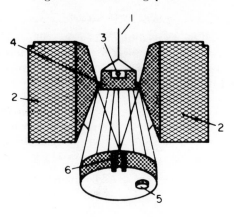

(1) ....

(2) ....

(3) ....

(4) ....

(5) ....

(6) ....

(3) Explain the following terms briefly:

Gravity: ....

....

....

Orbit: ....

....

....

Eccentricity: ....

....

....

Apogee: ....

....

....

Perigee: ....

....

....

Tracking stations: ....

....

....

(4) Name FOUR uses of artificial Earth satellites:

(i) ....

....

(ii) ....

....

(iii) ....

....

(iv) ....

....

(5) State ONE discovery resulting from Earth satellite technology:

....

....

....

....

Alternative lesson plans

Using the *learning phases/instructional events* model, we constructed a plan that would meet the needs of a traditional, orthodox class lesson. We followed this by giving two specimen lesson notes in Social Studies to show how lessons can be built up within this framework. You must remember, however, that neither the pattern arrived at nor the labels used (Presentation, Application, etc.) are fixed and rigid, but are determined by the lesson objective and the sequence of events leading up to it. The latter will be controlled by the particular phases of learning that the teacher wishes to use or select from the model. In order to show how different lesson plans requiring differing emphases may be derived from the model, we now give a few alternative outlines and briefly explain the significance of each.

A developmental lesson

A developmental lesson may be defined as a class lesson in which the emphasis is on developing new learning, making use of the previous knowledge of the children. Proceeding therefore from the known to the unknown, the teacher arranges the material in such a way that a child is able to understand the logic behind it. The chief problem is finding ways of linking the new material to the old; and the techniques of narration, questioning and explanation will figure prominently in overcoming it. One possible framework for a lesson of this nature is as follows:

Lesson note heading	
Content	*Method*
Stage 1: Introduction	
Stage 2: Development 　Sub-stage (i) 　Sub-stage (ii), etc.	
Stage 3: Continuation	

A lesson of this kind will make particular use of the *motivation, apprehending, acquisition* and *retention* phases from the model outlined earlier.

An appreciation lesson

An appreciation lesson in one or other of the arts is concerned as much with emotional reaction as with intellectual understanding. For children to get the most out of aesthetic experiences, two qualities need to be developed and encouraged – openness of mind and a willingness to explore. These features will dictate the broad features of a characteristic appreciation lesson for it will be more loosely structured and open-ended than other learning situations. The open-endedness arises from the fact that a child in this kind of lesson is presented with a new, original and unique stimulus (a poem, painting or piece of music, for instance) with which he must eventually establish his own relationship. The teacher therefore need not be too concerned to evaluate either the work of art or the children's responses. Nor need he be too anxious to achieve recall, or even retention, as his first task is to develop favourable and lasting attitudes to the subject in hand and to build up an acceptable system of aesthetic values. The emphasis of the lesson, therefore, will mainly be on the presentation and experiencing of the stimulus. In terms of the *learning phases/instructional events* model, the first two phases will figure most prominently, i.e. *motivation* and *apprehending*. A lesson note for an appreciation lesson, therefore, may be developed within the following structure:

Lesson note heading	
Content	*Method*
Stage 1: Introduction	
Stage 2: Presentation (with sub-stages as required)	
Stage 3: Continuation	

A reviewing lesson

Revising and reorganizing previous learning with a view to consolidation and greater understanding is the principal objective of a reviewing lesson. Such consolidation will be achieved by narration, questioning techniques, outlines, summaries, questionnaires, quizzes, multi-media approaches, written exercises, assignments and practical work. A lesson plan to meet these needs could be as follows:

Lesson note heading	
Content	*Method*
Stage 1: Introduction	
Stage 2: Consolidation Sub-stage (i) Sub-stage (ii), etc.	
Stage 3: Conclusion	

A reviewing lesson will, by definition, highlight the *recall, generalization* and *performance* phases of the model.

A skill lesson

There are many skills that have to be acquired and practised in the classroom or school context; consequently the plan of a skill lesson may take one of a number of forms. One of the factors determining the framework of the lesson will be whether the particular skill is a simple one or whether, being complex, it has to be broken down into its components. Another factor to be born in mind is that practice of the skill should come soon after its demonstration. Whatever the skill, and whether simple or complex, it will be the *performance* and *feedback* phases from the original model that will play an important part. Two alternative outlines are provided – the first for relatively simple skills, and the second for complex ones that require analysis into simple units.

Lesson note heading	
Content	*Method*
Stage 1: Introduction	
Stage 2: Demonstration Sub-stage (i) Sub-stage (ii), etc.	
Stage 3: Application	

Lesson note heading	
Content	*Method*
Stage 1: Introduction	

Stage 2: Presentation
 Sub-stage (i) Demonstration
                  Application
 Sub-stage (ii) Demonstration
                  Application
 Sub-stage (iii) Demonstration
                  Application, etc.	

A lesson involving pupil activities

Some class lessons involve a considerable amount of activity on the part of the pupils, so much in fact that the student may find it helpful to build it into the actual lesson note. To meet this need, the class lesson suggested earlier may be modified as follows:

Lesson note heading		
Content	*Method*	
Stage 1: Introduction		
Stage 2: Presentation		
Stage 3: Application	*Pupil*	
Teacher		
Sub-stage (i)		
Sub-stage (ii), etc.		
Stage 4: Conclusion		

A physical education lesson

A physical education lesson plan may take one of a number of forms. One such arrangement is as follows:

Lesson note heading		
Activities	*Organization*	*Teaching points*
(1)		
(2)		
(3) etc.		

A plan of this kind may be further subdivided horizontally and each section labelled depending upon what is to be included in the lesson, e.g. floorwork, apparatus, games, movement.

Group work

Again, there is quite a lot of variation in the way group activities are organized and recorded (e.g. vertical grouping, mixed ability grouping). One arrangement for planning learning activities is as follows:

THEME:

Organizational factors:

Group 1:	Objective		Group 2:	Objective
	Content			Content
	Method			Method
	Equipment			Equipment
	Evaluation			Evaluation

etc.

An integrated day

The following pattern is a possible way of recording work in a school operating an integrated day system:

(1) *Work for... day:*

Maths	Objective:	Art	Objective:
	content/method		content/method
	organization		organization
	equipment		equipment
English	Objective:	Project	Objective:
	content/method		content/method
	organization		organization
	equipment		equipment

(2) *Work matrix*

	Maths	*English*	*Art*	*Project*
a.m. 1st half	Group 1	Group 2	Group 3	Group 4
2nd half	Group 2	Group 1	Group 4	Group 3
p.m. 1st half	Group 3	Group 4	Group 1	Group 2
2nd half	Group 4	Group 3	Group 2	Group 1

(3) *Evaluative procedures*

Topics/projects/themes

The setting out of topic, project and theme work will vary according to such factors as the amount of time to be devoted to it, organizational factors and so on. Below, we give one plan which may be modified to meet most needs.

Objective:
Content:
Organization:
Equipment:
Methods of evaluation:

Lesson 1, Introduction: 1 Discussion of topic (project, theme) and related sub-topics.
2 Organization of topic (groups, leaders, allocation of sub-topics, organization of materials and equipment, time factor, how the finished work is to be presented and evaluated).
3 Introductory presentation.

Lesson 2, Development: Individual group work initiated. This may be set out with the matrix method, viz.

Theme					
Sub-theme	1	2	3	4	5
Group	1	2	3	4	5

Lesson 3, Conclusion: Presentation of work.
Evaluation according to specified criteria.

The completed topic, project or theme will have moved through the whole sequence of learning phases, beginning with *motivation* and concluding with *feedback*.

A composite lesson plan

Sometimes the presentation of two aspects of a subject within the confines of one lesson demand that two differing lesson notes have to be compounded. For example, a music teacher who only sees a particular class once a week may decide to devote the first half of a lesson to practical work (singing, say) and the second half to musical appreciation. An arrangement of this kind could be accommodated with the following lesson plan:

Lesson note heading	
Objective 1:	

Content	*Method*
Stage 1 Introduction	
Stage 2 Presentation	
Stage 3 Application	

Objective 2:	

Content	*Method*
Stage 1 Introduction	
Stage 2 Presentation	
Stage 3 Continuation	

Lesson plans – some related issues

So far in our consideration of lesson plans we have not mentioned the *time factor*. Not only must the instructional events of a lesson lead to the achievement of the objective, they must also fit into the time available.

Although the timing of your lessons will eventually become instinctive with experience and practice, in the early stages you will have to take the time factor seriously and gauge just how much you will need. One way of doing this is to begin by apportioning a time allocation to each of the lesson's sections as a notional guide (for instance, a forty-five-minute lesson could have a five-minute introduction, fifteen minutes for presentation, twenty minutes for application and a five-minute conclusion). Then visualize the setting for the lesson – the room, the children, the equipment needed and how it will be used, movement about the room, organizational factors and so on. Finally, mentally rehearse the lesson against this background in such a way that the whole conception is over quickly. In this way you will get the feel of the lesson's rhythm and will get into the habit of thinking of the content and method in relation to quanta of time so that eventually they will become inseparable.

It is important to distinguish in this connection between the prescribed and actual length of a lesson. There is sometimes a discrepancy between them – especially in secondary schools where classes have to move from room to room. In these circumstances, a prescribed forty-minute lesson can easily be cut to thirty-five minutes. When one realizes, while teaching, that a lesson is going to be shorter than anticipated, a quick adjustment must be made to the timing of events. If the lesson is an orthodox class lesson, for example, the application stage can be shortened without much difficulty.

One of the fears of beginning teachers is running out of material before the end of a lesson or of a lesson ending prematurely. What should you do in this situation? One way is to have a certain amount of material 'up your sleeve' that you can draw upon for 'fillers'. Marland[27] gives some useful examples of what a 'filler' may consist of:

> This can be based on old material from your subject presented in the form of question-and-answer, or a game, one side of the class against the other. It can be based on puzzles derived from your subject, or from words which are part of your subject. This is an excellent moment for a brief reading of a poem, incident or description that you know well and which in some way links with the class's interest. ... This is even a time when some aspect of school routine, future planning or class business can be introduced.

One final point. Having planned your lesson and taken all the numerous factors into consideration, do you have to stick rigidly to it? The answer is simple: of course not. The reason is that although you may have prepared your lesson note as thoroughly as possible, there will still be unpredictable happenings that determine the need for some modification of your plans. Perhaps the most important single factor likely to cause change will be the response of the class. If an activity is going well, you may decide to prolong it; if badly, there may be a case for cutting it short. Alternatively, a completely spontaneous happening in the lesson may determine a course quite different from the one you had planned. Be flexible, but stop well short of the kind of situation where events regularly control you.

Self-appraisals

Student teachers on teaching practice are normally required to review lessons they have taught in the course of a day and write a criticism of them. Some colleges insist that such a comment or criticism be written for *every* lesson taught. This would seem excessive and self-defeating, resulting in a rather empty and meaningless routine. It would be better for the student to select *one* lesson each day which he felt would best lend itself to close scrutiny and from which he could derive benefit. As regards the actual business of self-criticism, the reader is recommended to read the suggestions made on observation lessons in Part III (p. 106) as the principles outlined there will be of some relevance to him in the present task. He is also reminded that subjectivity is likely to be at its greatest when commenting on his own performance, particularly when he does so without any clear guidelines to go by.

Lesson criticisms may take one of three forms.

They may take the form of a *continuous report* expressing one's retrospective explanation and interpretation of the lesson in general terms. The report would then consider such factors as how far or to what extent the lesson objective had been achieved; the appropriateness of the subject matter of the lesson in relation to the age and ability of the children; the effectiveness of the teaching and learning methods; management and control; and perhaps some reference to the student's increasing awareness of the problems of teaching and learning.

Or they may be in the form of a *headed report* in which the student teacher selects particular aspects of the lesson that he wishes to highlight and then writes rather more specifically under each heading (he may use headings like *introduction to the lesson, control and management, organizational factors, questioning techniques, motivational factors, relationships*, etc.)

Alternatively, they may take a rather more *objective format* in the shape of a prepared schedule which permits a degree of quantification. The advantages of this kind of self-appraisal are that it is quicker to complete, more dispassionate and enables different lessons to be evaluated on a comparative basis. Thus, responding to a double art lesson with 3C every Thursday afternoon over a period of, say, six weeks allows one to

Box 15

	Self-appraisal schedule	
1 My attempts to motivate the class at the outset of the lesson were effective	:—:—:—:—:—:	My attempts to motivate the class at the outset of the lesson were ineffective
2 I had no discipline problems	:—:—:—:—:—:	I had too many discipline problems
3 I created a relaxed atmosphere	:—:—:—:—:—:	I created a tense atmosphere
4 I was satisfied with my questioning techniques	:—:—:—:—:—:	I was not satisfied with my questioning techniques
5 The class enjoyed the lesson	:—:—:—:—:—:	The class did not enjoy the lesson

record improvement or otherwise along particular dimensions (e.g. organization), thus establishing a comparative basis of criticism.

One way of devising a suitable schedule is to select a number of relevant contrasting phrases and have either a five-point or seven-point scale between each pair. The student then ticks the point he judges appropriate for a particular lesson. The selection of contrasting statements in Box 15 illustrates the principle.

The approach the student teacher adopts will, of course, depend on the nature of the lesson, its content, the teaching strategy he uses and the objectives he sets himself. But again, we encourage him to experiment with different ways in order to assess the relative strengths and weaknesses of each.

Organizing one's lesson note file

It is desirable that lesson notes and other relevant data be organized systematically in a hardbacked file with guide cards to indicate classes, groups, schemes of work, subject area and lesson notes. Impressionable tutors and external examiners take note of such organization. The content of the file may take the following format:

A *Title page*: this could provide the following information:
    (i) Date of the practice
    (ii) Name of the student teacher
    (iii) Name of the school, its address and telephone number
    (iv) Name of the headteacher
    (v) Name of the class teacher (if appropriate)
    (vi) Name of one's supervising tutor
B *Page 2* and following: details of the class(es) to be taught:
    (i) Number in the class
    (ii) Its composition, i.e. boys, girls, mixed
    (iii) Age ranges and grade(s) of ability (if appropriate)
    (iv) Names of the children
    (v) A seating plan
C A plan of the school
D The student teacher's copy of his own timetable
E Subject or class sections: schemes of work should precede lesson notes which should follow in chronological order
F Any further data required by either the college or the student himself (e.g. notes and information on the children, details of learning aids, examples of exercises, workcards, blackboard summaries, etc.)

A note on graded workcards and worksheets

Accompanying our second specimen lesson note earlier in this section on preparation and planning was a worksheet designed for pupils of similar ability, a streamed class in other words. Complementary to this kind of workcard or worksheet is the *graded* workcard or *graded* worksheet which can be used with mixed ability groups. As such these will allow the teacher to take into consideration the differential abilities and skills of pupils in such groupings. If the cards and sheets are to be successful in testing mixed ability groups, then the connection between their format and content and their respective lesson objectives for each of the groups must be drawn explicitly. It may be helpful initially for the student to have in front of him or her the differentiating objectives when composing the workcards or sheets until he or she has an intuitive grasp of the skills involved.

Broadly, there are two kinds of workcard or worksheet. First, there is the single worksheet or card that all pupils will receive but on which the questions are graded from the easy to the difficult, to cater for the composite nature of the class. Second, there is the form where two or more worksheets or cards are produced by the teacher on the same topic. Here, each will reflect a different level of difficulty corresponding to the broadly different levels of ability in the class – one worksheet for pupils of below average ability, another for those of average ability, and yet another possibly for the above average pupils. In designing worksheets or cards for mixed ability situations, it is helpful to bear in mind a number of guidelines or characteristics that enable such differentiation to be achieved. By way of example, we refer here to five possibilities – layout and presentation, choice and use of language, content, skills involved and testing techniques.

Layout and presentation

The layout and presentation of one's worksheets is important whatever the ability of the child. However, these features are especially important with pupils of below average ability. With such pupils it behoves one to take particular care with presentation and make the worksheet as visually attractive as possible. Space your questions and material well and use diagrams and pictures freely. By allowing the worksheet to breathe in this way you make the tasks for the less able a bit less daunting. It is also useful if you can use different colours. Providing opportunities for the less able to answer on the sheet itself (as opposed to an exercise book or another piece of paper) is also desirable: they provide the pupil with an immediate sense of achievement.

With the average and above average pupils there may be less need for diagrams and pictures to compensate for the increase in verbal information that will be needed. Where diagrams and pictures are used, they can be that bit more demanding than with the less able pupils. Whatever the child's ability, avoid the temptation to crowd too much material into a worksheet.

Choice and use of language

This is perhaps the most important feature to bear in mind where one is catering for differential abilities. For the less able, simplicity must be the keynote. Whatever information you wish to convey on your worksheet – written passages, questions or instructions – use simple grammatical constructions, a subject and a predicate, for example. Complex sentences involving subordinate clauses introduced by words like *but*, *if* and *although* should be avoided. Likewise, use short, commonly-used and easily-understood words. When you use words that may not be understood, as with technical or subject-specific language, give the meaning in brackets or in a footnote.

With average and above average pupils, simplicity and clarity are still important criteria, though one can allow a little more latitude and be more challenging with respect to sentence construction and choice of words. Longer passages and longer sentences with subordinate clauses can be introduced. You can also test and extend vocabulary by introducing longer words. Where unfamiliar words are used, give the meaning.

Whatever the ability, take particular care with written instructions. Strive at all times for simplicity and clarity.

Content

Worksheets for the less able will concern themselves in the main with factual and basic information directly stemming from or related to the topic. The emphasis will thus tend to be on the immediate, the particular and the concrete as opposed to the removed, the general and the abstract. The nature of the ability of such pupils may dictate that one way of arranging and sequencing the content is preferable to another.

With pupils of average and above average ability, you need not be quite so circumscribed in your approach to content. Assumptions can be made with greater confidence about background knowledge, previous learning or ability to seek out information required for completion of the set tasks. Again, care needs to be given to arrangement and sequencing.

Skills involved

The skills required of pupils of below average ability will tend to be of a simple order. The ability, for example, to read and understand, to perform simple tasks related to the topic, to identify and label, to tease out information from one part of the worksheet and transfer it to a diagram – such would be appropriate at this level of ability. Where analytical skills are introduced, they should be kept very simple. Tasks involving synthesis, inference or evaluation should be avoided.

With average and above average pupils one can make more demands on them in these respects. Greater demands on their reading and comprehension skills would seem appropriate, along with opportunities for analysis, synthesis, the making of inferences and evaluation. The ability to go beyond the worksheet and use reference material (books, libraries, catalogues, for instance) can also be tested. For some topics, the ability to distinguish between fact and opinion, and possibly to extrapolate from data provided on the sheet, might also be encouraged among the brighter pupils.

Testing techniques

Remember that there are numerous ways of gathering information from pupils. Do not restrict yourself to the basic question, valuable as it is. Structured questions are particularly useful with less able pupils, whereas unstructured or open-ended ones are of great value if you are testing brighter pupils' skills in divergent thinking, for example. Then there are a number of objective tests that can give variety to one's worksheets and at the same time meet the needs of different abilities – tests of recall, sentence completion, true–false items, matching pairs and multiple choice. For further details on these matters, read the appropriate section, pages 248–52.

Notes and references

1 Leeds Institute of Education (1974) *Teacher Education.* Windsor: NFER.
2 Jeffcoate, R. (1976) Curriculum planning in multiracial education. *Educational Research*, 18 (3), 192–200.
3 Shipman, M.D. (1972) Contrasting views of a curriculum project. *Journal of Curriculum Studies*, November.
4 Taba, H. (1962) *Curriculum Development: Theory and Practice.* New York: Harcourt, Brace and World.
5 Hargreaves, D.H., Hestor, S.K. and Mellor, F.J. (1975) *Deviance in Classrooms.* London: Routledge and Kegan Paul.
6 Davis, I.K. (1976) *Objectives in Curriculum Design.* New York: McGraw Hill.

7 Haysom, J. and Sutton, C. (1974) *Theory into Practice*. Maidenhead: McGraw-Hill.

8 Wheeler, D.K. (1967) *The Curriculum Process*. London: University of London Press.

9 Ashton, P., Kneen, P. and Davies, F. (1975) *Aims into Practice in the Primary School*. London: University of London Press.

10 Hirst, P.H. (1974) *Knowledge and the Curriculum*. London: Routledge and Kegan Paul.

11 Rowntree, D. (1974) *Educational Technology in Curriculum Development*. New York: Harper and Row.

12 Gerlach, V.S. and Ely, D.P. (1971) *Teaching and Media: A Systematic Approach*. Englewood Cliffs, New Jersey: Prentice-Hall.

13 Gronlund, N.E. (1970) *Stating Behavioral Objectives for Classroom Instruction*. New York: Macmillan.
Vargas, J.S. (1972) *Writing Worthwhile Behavioral Objectives*. New York: Harper and Row.
MacDonald-Ross, M. (1973) Behavioural objectives – a critical review. *Instructional Science*, 2, 1–51.
Mager, R.F. (1975) *Preparing Instructional Objectives*. San Francisco: Fearon.

14 Note: the original painting is in the Tate Gallery, London. A colour reproduction may be found in Bullock, A. (ed.), (1971) *The Twentieth Century*, plate 80, page 228. London: Thames and Hudson.

15 Tyler, R.W. (1973) *Basic Principles of Curriculum and Instruction*. Chicago: University of Chicago Press.

16 Shulman, L.S. and Keislar, E.R. (eds) (1966) *Learning by Discovery*. Chicago: Rand McNally.

17 Saylor, J.G. and Alexander, W.M. (1974) *Planning Curriculum for Schools*. New York: Holt, Rinehart and Winston.

18 Note: photographs of the house may be found in Scully Jr., V. (1960) *Frank Lloyd Wright* London: Mayflower. A colour photograph can be seen in Raeburn, M. (1973) *An Outline of World Architecture*, p. 116. London: Octopus Books.

19 Peters, R.S. (1966) *Ethics and Education*. London: Routledge and Kegan Paul.

20 MacDonald-Ross, M. (1973) Behavioural objectives – a critical review. *Instructional Science*, 2, 1–51.

21 Kibler, R.J., Cegala, D.J., Barker, L.L. and Miles, D.T. (1974) *Objectives for Instruction and Evaluation*. Boston: Allyn and Bacon.
Nicholls, H. and Nicholls, A. (1975) *Creative Teaching*. London: Allen and Unwin.
Davis, I.K. (1976) *Objectives in Curriculum Design*. Maidenhead: McGraw-Hill.

22 Gagné, R.M. and Briggs, L.J. (1974) *Principles of Instructional Design*. New York: Holt, Rinehart and Winston.

23 Mager, R.F. (1968) *Developing Attitudes toward Learning*. Belmont, California: Lear Siegler/Fearon.

24 Briggs, L.J. (1970) *Handbook of Procedures for the Design of Instruction.* Pittsburgh, Pa.: American Institutes for Research.
25 Gagné, R.M. (1974) *Essentials of Learning for Instruction.* Illinois: University of Illinois Press.
26 Brown, G.A. (1975) *Microteaching.* London: Methuen.
27 Marland, M. (1975) *The Craft of the Classroom.* London: Heinemann Educational.

PART III
Practising teaching

INTRODUCTION

Readers will recall that we began our *Guide to Teaching Practice* with a review of some of the changes currently taking place in education in Britain, changes that we believe have important implications for those entering teaching in the 1980s. We place these shifts in educational provision and control within a broad context of social and economic changes, identifying *inter alia* (1) the disappearance of traditional industries and their replacement by new technologies demanding different literacy and numeracy skills, (2) the changing nature of our society brought about by immigration, and (3) the pressing problems of permanent unemployment and its effect on young school-leavers.

Part III, *Practising teaching*, follows the pattern of our introductory chapter by focusing first on specific aspects of classroom management brought about by changes in the overall organization of secondary schooling. We then go on to look at related issues such as multicultural education, the development of curricula for children with learning difficulties, and the centrally important question of language in education. We also discuss the topics of classroom management and control, the classroom environment and situational factors, and finally, the place of extra-curricular activities in the life of the school.

One of the changes in the organization of the English education system that we refer to in Part I is the development of a comprehensive system of secondary schools whose purported aim is to offer a more egalitarian education by creating a greater mix of children from different social backgrounds and different levels of intellectual ability.

At the level of classroom organization and planning, one direct consequence of comprehensivization is mixed ability teaching. It is to this that we now turn.

MIXED ABILITY TEACHING

So many books and articles have been written about organizing mixed ability groups in schools and so many definitions of the term 'mixed ability' are now bandied about that it is quite impossible to discuss the topic of mixed ability teaching without bearing in mind that the term has different meanings for different people. It can be argued,[1] of course, that all teaching in school is mixed ability teaching since the moment a teacher has responsibility for teaching more than one child at a time, he or she is faced with the problem of planning worthwhile learning experiences for groups of children which take account of individual differences within the group. This does not get us very far, however, for as student teachers discover in their contacts with schools, there are teachers who appear to ignore or discount the manifest differences among the children they teach.

There is an important difference[2] between *teaching in mixed ability groups* and *mixed ability teaching* which we ought to get straight from the outset.

Mixed ability teaching implies a *certain kind of teaching* whereas any kind of teaching can, and does, go on in mixed ability groups. Elliott,[2] who makes this important distinction, identifies *mixed ability teaching* as occurring when a teacher attempts to regulate his treatment of individual differences by the principle of equality. For example, when a teacher adopts a teaching-to-the-whole-class approach (see Example 1 below) in a mixed ability situation he fails to regulate his teaching by the idea of equality because his teaching style assumes that individual differences do not exist.

In the sections that follow we review some of the more widely practised teaching strategies and learning styles that student teachers are likely to encounter during teaching practice. We begin with a formal, traditional approach, and lead on eventually to accounts of mixed ability teaching strategies.

Each of our presentations of classroom learning situations is accompanied by an extended definition where appropriate and by an outline of the important characteristics and the strengths and weaknesses of a particular approach, the intention being to help student teachers coming into contact with a particular methodology for the first time.

It is important to stress that in connection with the various teaching strategies we are presenting broad reviews. We do not take account of regional variations with respect to the interpretation (or assumption) of underlying philosophies, organization and administration of attendant practices, or even nomenclature. Nor, for the same reason, do we draw too fine a distinction between what is done with different ages of pupils.

Social structure and interaction in learning situations

There are a number of forms of interaction between teacher and pupils and among pupils themselves which may be found in school learning situations. The particular one operating at any given moment will depend upon the objective of the lesson, the nature of the task in hand and the implied educational philosophy. We now consider six characteristic learning situations which account for the principal patterns of interaction, both formal and informal, which may be found in the context of the school. Our analysis is based upon the work of Oeser.[3]

Situation 1: the teacher-centred lesson

The principle of interaction underlying the teacher-centred situation may be illustrated as in Example 1. Although only five pupils are represented in the diagram, this figure may vary, with perhaps a notional thirty pupils being a more representative number in this kind of situation.

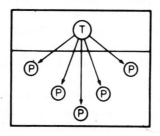

Example 1

The interaction pattern here is one in which the *teacher speaks and the pupils listen*. As Oeser notes, their relationship to him is confined to listening, perceiving and assimilating; and there is no interaction among the pupils themselves.

A social structure of this kind is found in its pure form in a radio or television broadcast. In a school context, it is found in the *talk* or *lecture* where there is a sharp distinction between the teacher and the class (depicted in the diagram by a continuous horizontal line), and in which the teacher's role is authoritarian, exhortatory and directive. This kind of interaction style may also form *part* of a class lesson as, for instance, at the outset when the teacher introduces new learning, or in the course of a lesson when he demonstrates a skill, or towards the end of a lesson when he sums up what has gone before. Preparation for a formal examination would present occasions when the teacher-centred approach would be an efficient means of teaching and learning.

Situation 2: the lecture-discussion

The second situation may be seen as a variant of the first, being one in which the pattern of interaction is not wholly dominated by the teacher.

It is represented diagrammatically in Example 2. Again, the number of pupils may vary, depending upon the circumstances.

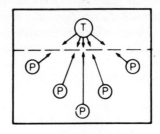

Example 2

Oeser points out that three of the most important aims of the educator are: to turn the latent leadership of a group in the direction of the educational process; to encourage the individual development of leadership; and to encourage co-operative striving towards common goals while discouraging the exercise of authoritarian leadership. The social structures evolving through situations 2, 3, 4 and 5 provide a framework for the achievement of these aims.

The arrowheads in the diagram indicate more or less continuous verbal interaction between teacher and pupils. Although as leader the teacher asks questions, and receives and gives answers, the initiative need not always be his; and competition may develop among the pupils. The sharp distinction between teacher and taught which was an important feature of the first situation and which was represented in Example 1 by means of a continuous horizontal line is now less obvious – hence the broken horizontal line in Example 2.

This kind of learning situation, the pattern of interaction depicted in Example 1, could develop into the pattern illustrated in Example 2.

Situation 3: active learning

Example 3 depicts a social situation in which the teacher allows discussion and mutual help between pupils.

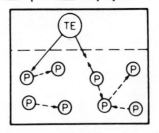

Example 3

Practical work in a science lesson would be an occasion for this kind of situation. The letters TE in the diagram indicate that the teacher now begins to assume the additional role of expert. As Oeser notes: 'He, of course, retains his other roles as well; but the emphasis in the teaching process now fluctuates between the needs established by the task and the needs of the individual pupils.' For this reason, the situation may be described as *task-* and *pupil-centred* and as one beginning to have a co-operative structure.

Situation 4: active learning; independent planning

Scrutiny of Example 4 shows how this fourth situation evolves logically from the preceding one. The pupils are now active in small groups, and the teacher acts more or less exclusively as an expert-consultant (indicated in the diagram by a wavy line).

As Oeser says: 'Groups map out their work, adapt to each other's pace, discuss their difficulties and agree on solutions. There is independent exploration, active learning and a maximal development of a task-directed leadership in each group.' The social climate is co-operative and the situation may be described as *pupil-* and *task-centred*.

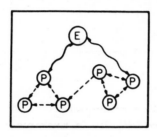

Example 4

Situation 5: group task-centred

A characteristic situation in which a smallish group of individuals is concerned with a particular topic, project or problem, is illustrated in Example 5.

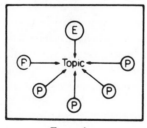

Example 5

A pattern of this kind may thus be found in a seminar or discussion session. The arrowheads indicate that the group as a whole is concerned with the task – its elucidation, clarification and solution.

The situation is clearly a *task-centred* ore in which there is an absence of hierarchical structure. Ideally, the role of the teacher here is simply that of a wise and experienced member of the group (depicted as 'expert' in the diagram). The more coercive roles traditionally associated with the teacher are out of place in this kind of social structure. The attitudes of members of the group to each other will tend to be co-operative and consultative.

Situation 6: independent working; no interaction

This final situation, illustrated in Example 6, arises when pupils are working quite independently and there is no interaction.

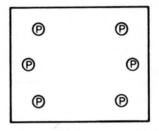

Example 6

This situation will occur when pupils are working at exercises 'on their own', or in a formal examination session.

In summary, Oeser observes that from situations 1 to 4 there is a progressive change from teacher-centred through task-centred to pupil-centred activities, from passive to active learning and from minimal to maximal participation, with a progressive diminution of the coerciveness of the teacher's roles. In situation 5, the situation is again task-centred, but the teacher's status as such has disappeared.

The six situations outlined above will help the reader not only to understand classroom-based social and learning situations, but also patterns of interaction occurring outside the classroom.

It is of great importance that the student teacher be aware of the sort of situation he wants in a lesson, or at a particular point in it. This will be chiefly determined by his lesson objective together with the kinds of factors isolated by Oeser which will contribute to defining the overall situation. These include: (1) high–low teacher dominance; (2) large–small number of pupils; (3) high–low academic level of class; (4)

active–passive pupil participation; (5) individual–co-operative effort; (6) contentious–non-contentious material; (7) strong–weak needs; (8) task and learning oriented–examination oriented; and (9) directing–helping (counselling).

Teaching strategies in mixed ability groups*

Having presented a broad outline of teaching strategies, we turn now to consider the question of mixed ability teaching in more detail.

It is axiomatic that the adoption of mixed ability grouping requires the teacher to employ methods and means of class management that are compatible with it. Using methods that depend for their success upon a more or less homogeneous range of ability invites difficulty and failure.

Much of the time spent teaching mixed ability classes will be devoted to individual and small group work. The advantage of individualized learning in this context is that each child is able to work at a pace best suited to his needs and ability. He is therefore not stretched beyond his capabilities, nor prevented from fully realizing his potential in a particular direction. One of the most efficient means of achieving individualized learning is through preparing individual programmes for the children concerned. This is especially the case in certain basic subjects like mathematics. The implications of this approach for the student teacher are twofold: (1) a high work load, particularly *before* a lesson; and (2) a considerable amount of record-keeping. Using Oeser's notation we can diagram *individualized learning* in mixed ability groups as in Example 7.

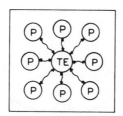

Example 7

The use of *themes* caters for individual and small group needs, especially among older children. A theme in this context may be seen as

* This section draws on material from Cohen, L. and Manion, L. (1981) *Perspectives on Classrooms and Schools*. Eastbourne: Holt, Rinehart and Winston. Chapter 7.

a central idea (e.g. animals, fire, witches and spells) used as a starting point for learning and one which will engage the children's interests. The main advantage of the theme approach is that it offers a framework within which to operate yet at the same time a considerable degree of freedom to both the children and teacher.

The successful outcome of a theme approach depends very much on the right choice of theme at the outset. It should be neither too narrow in scope nor too general; and sub-topics subsumed under the theme must have coherence arising from their logical interrelationships.

The factors that need to be borne in mind when choosing a theme include the ages, interests, aptitudes and abilities of the pupils involved in the enterprise. We suggest, too, that the student finds out in advance which children are slow learners, poor readers or potentially disruptive. Another fact that must not be overlooked is the competence of the student himself. He should not select a theme outside his own limitations, nor one that will demand more time in preparation than he is able or willing to give. Yet another factor concerns the objectives the student has in mind. These must be carefully specified to ensure the successful organization of the undertaking.

Once a theme has been chosen, the next decision concerns whether all the children will work on the same things and engage in the same activities, or whether they will be allowed to choose their own sub-topic from the theme and devote their attention to that. The decision will be influenced by the teacher's objectives, but most likely he will want to make use of one or other of two techniques: the *circus approach* and the *selective approach*. With the former, a pupil will work at each of the sub-topics embraced by the theme in sequence; with the latter, he will select one or two sub-topics and give his attention exclusively to these.

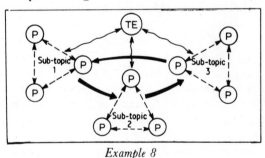

Example 8

Again, using Oeser's notation, the *circus approach* to a theme in small group work can be diagrammed as in Example 8. The thick shaded arrows show that each small group engages in each of the sub-topics of the theme.

The *selective approach* to a theme in small group work can be represented as in Example 9.

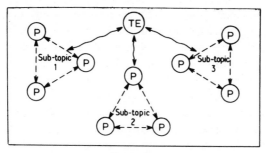

Example 9

A theme can be initiated by means of a lead lesson, for this is one of the more successful ways of arousing interest. A second means of stimulating interest, if pertinent to the chosen theme, is to visit places in the locality having bearing on the work to be explored – a museum or television studio, for example. To make the most of a visit of this kind, the teacher must plan and prepare carefully so he can bring as much as possible to the attention of his pupils. A third means of capturing interest would be to surround the children with examples, materials and resources relevant to the theme and suggest what they might possibly do with them. This approach has proved especially useful with primary children.

The organization of the theme approach can be particularly daunting for student teachers. No matter how much the children's interest has been aroused, it will be to little avail if the organization is faulty and does not permit the theme's thorough implementation. This can only be achieved by careful preparation and planning.

Once matters are underway, the teacher's main task is to keep a careful watch on the progress of each pupil. This will mean checking that he has adequate materials and resources, striving to maintain the original motivational level and suggesting ways in which an individual child's efforts may develop. If the work of the class is to be an educational experience, the teacher will find that he has to work just as hard as he would in a more traditional lesson.

One final point arises with subjects which at first glance do not appear to lend themselves to the theme approach. Languages, mathematics and science, for example, generally require a 'linear' approach, that is, knowledge in these areas has to be developed step by step and cannot easily be approached obliquely from a child's own interests. Where this is the case, provision is usually made in the timetable for either formal teaching or individualized work. However, a change of objectives even with subjects of this nature very often discloses potential for a theme approach.

Let us summarize some of the points we have been discussing concerning the organization of group work in mixed ability classes. Box 16 identifies some of the organizational skills that make for successful teaching in mixed ability groups.

Box 16

Skills needed for mixed ability group work

1 *Decide beforehand* how your group will be made up: self-selected, or selected by you, and if so on what criteria?
2 *Decide if your groups will be static* or regrouped for different activities.
3 *Have the lesson carefully prepared* and everything ready beforehand.
4 *Ensure that each group* has appropriate *subject material* and activities.
5 *Go round from group to group quickly.* Make sure you are still visible by, and still watching, other groups.
6 Do not forget to *look behind you* as you go round.
7 *Be prepared for early finishers* and have things ready for them to do.
8 *Watch for signs* that pupils are unoccupied – unnecessary movement and too much chat, incipient rowdiness.
9 Have a good way of *ending the lesson.*

Source: adapted from Kerry and Sands[4]

Slow learners and bright pupils in mixed ability classes

The various definitions[5] of mixed ability organization in the literature share one thing in common and that is their recognition that mixed ability classes contain a span of ability ranging from significantly below to significantly above the average.

Arguably, it is at the extremes of the ability range where children have most need of individual attention. For student teachers, it is absolutely vital that they should plan for the bright and the slow in planning their teaching programmes. Kerry and Sands[4] identify some *common problems* which experienced teachers face when dealing with slow learners and bright pupils in mixed ability classes. They are to do with:

Dead time This is the time between a pupil finishing one activity and starting another. Bright pupils complete work quickly because tasks are often too easy for them. Slower pupils can often manage only a sentence or two, and then they feel they have exhausted the topic.

Boredom   This may result from spending too much time waiting for the teacher to correct work, approve progress to the next step or take remedial action.

Lack of motivation   Children who are often unoccupied and bored can easily lose interest.

Disruption   The creative mind continually seeks new diversions. The less able may simply be looking for something more relevant to do! The bored pupil is always a potential trouble-maker.

Provision of special work   The previous four problems imply that the teacher must of necessity provide special work for pupils at both ends of the ability spectrum.

Increased preparation time by the teacher   Implicitly, providing special work means spending more time in preparing lessons.

Linguistic and cognitive levels of worksheets and texts   One perennial problem of mixed ability classes is that teachers tend to 'teach to the middle'. Part of the 'special provision' for exceptional pupils is to cater for bright pupils who need to be stretched intellectually and to cope with slow learners for whom the language of text or instructions may not be clear.

Emotional and pastoral problems   Finally, both sets of pupils may (but not necessarily) have problems of a social nature, e.g. concerning peer-group relations. Bright pupils are sometimes rejected as 'teacher's pet', and slower learners are labelled 'thick'. The teacher needs to bear relationship problems in mind when organizing classroom work and activities.

Having identified some of the *common problems* that experienced teachers face when dealing with slow learners and bright pupils, let us now examine some of the specific solutions that have been proposed for dealing with these two groups of children.

Slow learners

'How can one use worksheet assignments when half the class can't read?' This must surely be one of the most frequently voiced comments by teachers in any discussion of mixed ability teaching. Despite the exaggeration of the proportion of non-readers in that rhetorical question, a small but sizeable number of children in the classes of most secondary schools which have a truly comprehensive intake will lack basic skills in reading and in number. What is to be done with these pupils? A number of solutions suggest themselves. First, slow learners (and most poor readers constitute this category) might be winnowed-out at the beginning of their secondary schooling to form a separate group for whom special courses are devised and taught by trained remedial staff. Second, a programme of part-time extraction might be devised in which children needing special help in literacy and numeracy are withdrawn to receive that tuition. Third, teachers might be encouraged to meet the needs of slow learners entirely within the context of mixed ability groups.

The appeal of the first solution, that is, the total extraction of pupils needing remedial help, lies in the benefits that they might enjoy as a result of working in small groups with sympathetic and specialist remedial teachers. The disadvantages, however, may well outweigh the advantages. All too frequently such a degree of separation from fellow pupils generates anti-school attitudes and behaviour problems in remedial groups. Part-time group extraction for remedial reading is widely practised in many secondary schools. Davies[6] shows how such a solution can be accomplished:

> Pupils needing remedial attention will be scattered across the whole year group when placed initially in forms under the care of a form tutor. These forms will be permanent units which for three, four or five years will be registered together . . . and whose needs will be the concern of the form tutor having responsibility for helping with their problems and keeping their records. These mixed ability units are retained for certain lessons – e.g. Art, Handicraft, Housecraft, Music, Physical Education. For all other lessons the year group will be setted into more homogeneous groups. In this way children of all abilities might work together for perhaps a quarter of their time at school.

While this pattern of remedial help has much to commend it, contributing as it does both to the educational and the social objectives of mixed ability teaching, it has been argued that it serves to minimize rather than to remove the problems of teaching slow learners. Placing children in mixed ability groupings for only 25 per cent of the school day, Davies suggests, is a guarantee of creating sub-cultures within the student body as a whole, with all the attendant problems that such smaller groupings can generate.

In arguing for the total retention of slower pupils within mixed ability groups, both Kelly[7] and Davies[6] are aware of the enormous demands that such a solution imposes upon most teachers. For Kelly, the social and the emotional advantages to be derived make it unwise and undesirable that non-readers should be excluded from mixed ability work. Kelly's solution is to give these pupils individual assignments in group projects that capitalize upon what strengths they have, such assignments being based upon as many resources that can be used without reading skills as can be obtained or made. It is doubtful that Kelly's solution arouses much enthusiasm among teachers as a whole. Davies' proposal, based as it is on actual practice, is more realistic:

> At one stage, itinerant remedial help was brought into the mainstream classroom, with a pair of teachers operating in harness, using carefully devised assignments wherein every pupil was guided to tasks with which he or she could cope initially via the use of resources suited to his or her capabilities.

However desirable Davies' solution, it is contingent upon a relatively small number of pupils needing remedial help and the availability of a large number of remedial staff. In most schools today this is scarcely a viable proposition. By and large, it is the practice of part-time extraction which is chosen as the way of dealing with slow learners in mixed ability teaching situations.

Bright pupils

What of the fast learner and the gifted child? The following extract from a fourteen-year-old's essay entitled 'My dream world' well illustrates the problem of the gifted child who feels underchallenged in a mixed ability teaching situation:

> Ever since I can remember I have enjoyed learning. At H.L. (her primary school) I had every encouragement. I was allowed to work at lunchtimes; there were adequate text books which we could bring home, and we were 'set' according to ability and speed of working. That meant that those of us with academic ambitions could help and encourage each other. Those less quick to comprehend had lessons geared to their pace.
>
> Since I have been at R. (secondary comprehensive) I have begun to despair of my dream becoming reality (university degree and a teaching diploma). It is hard to find satisfaction in working from worksheets. Without text books, except for Maths and French, I cannot pursue an idea which interests me, or revise except from my own notes. We have no library at W.E. (her home village) and the public library in L. (nearest town) leaves much to be desired. Why cannot I have text books to bring home? Why was it so outrageous for me to ask to take home an atlas to finish some work? Why must I be taught with pupils who have no desire to learn?

The Report of Her Majesty's Inspectors entitled *Gifted Children in Middle and Comprehensive Schools*[8] highlights the problem of the gifted pupil. Unlike *the handicapped* or *the backward*, groups for which criteria of identification have been established and forms of provision planned, *giftedness* is an ill-defined term. For the vast majority of schools and their teachers, the report concludes, giftedness is neither implicit nor explicit in the day-to-day dialogue of school life. The irony is that whereas gifted children can, and frequently do, work below their potential from lack of challenge or from personal choice, and pass unnoticed, slow learners can less easily disguise their inability to work at the level and pace of their fellows. This latter observation is supported in the findings of a study[9] of able children in mixed ability classes in which heads of departments were asked to comment on the problems that mixed ability teaching posed, for bright pupils. They identified the following:

1 Teachers spend too much time with slow learners.
2 Good pupils can get away with not working at an appropriately fast pace.
3 It is hard to cater for the very bright in a mixed situation.
4 Bright pupils fail to cover enough subject content for their needs.
5 Teachers are not doing their best for top pupils – work is aimed at the middle band.
6 The top third of pupils are not stretched.
7 Bright pupils are more difficult to teach than other pupils.

The research concluded that for bright pupils, the following three needs are paramount. First, teachers must help bright children to develop appropriate study skills. *Inter alia*, this will involve producing genuinely graded worksheets and instructing able children in methods of self-testing. Second, teachers need to encourage bright pupils to develop skills of higher level thinking. This will involve teachers in looking critically at classroom interaction and at their own questioning skills. Third, teachers must come to accept the 'normality' of bright pupils, particularly on the emotional level, even though they may seem 'old for their age'. The desire not to be different on the part of bright pupils sometimes triggers off underachievement on their part. Bright pupils need to be rewarded for scholastic achievement and at the same time to retain their identities with the class group.

Resources

Mixed ability organization raises a number of practical problems not the least of which is the development and utilization of adequate resources to sustain this system of teaching. Unlike traditional whole-class teaching, a mixed ability regime requires a far greater quantity and variety of learning resources. Most schools that have organized along mixed ability lines have developed some sort of resource centre system either localized within individual subject departments or centralized so as to serve the needs of the whole school.

A resource centre involves six essential elements:

1 Production of home-made resources.
2 Selection and acquisition of other resources.
3 Classification and indexing for retrieval.
4 Storage.
5 Use, including guidance and lending, etc.
6 Evaluation and weeding.

The average school resource centre today is likely to contain most or all of the following materials: books, periodicals, maps, models, posters, filmstrips, pictures, records, audio-tapes, slides and worksheets. Probably the most commonly-used resource is the worksheet or workcard. One inquiry[10] into the use of worksheets revealed that, at any one time, there were several basic types in operation in the particular school. For example, there was a *single workcard* used by the whole class which, because it lacked structure, failed to satisfy the extremes of ability. Second, there was a *single structured workcard* which started from concrete problems that were within the grasp of the majority of pupils in the group and proceeded in both depth and breadth to more abstract problems. This type of workcard had the effect of frustrating the least

Box 17

Preparing workcards for mixed ability teaching

1 Decisions must be made about the starting point for the programme. This may require a degree of pre-testing or a knowledge of pupils' background information from other subjects or from outside the school.
2 The card must start from the pupils' own experience (not what we think is their experience).
3 The programme must move from the concrete and particular to the abstract and general.
4 The card must be developed so that the programme progresses in small manageable steps.
5 Success points must be found for all pupils in the scheme of work, i.e. by the use of self-checking systems or discussion with the teacher as a means of offering encouragement or support.
6 The most able pupils must be extended by the use of problem-solving techniques which are not always within their capabilities, therefore demanding the teacher's active involvement.

Source: adapted from Wyatt[10]

able children who found little success in this arrangement. A third approach involved *a series of shorter workcards* that were designed to complete the whole programme. The cards were graded in difficulty, the earlier ones presenting concrete problems and providing a series of success points for the less able pupils. The later series were designed to extend the more able children and presented them with open-ended, problem-solving tasks. The appeal of this third approach to workcard development is that it allows for a whole range of resource materials to be used as a supplement to the basic programme. Whatever method is adopted, the author (an experienced teacher) identifies certain basic criteria that need consideration. We summarize these in Box 17.

Finally, the oft-quoted description of mixed ability teaching as 'death by a thousand workcards' points to the injudicious use that some schools make of this key learning resource. The workcard is best seen as one of a number of teaching resources that are appropriate to mixed ability teaching. An unrelieved diet of workcards is a certain recipe for boredom and indiscipline in any classroom.

Implications for student teachers

By now it is abundantly clear that successful teaching in mixed ability classrooms involves a wide range of preparation and a variety of professional skills. Is it possible, one might ask, to identify specific factors that make for effective mixed ability teaching? In proposing a ten-point attack on the challenge of mixed ability teaching, Wragg[11] has the particular needs of student teachers in mind. Box 18 identifies his proposals which we then present in greater detail.

Individual differences

Mixed ability teaching requires a thorough understanding of individual differences. Teachers need to anticipate difficulties by identifying, for example, those who require more time, those who lack self-confidence and those who are impulsive.

Language in the classroom

Unless teachers are aware of the crucial importance of language, much of the teaching in mixed ability classes will be misguided. The effective preparation of worksheets, charts, and wall displays too, is contingent upon the use of appropriate language.

Box 18

Ten sets of skills for mixed ability teaching

Preparatory skills

  1 Understanding individual differences among children in the class.
  2 Understanding the importance of issues to do with language in the classroom.
  3 Ability to be a member of a team.
  4 Devising and preparing appropriate curricula.

Teaching strategies

  5 Using whole class teaching judiciously.
  6 Handling small groups.
  7 Interacting with individual children.
  8 Developing flexibility and adaptability.

Evaluation

  9 Monitoring pupils' progress and keeping records.
10 Evaluating one's own teaching and undertaking professional self-development.

Source: Wragg[11]

Team membership

Considerable interpersonal skills are required in mixed ability situations where teachers are frequently required to work in teams in the planning and preparation of course work materials.

Devising and preparing curricula

Because mixed ability teaching poses more planning problems than other forms of classroom grouping, teachers need to acquire the inventiveness, the sensibility and the determination to devise and prepare appropriate curricula.

Using whole class teaching

Contrary to popular belief, mixed ability teaching requires the judicious use of whole-class teaching. Stand-up-and-talk skills are therefore very important. Teachers need to be able to command attention, to explain clearly, to speak audibly and distinctly, and to chair proceedings with large groups.

Handling small groups

Teachers need to develop the ability to handle several groups at once. In mixed ability teaching such groups often differ in size, constitution and task in hand. Teaching them requires 'with-it-ness', that is, the ability to work with one group while keeping a vigilant eye on others in the classroom.

Interacting with individuals

Interacting with individual children is a vital skill in mixed ability teaching. Teachers need to be able to secure a high degree of industry from children working on their own. This involves designing appropriate individual assignments and monitoring individual progress.

Developing flexibility and adaptability

Mixed ability teaching requires numerous decisions to be made during the course of any lesson in which, typically, groups and individuals are engaged in several different activities. Success under such conditions demands flexibility and adaptability on the part of the teacher.

Monitoring pupil progress

In mixed ability teaching, regular assessment and recording of children's progress is, if anything, more important than in traditional forms of classroom grouping. Teachers need to learn a wide range of assessment techniques and to develop an awareness of when and why to make evaluative judgements.

Evaluating one's own teaching

More important, perhaps, than evaluating pupils' work is the teacher's assessment of his/her own performance. Ultimately, improvement in teaching only takes place when teachers decide for themselves to change the ways in which they plan, prepare and initiate learning activities.

WATCHING HOW OTHERS MAKE LESSONS 'HAPPEN'

All that has been said so far about mixed ability grouping is so much claptrap unless student teachers are able to profit from the advice and translate it into successful classroom practice. For this reason we devote a major part of the text (pages 177–218) to a range of issues to do with management and control in classroom settings. Suffice it at this point, therefore, to look at what students can learn by observing how experienced teachers of mixed ability groups succeed in making lessons 'happen'.

Observing others teach often makes up an important part of a student's commitments in the course of school visits, school experience and teaching practice. Such opportunities to witness more experienced teachers in action can be rewarding providing that the student teacher knows *how* and *what* to observe. If, however, he is merely content to view passively all that contributes to the flux of classroom life without serious attempt at analysis and explanation, then the experience will be at best valueless and at worst detrimental.

Let us consider first why the experience could be detrimental. A student teacher viewing a lesson in the manner described is simply continuing what he has been doing for the past twelve years (assuming he went from school to university or college); and in doing so, will probably increase the likelihood that he in turn will teach as he himself was taught, a state of affairs to which Skinner[12] draws attention in his criticisms of current practices in teacher education. Even if the student's models have been reasonably good ones, he is still only perpetuating an ossified system which may be inappropriate for the future. The results of one investigation[13] support this view. There, the researchers inferred from their observations that students tended to borrow the practices of other teachers whom they had observed rather than think out original approaches of their own.

How then, the reader may well ask, can one make an observation session constructive and purposeful? The answer will depend upon the observer's knowledge and grasp of what Dearden[14] refers to as the 'theoretical concepts' of disciplines relevant to the classroom situation, viz. psychology, social psychology, sociology, philosophy and the particular subject being taught. Such concepts are valuable because they 'organize in highly systematic ways our ordinary, "commonsense" experience, and in so doing greatly increase our understanding of it.'

Many students during observation lessons merely interpret what they see in commonsense terms. A commonsense interpretation has structure, of course, but it is the structure of the layman and as such will be tied to the concrete reference points in time and space which bind the perceptions to the here and now. An observer adopting a commonsense perspective would thus perceive the gross external features of a lesson – the way the room is arranged, the teacher's voice, the noise, the fish tank in the corner, a fight between two boys at the back of the class. What he will not do, however, is to attempt to relate them to each other, or use classroom features or events of this kind to explain subsequent experiences more systematically, for commonsense is simply content with a miscellaneous collection of information – as Cohen and Nagel[15] observe.

The relevance of 'theoretical concepts' in this and other contexts lies in the fact that by a process of abstraction they permit us to develop *inner meanings* that are not tied to such concrete reference points. As Brown and Ghiselli[16] say: 'Conceptual meanings are then freed from the perceptual events that gave them birth, and through reasoning they are combined and re-combined in all the diverse relational ways that human imagination can conceive.' It is the 'theoretical concepts', then, which 're-structure "commonsense" experience in accordance with a particular theoretical interest' (Dearden) and enable us to reflect on 'the brute immediacy of our sensations' (Cohen and Nagel). This kind of re-structuring and reflection is the hallmark of the professional.

An illustration may perhaps make clearer this distinction between a *professional* and a *lay* observation of a particular experience. A student teacher intent on probing the inner significance of a lesson's external events may begin at the psychological level by taking a concept like *motivation*. We have suggested elsewhere that two kinds of motivation may operate in the initial stages of a lesson – intrinsic motivation and that which has to be established by an external source. The student could begin therefore by taking note of the kind the teacher utilizes. Does he build on the children's inherent interests? Does he establish the motivation himself? And if so, how? Does he revive motivation established on previous occasions? Or is he totally insensitive to such means of induction? Other questions will follow naturally. How does the teacher maintain a reasonable level of motivation once the lesson has got underway? How does the class respond to the teacher's efforts in this respect? What are the consequences of his complete disregard of the need to stimulate and maintain interest?

In a similar manner, the student observer could relate the concept of *memory* to the same classroom situation. To make the problem more tractable and his powers of observation more acute, he may chose to break the concept down into related sub-concepts – *acquisition, retention* and *recall*. He is now in a position to pose fundamental questions like: how does the teacher set about assisting and facilitating the class's acquisition of new learning? What cues and devices does he employ to assist retention and encourage recall? How successful is he with these?

The question of discipline could likewise be scrutinized using one or more of the concepts developed by Kounin.[17] The student could select the concept of *with-it-ness*, for example, and assess the extent to which the teacher is aware of what is going on in the classroom, of how the children are reacting to him and to the lesson.

So far, we have framed a series of questions arising from three concepts relevant to the classroom situation. Does the professional observer's task stop here? No, desirably, for the next stage will be for him to organize the selected concepts by examining the relationship between them. The experience he is observing can then be partially explained by the resulting plexus of interrelated concepts, and the more concepts he selects, the fuller his explanation. Such relationships may be causal, or simply correlative, and the observer will have to rely on inference and reasoning for his conclusions. Thus, having answered the questions stated above to his satisfaction, the observer could arrive at the following conclusion:

> *Failure of the majority of the class to learn the material adequately was due in part to poor motivation at the outset of the lesson; and the teacher's subsequent inability to sense the class's frustration resulting from this failure led to discipline problems towards the end of the lesson.*

A second observer viewing the same lesson from a lay stance, that is without an appropriate conceptual framework and dependent upon commonsense structuring, might have concluded thus:

> *The lesson got off to a slow start; the children seemed apathetic; one boy broke a chair; and the class got progressively more noisy and restless towards the end.*

The difference between these two conclusions is this: the first offers a plausible explanation and opens up a vista of supposition; the second dies on itself. The one searches for relationships and attempts to impute meanings in an effort after understanding; the other is content to record events chronologically and discretely. The professional concentrates his perceptual efforts deliberately and systematically on a restricted and predetermined number of events; the free observation of the layman, however, simply takes events as they come, and involves attending to the most impressive occurrences at the expense of the less dramatic features which are probably more significant in terms of explaining the situation.

Of course, this is a comparatively simple example using only three psychological concepts to illustrate the principle. In actual observational situations, the student would work towards fuller explanations by drawing upon a wider range of behavioural, educational and organizational concepts within a predetermined framework.

The reader will find additional information and guidance on classroom observation in Cartwright and Cartwright,[18] Goodlad, Klein and associates,[19] and Walker and Adelman.[20]

Finally, we recommend that the student who is going to observe other teachers' lessons bears the following points in mind:

1 The difference between a *professional* observer and a *lay* one in a given setting lies chiefly in the former's understanding and use of appropriate and relevant 'theoretical concepts'.

2 The student teacher who wishes to get the best out of his observation lessons should acquire as thorough a grasp as possible of a few basic concepts in psychology, social psychology, sociology and philosophy, at least in so far as they relate to the classroom. He should also acquire a comparable understanding of concepts in his own academic subject(s), and also in educational organization.

3 No one can possibly attend to the totality of the classroom situation, so complex is its make-up. One can only be aware of a limited number of relationships in any one situation.

4 In the light of (3) above, one possible way of approaching the task of observation could be as follows:

(a) Begin by structuring the situation. This may be done by selecting *one* of the following categories as a framework: the physical environment; the emotional environment; organization and management; instructional procedures; learning activities; subject matter and content; materials and equipment; use of audio-visual resources; pupil involvement; interaction and relationships; levels of expectancy; motivation; language and communication; situational factors; control and discipline; and feedback.

(b) Having chosen one of these categories, select a limited and appropriate number of concepts relevant to the category and frame a number of questions (see Box 19 for a set of questions on *motivation*). Although the student's choice of concepts will generally be determined by context, interest and purpose, he should aim to meet the *criterion of fertility*, that is, the selected concepts should permit him to make a reasonable number of worthwhile inferences.

(c) As the observer becomes more experienced, he can select two or more related categories from the suggestions given under (4)(a), frame suitable questions for each, and then attempt to relate them to each other. Thus, having studied *motivation*, for instance, in his first observation lesson, the observer can go on in his second lesson to examine *motivation* and *subject matter and content*. He can subsequently add other categories such as *language and communication*, *control and discipline*, and so on.

5 Although the observer is encouraged to select a limited number of concepts for study, it must be stressed that the more evidence about the teacher, the children and events that he is able to collect, the fuller will be his explanation and the more reasonable and justified will be the inferences he draws from that evidence.

6 The student's efforts to develop observational skills will be wasted unless he is prepared to express his findings in writing. This may take one or both of two forms:

(a) A written answer to each question treated separately; and

(b) A summary account drawing together the various threads in an attempt to explain features of the lesson observed.

Such an undertaking will demand a certain amount of reflective analysis without which understanding cannot be achieved.

Box 19

Motivation

Questions for use in an observation lesson

1 What techniques and approaches, if any, did the teacher use at the outset of the lesson to engage the class's interest?
2 How did he sustain the interest, once aroused?
3 How did he deal with the problem of flagging motivation?
4 In what ways did the teacher capitalize on the children's own interests?
5 Could any parts of the lesson be explained in terms of the concepts of intrinsic and extrinsic motivation? Did the teacher, for example, arouse the children's curiosity, challenge them or offer them some form of reward?
6 What part did *feedback* play in the lesson? How was it conveyed? And what was its effect on the class?
7 Could you establish any relationship between motivation and (a) social class; (b) ability; (c) age; (d) sex; or (e) aspects of the subject being taught or investigated?
8 What effect did the *personality* of the teacher appear to have on the overall success (or failure) of the lesson?
9 Were threats used as a means of motivating the children?
10 Examine the relationship between motivation and the instructional approach or approaches used by the teacher, e.g. formal class teaching; discussion; group work; guided instruction, etc.
11 How would you describe (a) the teacher's attitudes towards his class, and (b) his expectations of their performance? Could either of these be seen to affect his class's motivation?
12 Which forms of motivation did the class appear to respond to best?

Notes and references

1 Ridley, K. (1982) Mixed ability teaching in the primary school. In Sands, M. and Kerry, T. (eds) *Mixed Ability Teaching.* London: Croom Helm.
2 Bailey, M. Mixed teaching and the defence of subjects, cited in Elliott, J. (1976) The problems and dilemmas of mixed ability teaching and the issues of teacher accountability. *Cambridge Journal of Education*, 6 (2), 3–14.
3 Oeser, O.A. (1960) *Teacher, Pupil and Task.* London: Tavistock Publications.

4 Kerry, T. and Sands, M. (1982) *Mixed Ability Teaching in the Early Years of the Secondary School*. London: Macmillan.

5 See, for example, Reid, M., Clunies-Ross, L., Goacher, B. and Vile, C. (1981) *Mixed Ability Teaching: Problems and Possibilities*. Windsor: NFER-Nelson.

6 Davies, R.P. (1975) *Mixed Ability Grouping*. London: Temple Smith.

7 Kelly, A.V. (1974) *Teaching Mixed Ability Classes*. London: Harper and Row.

8 Great Britain, Department of Education and Science (1977) *Gifted Children in Middle and Comprehensive Schools*. London: HMSO.

9 See Kerry, T. (1978) Bright pupils in mixed ability classes. *British Educational Research Journal*, 4 (2), 103–11.
Bradley, H.W. and Goulding, J.G. (1973) Handling mixed ability groups in the secondary school. University of Nottingham: School of Education.
Lydiat, M. (1977) Mixed ability teaching gains ground. *Comprehensive Education*. 35, 12–19.

10 Wyatt, H. (1976) Mixed ability teaching in practice. *Forum* 18 (2), 45–9.

11 Wragg, E.C. (1978) Training teachers for mixed ability classes: a ten-point attack. *Forum*, 20 (2), 39–42.

12 Skinner, B.F. (1965) Why teachers fail. *Saturday Review*, 16 October, 80–1, 98–102.

13 Joyce, B.R. and Harootunian, B. (1964) Teaching as problem-solving. *Journal of Teacher Education*, 21, 192–223.

14 Dearden, R.F. (1968) *The Philosophy of Primary Education*. London: Routledge and Kegan Paul.

15 Cohen, M.R. and Nagel, E. (1961) *An Introduction to Logic and Scientific Method*. London: Routledge and Kegan Paul.

16 Brown, C.W. and Ghiselli, E.E. (1955) *Scientific Method in Psychology*. New York: McGraw-Hill.

17 Kounin, J.S. (1970) *Discipline and Group Management in Classrooms*. New York: Holt, Rinehart and Winston.

18 Cartwright, C.A. and Cartwright, G.P. (1974). *Developing Observation Skills*. New York: McGraw-Hill.

19 Goodlad, J.L., Klein, M.F. and associates (1974) *Looking Behind The Classroom Door*. Worthington, Ohio: Charles A. Jones.

20 Walker, R. and Adelman, C. (1975) *A Guide to Classroom Observation*. London: Methuen.

OPEN CLASSROOMS

Introduction

In the recent past, traditional classrooms, our concern in the preceding section, have come to be contrasted in terms of theory and practice with open classrooms, the focus of interest in the present section. We have listed in Box 20 some of the more important differences between the two that were identified by Bennett.[1] Although the concept of the open classroom is not the exclusive preserve of the primary sector,[2] much of what we say in the pages that follow will have more or less immediate relevance to that sector.

In spite of its place in modern education, there appears to be little agreement among theorists as to the precise nature of open education.[3] One writer[4] spoke of it as being 'an approach to education that is open to change, to new ideas, to curriculum, to scheduling, to use of space, to honest expression of feeling between teacher and pupil and between pupil and pupil, and open to children's participation in significant decision-making in the classroom.' Other writers, seeing open education in a wider context, believe that open schools should be more sensitive to the needs of the local community than is the case with more traditional schools. Pluckrose,[5] for instance, writes of the necessary criteria for an open school thus: 'It should meet the needs of and serve local society, be aware of its attitudes, and be able to link them to school life and work as the need arises.' For him, the open school is a way of extending the school's human dimension.

Although defining open education is problematic, it is possible to identify its principal characteristics. Stephens,[4] for example, in her study of open classrooms in both Britain and the United States, identified the following which may be seen to constitute the basic model of an open classroom: (1) a minimum of lessons to the whole class, most instruction being geared to small groups or individuals; (2) a variety of activities progressing simultaneously; (3) flexible arrangements so that children can engage in different activities for varying periods of time; (4) an environment rich in materials and equipment; (5) freedom for children to move about, converse, work together and seek help from one another; (6) opportunities for children to make decisions about their work and to develop responsibility for setting and meeting their educational goals; (7) lack of rigid, prescribed curriculum and provision for children to investigate matters of concern to them; (8) some integration of the curriculum, eliminating isolated teaching of each subject; (9) emphasis on experimentation and involvement with materials; (10) flexible learning groups formed around interests, as well as academic needs, and organized by both pupils and teachers; (11) an atmosphere of trust, acceptance of children and respect for their diversity; (12) attention to individual intellectual, emotional, physical and social needs; (13) creative activities valued as part of the curriculum; (14) a minimum of grading and marking; and (15) honest and open relationships between teacher and pupil and between pupil and pupil. Of course, open environments will vary greatly in the way they select, interpret and implement these characteristics which, for convenience, may be roughly summarized by the concepts of *freedom*, *activity* and *discovery*. Indeed, it may not be an exaggeration to say that each school will represent a different version of open education.

Box 20

Characteristics of traditional and open classrooms	
Traditional	*Open*
1 Separate subject matter	1 Integrated subject matter
2 Teacher as distributor of knowledge	2 Teacher as guide to educational experience
3 Passive pupil role	3 Active pupil role
4 Pupils have no say in curriculum planning	4 Pupils participate in curriculum planning
5 Accent on memory, practice and rote	5 Learning predominantly by discovery techniques
6 External rewards used, e.g. grades, i.e. extrinsic motivation	6 External rewards and punishments not necessary
7 Concerned with academic standards	7 Not too concerned with conventional academic standards
8 Regular testing	8 Little testing
9 Accent on competition	9 Accent on co-operative group work
10 Teaching confined to classroom base	10 Teaching not confined to classroom base
11 Little emphasis on creative expression	11 Accent on creative expression

Source: adapted from Bennett[1]

Other features underscoring these characteristics include an optimistic view of human nature, a concern with *process* as opposed to *content*, and a desire to broaden concepts such as *education*, *learning* and *responsibility*, which in traditional education have a more restricted meaning.

Before turning to the curriculum in open classrooms, we refer to *open plan* schools.[6] These are schools in which the traditional architectural arrangements have been replaced by an arrangement of learning bays and teaching areas that lend themselves to learning and teaching in a more flexible and informal manner. With its emphasis on space, a design of this nature facilitates a freer flow of children and assists teachers in implementing progressive concepts such as the integrated day, team-teaching and vertical grouping. In theory at least, all the amenities of the school and all its teachers are available to all the children. In practice, however, the position in most open plan schools is that each group has its own teacher and base, but is free to move into other parts of the building and approach other teachers for help.

Ideally, open education should be practised in an open plan school. In practice, however, this is not always the case, for some open plan schools have been determined by economic necessity, not educational philosophy. It is therefore possible to find traditional teaching methods being used in open plan environments.

The curriculum in open classrooms

Any consideration of the curriculum of open education must be preceded by some reference at least to the assumptions about children's learning and the nature of knowledge which underlie the movement. In Box 21 we list a set of assumptions concerning children's learning in open

Box 21

Assumptions about children's learning

1 Children are innately curious and display exploratory behaviour quite independent of adult intervention.
2 Exploratory behaviour is self-perpetuating.
3 The child will display natural exploratory behaviour if he is not threatened.
4 Confidence in self is highly related to capacity for learning and for making important choices affecting one's learning.
5 Active exploration in a rich environment, offering a wide array of materials, facilitates children's learning.
6 Play is not distinguished from work as the predominant mode of learning in early childhood.
7 Children have both the competence and the right to make significant decisions concerning their own learning.
8 Children will be likely to learn if they are given considerable choice in the selection of the materials they wish to work with and in the selection of questions they wish to pursue with respect to those materials.
9 Given the opportunity, children will choose to engage in activities which will be of high interest to them.
10 If the child is fully involved in and having fun with an activity, learning is taking place.
11 When two or more children are interested in exploring the same problem or the same materials they will often choose to collaborate in some way.
12 When a child learns something which is important to him he will wish to share it with others.

Source: Barth[7]

classrooms that have been identified by Barth.[7] The classification is based on his own classroom observations and on discussions with experts in the field. These assumptions need to be studied in conjunction with a further five postulates specified by Barth which relate to children's intellectual development. These claim that: concept formation proceeds very slowly; children learn and develop intellectually not only at their own rate, but in their own style; children pass through similar stages of intellectual development . . . each in his own way, and at his own rate and in his own time; intellectual growth and development take place through a sequence of concrete experiences followed by abstractions; and verbal abstractions should follow direct experience with objects and ideas, not precede them or substitute for them.

What assumptions does open education make about the status of knowledge? Knowledge plays a significant part in the aims and thinking of *traditional* education, where it is seen as a worthy end in itself. Its possession is highly prized in all fields of learning. The philosophy of open education, however, questions the value traditionalists place on it. Barth[7] explains why:

> Implicit in the ideas of open education are assumptions that bring into question not only the importance of knowledge *qua* knowledge, but also its meaning for the learner. Rather than an end in itself, knowledge is seen as a vehicle for the development of processes of thinking such as logic, intuition, analysis and hypothesis formation and as a catalyst that facilitiates the individual's development towards the ultimate goals of education – self-esteem, dignity and control over himself and his world.

From this perspective, Barth promulgates five assumptions thus: the quality of being is more important than the quality of knowing; knowledge is a means of education not its end. The final test of an education is what a man is, *not* what he knows. Knowledge is a function of one's personal integration of experience and therefore does not fall into neatly separate categories or disciplines. The structure of knowledge is personal and idiosyncratic, and a function of the synthesis of each individual's experience with the world. There is no minimum body of knowledge which is essential for everyone to know. And it is possible, even likely, that an individual may learn and possess knowledge of a phenomenon and yet be unable to display it publicly. Knowledge resides with the knower, not in its public expression.

Given these perspectives on children's learning and the nature of knowledge, then, how do open educators see the curriculum? Do they admit of the concept? Is there a place for it in the open classroom? What does the word mean to open educators? Certainly, it does not have the meaning that traditional educators impute to it, that is, a content of information and skills determined by adults and sequenced from the simple to the complex, from where the child is to where the adult would have him.

In contrast to the traditional curriculum, the curriculum of the open classroom has both a teacher *and* a pupil aspect. Indeed, it is the interaction between the teacher and pupil which produces what open educators claim is its dynamic and flexible character. As Stephens[4] explains:

> Teachers bring to curriculum development a general knowledge of areas to be included and skills appropriate for certain age-groups, plus their own previous experiences and interests. From this background they design the outlines of their curricula. Children in turn help to shape their curricula by their reactions to materials, their changing needs, their blossoming interests. The open curriculum is both planned and unplanned. It is planned in the sense that teachers do not simply drift from day to day, waiting for things to happen. The environment is carefully structured, materials are chosen to provide particular experiences, lessons are planned in response to individual and group needs. Yet the curriculum can also be unplanned in the sense that directions are not always prescribed; there is room for unseen exploration.

That the curriculum is, therefore, a joint responsibility having the quality of both adult and child initiation is its most distinctive feature.

Organizational features of the timetable and curriculum in open classrooms

Two key concepts at the heart of educational practice in open classrooms are the *integrated day* and the *integrated curriculum*. As both are subject to wide interpretation and varied practice we refer to each in general terms only.

The *integrated day* has been described by Dearden[8] as an organizational concept, implying that 'set timetables, or other formalized ways of changing from one activity to another, are abandoned. Instead, the flow of children's learning activities is broken and changed informally and often individually, with a large element of the children's own choice governing the matter.' In consequence, Dearden adds, a variety of contrasting activities are likely to be in progress simultaneously in the room or area. 'Some children may be reading or writing, others weighing or measuring, some painting, experimenting or modelling, while yet others may be in a group being instructed or questioned by the teacher, or out of the room altogether.'

Dearden considers that at least three things may be said in favour of having an integrated day. First, it allows for more individualized learning in content and pace and this makes for more interest and involvement: 'when curricula and methods are more precisely tailored success is more likely.' Second, because the amount of time a teacher can devote to a particular child is strictly limited, children learn how to learn on their own in those areas of work where this is possible: 'at the primary stage, this principally means acquiring various information-getting skills such as are involved in using reference books, using libraries and writing to relevant people. It also involves acquiring habits of initiative and persistence, so that available opportunities to find out for oneself are not shied away from . . .' Third, more individualized learning and developing skills of learning for oneself are closely related to the development of personal autonomy and self-direction.

Advocates of open education object to the sharp division among subjects found in traditional classrooms. They argue that learning cannot always be neatly wrapped up in separate packages. Many activities involve knowledge of, and skill in, a variety of subjects. Open educators therefore recommend an *integrated curriculum* in which subject boundaries are less distinct. The work of a class is organized around broad unified themes which encompass a number of subject areas. Skills are studied as they are needed by the activity and are practised in the course of significant tasks, rather than in isolation. In this connection, Dearden[9] writes:

> Integration logically presupposes differentiation, the differentiated elements being subordinated to some unitary whole. In what might be called 'loose' integration, the subordination of elements is no more than their selection according to relevance to a topic, theme or centre of interest. Thus geography, history, science, music and art may be selectively drawn upon for the contribution they can make to some such theme as canals, the sea, railways, flight, India or whatever. If the theme is the sea, then there may be maps of oceans, the history of voyages of discovery, experiments on floating in salt and fresh water, the painting of scenes beneath the sea, the playing of 'Fingal's Cave', the singing of sea shanties, *Treasure Island* may be read and the economic uses of the sea may be studied. No doubt the justification for such a 'loose' integration of subjects would be that it naturally follows the course of an interest without any arbitrary interruptions or divisions. And a good deal of such general knowledge is acquired in areas where it is difficult to argue that this rather than that must be

known, or that this rather than that must be covered. The strongest argument for loose integration is thus motivational.

Inevitably, in most integrated days there has to be a certain amount of formal timetabling. This usually occurs, as Dearden notes,[8] where the use of common or shared resources, such as in music or television programmes, is involved. Similarly, even though an integrated curriculum may be in operation, a certain amount of differentiation must needs occur. As Dearden explains,[9] 'Physical education for practical reasons, mathematics for reasons of sequence, and language skills because of their arbitrary social conventions all have to be differentiated out, at least for some of the time.'

From the child's perspective, integration in learning is natural during the early years of life. At this stage in his mental development, the child does not see what he learns as classifiable into distinct subject areas or isolated skills. He reads, records, calculates in pursuit of his current interests, and not until the age of nine or so does he begin to classify what he learns into subject compartments. Integration stems from the child and from the natural ways in which he learns. It is the child who integrates, not the teacher.

Grouping in open classrooms

As a school's philosophy is reflected in its organization, one can expect that the open school will have an 'open' approach to grouping and that different methods of grouping may be used as the circumstances demand. Stephens[4] notes that there are two broad perspectives from which grouping for instruction can be viewed – *the intra-school* and *the intra-class*. The former concerns the way children are arranged *within the school* and may include *horizontal* (or *chronological*) *grouping* or grouping children of the same age-range, *vertical grouping* or mixed age-grouping, and *transitional grouping*, a combination of horizontal and vertical grouping. Intra-class grouping, on the other hand, is concerned with organization *within* a class or group. In this category, Stephens[4] identifies three kinds of groups: *instructional* or *interest* groups formed around areas of the curriculum; *organizational groups* related to seating arrangements, administrative concerns and so on; and *social groups* formed for the purposes of play or talk. In contrast to groups in traditional classrooms, these tend to be flexible, loosely structured, formed and led by pupils as well as by teachers, and relatively impermanent. Of course, as we have indicated earlier, these arrangements do not in any way preclude the need for class teaching, as in story or music.

Because of the importance of intra-school groupings, we look at each of these in more detail.

Horizontal (or chronological) grouping

Horizontal grouping, as we saw above, refers to classes in which children are of the same age-range. This may vary from three months to possibly one year depending on the size of the school. Allen and her colleagues[10] have identified a number of advantages and disadvantages of horizontal grouping. The advantages are that: (1) the narrow age-range may enable teachers to feel more secure and the narrower range of ability may appear to make their task simpler; (2) children and teachers are both able to make a completely new beginning with each new school year; and (3) classes grouped in this manner show greater social cohesion and interaction because they are at similar levels of intellectual, social and emotional development and have similar interests.

Some of the disadvantages are as follows: (1) as the class is new at the start of each school year, there is no continuity with the previous year; (2) there is the possibility that children in the younger parallel classes may underachieve because they are known to be younger and appear less able; (3) a teacher who sees his class as a fairly homogeneous group may be in danger of not noticing the exceptions; and (4) teachers who tend to specialize in one age-group for a number of years will automatically restrict the range of their experience.

Vertical grouping

Because of the importance of vertical grouping in the primary school, we explore this concept in a little more detail. Vertical grouping may be defined as a method of organizing children in such a manner that each class contains children from each age-group in the school. At the present time, vertical grouping is found chiefly in infant schools, and in ones so organized all classes will be parallel and each class will contain an equal proportion of children of all ages from four-plus to seven-plus. The children will subsequently remain throughout their infant school life in the same class under the supervision of the same teacher. Each child will then 'run his own race' in a stable community guided by one teacher. Variations in this pattern abound in the primary sector. Thus, in some areas it is more common to find the reception class or the top infants being taught separately. Such structuring is sometimes termed partial vertical grouping or transitional grouping. We consider this variant more fully shortly.

The full name for this kind of organization is *vertical all-age grouping* although the shorter term *vertical grouping*, being more frequently employed, is perhaps preferable. It is sometimes referred to as *vertical streaming*, but this is perhaps better avoided as 'streaming' connotes ability grouping. Vertical grouping is also known as *family grouping* because the age-range of a class so structured resembles that found in a typical family. The term is an acceptable alternative provided it is not interpreted too literally, implying that members of one family are necessarily found in the same class (though, of course, this may be the case in some rural areas).

Vertical grouping thus implies a flexible organization which provides a wide basis for a child's emotional, social and intellectual development. Although a class so structured contains roughly equal proportions of each age, it does not mean that the class is rigidly stratified on this basis. The distinctive strength of this arrangement lies in its fluidity, for individual, group and class work are all possible. Indeed, it is the individual needs and interests of the children, and not their ages, which lie at the basis of group formation and re-formation.

In addition to the flexible organizational structure noted above, vertical grouping possesses a number of additional advantages (some of which it shares with horizontally grouped children being taught on an individual or group basis) that may be listed thus: (1) a more natural and relaxed atmosphere can result from this same flexibility; (2) the organization minimizes problems arising from a child's entering the infant school for the first time – moving into a stable and secure community, the new entrant is able to adjust more quickly and successfully; (3) the organizational flexibility relates more effectively to the children's motivation, to the content of learning, and to the integration of the curriculum than is the case with more traditional approaches; (4) children are better able to learn from each other as well as from the teacher; (5) the structure allows more effectively for variations in personal growth and development than is the case with more rigid organizational structures, fixed age-groups and set instructional procedures; (6) the organization increases the likelihood of children interacting with the environment; (7) a wider range of social experience is possible, together with resultant benefits such as a greater sense of belongingness, support and security; (8) should problems arise, a child can be moved to another class without much difficulty; (9) older children develop a sense of responsibility towards the younger ones; (10) the teacher is in a better position to deal with the children individually; (11) communication between teachers benefits, as each teacher is confronted with similar problems of the various age-groups; and (12) teachers using vertical grouping tend to speak favourably of it.

Critics of vertical grouping, however, raise the following objections: (1) the duties of the teacher become excessively onerous; (2) personality clashes between a teacher and child may make it undesirable for a child to spend two or three years in the same class; (3) older children may help younger ones too much, thus hampering their own progress; (4) children on the point of entering the junior school may be given preferential treatment; (5) the noise created by the younger children may disturb the older ones (partial vertical grouping can solve this problem); (6) the structure presents difficulties for activities such as stories and poems, religious education, and those areas such as music and movement and physical education where skill depends on maturation; (7) groups whose teachers are uncommitted or weak will be disadvantaged by a vertically grouped structure; and (8) hostility from parents (though this often arises from misunderstandings).

Mycock[11] has listed *four basic educational principles underlying the practice of vertical grouping*. These may be briefly summarized as follows: (1) being a stable and secure community, the school embodying the principles of vertical grouping provides the continuity and coherence necessary in a child's educational life; (2) a vertically grouped situation caters for a wide age-range in its own right, provides for individual motivation, tempo and maturation, and thus facilitates maximal individual growth; (3) a vertically grouped structure provides for the acceptance of the child as an agent of his own learning. It meets a child's natural urge to explore and discover, and provides a school environment that promotes and develops a child's ability to think by involving him in the selection and rejection of ideas, by developing discrimination and by forming value judgements; and (4) such an organization provides for the fullest development of the balanced personality. It meets the need for a holistic view of child development which will foster attitudes, qualities and abilities that will enable a child to live a happy, well-adjusted life in a complex and changing social environment.

Although the one essential characteristic of vertical grouping is the age-grouping, some teachers identify two further characteristics. These are: (1) the *integrated* or *unstructured day*. This they perceive as crucial to the successful working of vertical grouping. In so far as it is possible, a school is thus stripped of all artificial divisions. In practice, however, there is a considerable amount of experimentation in this respect. As a general rule, much of the day is left unspecified for both individual and group work, with all the children coming together from time to time for set teaching periods; and (2) a *structured environment*. An unstructured day is only made possible by having a highly organized classroom, and success in vertical grouping rests to a large extent on a highly structured environment. Space and opportunity to spread out are essential; and every classroom should have a good range of basic equipment.

The role of the teacher in a vertically grouped structure, as in other integrated situations, is a complex and subtle one. A selection of her functions, though by no means exclusive to vertical grouping, may be itemized as follows: (1) she promotes a relaxed and tension-free atmosphere that is conducive to happiness, mutual and self-help; (2) she establishes and maintains an appropriate and flexible environment in which children can learn chiefly through their own activities; (3) she ensures provision of materials and apparatus; (4) she arranges learning situations and opportunities; (5) she recognizes the needs of each individual child and sees that these are met; (6) she is a teacher, guide, source of reference and motivator; (7) she establishes standards; and (8) she evaluates and records individual effort and progress.

After a prolonged study of a wide variety of primary schools in rural, urban and suburban areas, Allen and her colleagues[10] concluded that the advantages of vertical grouping seem on balance to outweigh the disadvantages. They felt that the system could be a very positive gain in schools with a large number of immigrant children or in ones situated in deprived areas, in both of which a sense of security among the children was required.

Transitional grouping

It has been suggested that transitional grouping may be perceived as a compromise between horizontal and vertical grouping. Arrangements for transitional grouping in infant, junior and first schools are extremely flexible. One such arrangement in an infant school would be to have the five- and six-year-olds vertically grouped in parallel classes and single-age classes for the seven-year-olds. Allen and her colleagues[10] found in first schools that the fives and sixes were vertically grouped and then proceeded to further vertically grouped classes containing seven- and eight-year-olds.

Transitional grouping has arisen in recognition of the differing intellectual and social needs which distinguish six- and seven-year-olds. Allen and her colleagues point out that the younger child is largely engaged in the formation of concepts relative to physical and social reality and in learning to separate fact from fantasy and desire. He tends to be adult-oriented and to regard his peer group as rivals.

The seven- or eight-year-old, by contrast, is 'normally engaged in learning to manipulate fact, in acquiring skills and the concepts essential to everyday life. He is learning to be peer-group related and to adopt the appropriate personal and sex role within the group.' Transitional grouping thus caters for these and other differences.

Allen and her associates[10] have further recorded both the advantages of transitional grouping and the disadvantages. Advantages include: (1) with transitional grouping, children have the experience of changing to a single-age class within the security of the same school; (2) transitional grouping allows children more variety of adult contact; (3) separating children at seven appears to eliminate the need to cater for physical education, story and music at a separate level for certain ages as within the vertically grouped class; (4) it helps with the problem of younger children trying to follow too closely the lead of the older children, and losing experience of activities such as fantasy play or the investigation of the properties of materials; (5) older children also benefit in that they can expect more opportunity to use materials creatively and more teacher's help with the practice of basic skills; (6) some teachers are happier with older children, and others are more suited to younger ones; and (7) the system appears to be particularly advantageous in a socially deprived school.

Three disadvantages identified by the authors may be listed thus: (1) where an individual child has not emotionally or intellectually reached the level of his companions, this is obviously more noticeable on transfer to a seven-year-old class or a vertically grouped seven-to-eight year-old class; (2) as with vertically grouped situations, there may well be misunderstandings by the parents which need sympathetic explanation by the school; and (3) where children have made friends with older or younger children in their vertically grouped class and are now separated, there may be distress on the part of the children which needs to be understood by the school.

We continue by examining some of the principal teaching and learning styles to be found in open classrooms. The latter will include both formal and informal approaches on the part of the pupils.

Teaching and learning styles in open classrooms

A visitor to an open classroom would, within a comparatively short space of time, be struck by the range and variety of teaching and learning styles that characterize the work in a typical day. Our review of these aspects of the open classroom includes individualization, individual attention, discovery learning, the place of play and talk, topics and projects, and team-teaching. We conclude with short descriptions of pupil types in primary classrooms.

Individualization

Individualization of instruction is based on recognition of the fact that not all children can be expected to learn at the same rate. The approach is used in both traditional and open classrooms though its relationship to the content of learning is different in each case. In the traditional classroom, individualization is achieved by varying the pace or duration of learning, by varying the mode of teaching or by modifying the set curriculum in some way. What these variations have in common, however, is the belief that all children must master a specified curriculum determined by the teacher or the system. A consequence of this is the need for frequent evaluation and testing to check the children's progress. In open classrooms, where individualization is a key concept, children collaborate in formulating their own curricular goals. As Stephens[4] explains, 'The teacher's responsibility is not to decide in advance exactly what each child will study but rather to provide a climate in which individual children can make choices about the curriculum and explore matters of interest to them.' This does not mean that the child does as he likes, or that the teacher abandons all responsibility in this connection, but that the curriculum is freed from the constraints of the traditional approach and now more appropriately meets the unique needs, interests and abilities of each child. Individualization is sometimes misinterpreted as meaning that each child works on his own in a physical sense. But this is not the case. It simply means that his individual needs are taken into account. More often than not, these can be most effectively met by grouping – a topic we have already considered on an intra-school and intra-class basis.

Individual attention

Individualization involves encounters with the teacher, and her contribution to the teaching–learning process in the open classroom can be considered in terms of *individual attention*. In a classroom environment characterized by high openness, the burden of informal encounters between the teacher and child can be very onerous, sometimes totalling as many as a thousand interpersonal contacts a day. For this reason, individual attention can be one of the more problematic concepts in an open environment for it is never far removed from its polar opposite – individual neglect. Two earlier studies conducted in the United States, for example, show that in any given period certain children received most of the attention while others were largely ignored.[12] A British study conducted in the early 1970s[13] revealed that two main groups of children received attention – the active hard workers and the active miscreants. It was concluded that the *average passive* child missed out in this respect, not through any rational policy on the part of the teacher, but because the on-going classroom pressures limited pupil contact to the two categories identified above. Further, for the neglected child who was also diffident and therefore unlikely to talk even to those other children in his group, the classroom became 'bereft of language, either written or spoken'. Boydell[14] graphically describes the possible consequences of individual neglect:

> Isolation from the teacher, coupled with a fairly high probability that contacts will not be work-oriented when they do occur, is as much a classroom reality for many children as the exhausting never-ending series of individual work conversations are for the teacher. 'It's time to pack up' said by a weary teacher at the end of the afternoon may be all some children have heard her say to them all day!

More recent research[15] in this connection offers more hope, however. In dividing the pupils into three sub-groups – high achievers, medium achievers and low achievers – the researchers found that there was, in fact, very little difference in the distribution of teacher–pupil interaction between the three groups of pupils; overall, they found, it was almost identical. They found no evidence that there was any discrimination either in favour of or against any particular group of pupils according to their achievement level.

Discovery methods

A concept arising from the strategies of topic and project work which we shall be considering shortly, and one of central importance to the pedagogy of open classrooms, is that of *discovery learning*. Dearden[9] suggests that by its means we may reasonably expect children to learn something new; and to do so through some initiative of their own. He goes on to identify three other points to be borne in mind in any discussion on learning by discovery. First, what is involved primarily is the learning of facts, concepts and principles rather than skills, techniques or sensitivities; and that the subjects most relevant to discovery learning are mathematics, science and environmental studies. Second, discovery learning may be contrasted with the sort of learning usually associated with the traditional classroom, i.e. learning by instruction or demonstration. And third, learning by discovery does not just happen: it comes about as a result of a particular teaching method or strategy. Numerous strategies can be distinguished in this connection; perhaps the commonest one to be found in open classrooms is that of *guided discovery*. By this means, a teacher supports a child's self-chosen activity with questions, commentary and suggestions.

From time to time, discovery learning, as with other features of the open classroom, comes under fire from those holding entrenched traditionalist positions. Such attacks are best countered with the kind of sentiments expressed by Dearden in his concluding remarks:

Learning by discovery characteristically aims to engender intrinsic interest, both in what is learned and in the process of learning it. It also emphasizes the satisfactions of learning independently. But the development of both intrinsic interest and independence in learning are extremely important liberal education aims. If a method in the hands of some teacher is successful in achieving these aims, then it has much to be said for it, at least as one valid method amongst others.

Play and talk

The educational significance of *play* for younger children has been a persistent theme in the writings of theorists from as early as Plato. The prominent role accorded it by initiators of the progressive movement in education has now assumed one of pre-eminence in the thinking and practice of open educators. Indeed, one writer goes as far as to say that the 'role of play in children's learning is central to an understanding of open education'.[4] It is not easy to determine from the literature on open education precisely on what the significance of play rests. Scrutiny of comparatively recent writings on the subject lead one to infer that it serves a twofold purpose in the thinking of open educators. First, it seems to cater for a fairly wide range of *children's needs*, including psychological, personal, social and educational ones. In this capacity, play will be an important source of knowledge in the sense that open educators imply, that is, the child's 'personal capacity to confront and handle new experiences successfully'.[7] And second, it appears to be an important *integrative factor*, a vital means of breaking down traditional divides. Thus play merges with, or becomes indistinguishable from, work; and the boundaries between other traditional dualisms such as doing and knowing, or intellect and emotions, are similarly blurred by the concept.

Talk in the open classroom likewise occupies a strategic position. Indeed, many open educators regard talk as an important index of the degree of openness in a classroom. Adelman and Walker[16] express the point thus:

> What should we look for in classrooms as indicating openness? We consider that the nature of talk is the crucial factor, for talk is the only readily available manifestation of the extent and process by which mutual understandings of what counts as knowledge in any context are transacted.

Openness then by this yardstick is reflected by the quality of action and the significance and nature of the talk taking place in the classroom, and this is best achieved at the individual and small group level. The fundamental problems of openness, as Adelman and Walker point out, therefore revolve around the difficulties of asking and answering questions, of knowing when to disclose and when to withhold information. To this end the open classroom, much more than its traditional counterpart, demands of the teacher an awareness of the child's mind and viewpoint, and this means that 'the amount of thought sensitivity and empathy that the teacher has to mobilize and accomplish "openness" makes his task more challenging, vulnerable and exhausting than in a "closed" classroom where the rules for access to knowledge are set rather than negotiated.'

Topic and project work

The use of topics, projects, themes and centres of interest is a key feature of the work of the open classroom. We have already touched on some reasons for this – their value in integration and discovery learning, for example. Of course, their use is not confined to the open classroom since they may play an equally important role in the work of traditional and 'mixed' classrooms. The terms themselves lack precise definitions, but they do possess similarities which have been identified by Rance.[17] Thus, they all attempt to break away from the conventional methods of teaching and place more emphasis on the child than on the subject; they endeavour to allow the child to construct his own methods of approach to knowledge; they give him the opportunity to 'learn how to learn'; they break down barriers between school subjects; and they all utilize a child's own interests. We look in particular in this brief review at topics and projects.

Topic work may be defined as the individual and group investigations, recordings and presentations which children undertake when pursuing a topic. As Rance[17] writes:

> It requires the content of normal curricular subjects to be used so that the pupil can develop a simple but logical method of systematically seeking, absorbing, organizing and recording knowledge. This process should be allowed to flourish in a situation which enables the child to make a free choice, within predetermined limits, of the subject he wishes to study and encourages him to create an end-product commensurate with his mental and physical abilities.

Rance further elucidates the terminology used in topic work. Thus, there are two types of topic: *the graded topic* in which the teacher aims at teaching children new methods for obtaining, selecting, recording and presenting knowledge, the emphasis being on method; and *the subject topic*, the chief aim of which is to encourage children to acquire a wide range of information concerning a particular subject. The emphasis here is on content.

An individual topic is carried out by one child; a group topic is undertaken by a group of from four to six children; and a class topic by the whole class. An independent group is a self-sufficient unit contributing to one independent section of the topic; and a linked group collaborates with one or more other groups.

Generally speaking, topics should be freely chosen by the children on the basis of their own interests. They may initially require some suggestions and the teacher can help here with a compiled list of possibilities. The children, however, should be allowed to make the final choice.

The methods of undertaking a topic vary considerably with its nature and the maturity and experience of the children. The following five-stage-plan by Rance, however, would serve as an organizational basis for student teachers embarking on a topic perhaps for the first time:

1 The teacher's preparation of the subject.
2 Introduction of the subject(s) to the class.
3 The organization of the subject(s) with the class.
4 The children's research into the subject matter.
5 The end-product.

Rance points out that (a) the form the end-product takes can be discussed during stage 3; and (b) once the five stages have been carried out, it is usual to have a discussion session in which the topic is reviewed and in which improvements for subsequent topics are suggested.

The teacher's functions throughout the sequence of stages are numerous. She introduces the work, arouses initial motivation and is subsequently available as a consultant and resources person. She should be careful not to direct too closely or obviously the actual course of the investigation for, as far as possible, the children themselves should determine how they wish to pursue their research and presentation. From time to time the teacher will need to re-stimulate interest and perhaps suggest new or alternative avenues of approach and exploration to the children as they work on their topics. She must constantly be on the alert for waning interest.

The importance of having a *well-defined end-product* agreed at the organizational stage cannot be overstressed. No matter how well motivated children are initially, they can easily lose interest as the topic gets underway. If or when this happens, the defined end-product will assist in re-focusing attention and sustaining interest. What form the end-product takes will depend on a number of factors. Common forms of display and presentation include an exhibition, presentation in booklets and folders, displays and murals, tape recordings, mimes and plays, a talk by one or more members of the group, movies and filmstrips, models, collages, a magazine, a festival, spoken prose and poetry — or any combination of these.

Readers seeking additional information on the subject of topics are referred to Rance's book[17] which provides a detailed consideration of the subject. In particular, they are advised to read chapter 10 which examines the special problems of the student teacher when attempting topic work. Another useful source of information in this respect is the book by Lane and Kemp.[18]

In conclusion, the reader is reminded that the chief points to bear in mind are: (1) her own thorough preparation, and especially the preliminary reading and research she needs to undertake; (2) the organization of the topic with the class (organization of resources and definition of end-product are important here); (3) making sure that the children enjoy the work; and (4) establishing and maintaining a reasonably high level of motivation and anticipating the points where it can be expected to flag.

It is difficult to establish a clear-cut distinction between topic work and project work. Invariably, a project involves a large group or the whole class and usually takes longer to accomplish than a topic. It is possible, for example, to spend a whole term on a project.

Much of what was said on topic work will apply to projects. The choice of subjects will be determined where possible from the children's own interests, with encouragement and suggestions from the teacher. One useful technique is for the teacher and class to arrive at a theme by discussion and then by means of a series of basic questions, the teacher can construct a *flow chart* on the blackboard. An example of a completed flow chart on the theme 'The Sea' is given in Box 22. When the flow chart has been completed, the class can then be divided into groups, each group undertaking a suitable area of investigation selected from the possibilities presented by the chart. Social studies, environmental studies and science lend themselves particularly well to class projects and flow chart treatment.

A suggested scheme for assessing project work is given in the section on evaluation and assessment. The major categories of assessment include: (1) *strategical considerations*: suitability of the overall plan; use of source materials; and ways of obtaining information; (2) *selection criteria*: basis for inclusion/exclusion of materials; organization and selection of materials; criteria employed; and the balance of the various sections of the project; (3) *presentation*: overall quality; general neatness; and aptness of illustrative material; and (4) *attitudinal considerations*: enterprise; perseverance; and co-operation with others.

For further information on project work in the primary school, we refer you to Haslam.[19]

Box 22

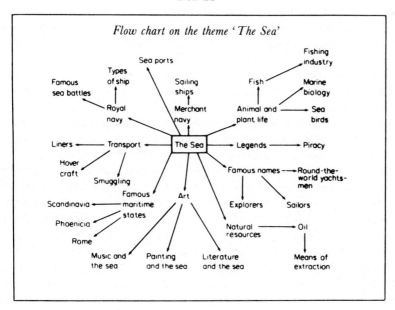

Flow chart on the theme 'The Sea'

Team-teaching

Another instructional procedure available in open schools is team-teaching. This implies that two or more teachers share collective responsibility for all or a significant part of the instruction of the same group of children. The notion can only be described in a general way, and Warwick[20] offers the following definition: 'A form of organization in which individual teachers decide to pool resources, interests and expertise in order to devise and implement a scheme of work suitable to the needs of their pupils and the facilities of their school.'

Warwick observes that the concept of team-teaching enshrines two distinct schools of thought. To some, it is perceived in pragmatic terms, as an economic and democratic way of organizing a school. From this perspective, if offers a convenient administrative framework within which existing structures can survive with some modifications. To others, however, team-teaching represents far more. They perceive it as a reorientation of the curriculum in such a way that the needs of both teacher and taught are more fully met.

Team-teaching, in contrast to the assumptions underlying traditional approaches to education, takes as its starting point the needs of the children and attempts to structure them as fully as possible into the work of the school. It questions the notion that the requirements of either teacher or pupil are best served by an arbitrary division into subject departments, each working in isolation from the others. It does not assume that the only contribution to the classroom situation comes from the teacher directing the children from the front of the class, and seeks new forms of organization in which the individual and the group can play a much greater part.

Advocates of team-teaching would argue that as long as traditional academic structures remain, teachers will feel impelled to work in isolation – in their classrooms, departments and preparation. But as soon as they think and act co-operatively, the possibilities of team-teaching can become a reality.

As regards the *organizational aspects* of team-teaching, because the possibilities are quite numerous, we can only indicate one or two alternatives in this connection. In the primary school, for instance, where team-teaching developed in order to meet the needs of vertically grouped classes and of working an integrated day, a team may consist of from two teachers to possibly the whole staff. Allen and her colleagues[10] have observed from their researches that the size of the team is often related to the layout of the building, and also to the compatibility of the teachers. Each teacher may then be responsible for a particular aspect of the curriculum – languages or mathematics, for example. In schools where teachers do not want to teach only one subject, they change their activities fairly regularly.

Of the group involved in a team-teaching enterprise, Allen and her colleagues say that:

It may consist of all the children in one age-group in a school, or it may be vertically grouped as would be the case if the whole school formed one team. Experience has shown that the reception class children benefit from a term on their own to establish themselves securely in school, though where there is a nursery class this is not as necessary.

Although the children may move freely from one work area to another, they should have a base where they can keep their belongings and a particular teacher of their own.

For team-teaching to be effective, there must be co-operation between teachers who should be in frequent contact with each other. One way of organizing team-teaching in the primary school is to have a short meeting of all those involved so that the pupils can be informed of the activities they will be taking part in during the day. Each teacher can then take the opportunity to explain any new activities for which she will be mainly responsible. Allen and her colleagues[10] refer to this as a 'catching of interest' time which is very similar in its intent to the 'lead lesson' approach adopted in some secondary schools (see below). After this the children take up the activity of their choice.

Activities such as physical education, music and movement, story or television programmes can be accommodated by taking groups out of the team. As Allen and her colleagues point out, 'It may be possible for the whole team to lay down tools and go to another activity at the same time. Alternatively it may be necessary for a room to be closed for a period while the teacher takes a group for one of these activities.'

The authors also observe that behaviour problems may arise with those children not able to cope with the freedom that team-teaching places on them. The solution suggested is for them to be directed to particular activities at set times until the established routine gives them sufficient confidence and security to manage more freedom of choice.

One approach to team-teaching, particularly useful in the secondary school, is structured around two basic concepts – the *lead lesson* and *follow-up* work. We look briefly at each.

The *lead lesson* initiates a sequence of work. It is intended to stimulate interest and capture the imagination. As the work of the period(s) following depends on it, it is essential that it has drive, impact and variety. As Freeman[21] says, 'If (the lead lesson) fails the follow-up work will be difficult because pupil interest will be low and the purpose and direction of follow-up work unclear.' To ensure success, then, a wide range of techniques and teaching aids needs to be used – possibly film, filmstrips, slides, tape recorders, television, etc. The lead lesson also serves as a key presentation, bringing together the full group, or a large part of it, ensuring continuity and, where necessary, providing direction. Although some schools allow an hour or so for a lead lesson, most schools devote twenty or thirty minutes to it. The occasion itself is usually shared among team members according to their particular interests and expertise. Freeman records that all accounts referring to lead lessons emphasize the importance attached to their preparation and organization.

Follow-up work should be given the same care and attention as the lead lesson. Maximum benefit will not be derived from the lead lesson unless this is so and the scheme will suffer as a consequence. An average of three to five follow-up sessions are necessary each week. The first of these should, ideally, come directly after the lead lesson to enable immediate recapitulation and consolidation of the material and a running through of the work schedule for the week. It is therefore helpful if the lead lesson can be timetabled for the beginning of a longish session or a double period. This allows for such immediate follow-up work. Freeman considers that schools tend on the whole to arrange follow-up work either in classes of normal size (20–40 +), or in a system of individuals or small groups (6–15).

The *role of the teacher* in a team-teaching situation is worth noting. Once the work is underway, the teacher acts in an advisory capacity. She knows what material and equipment are available and where various pieces of information can be obtained. Earlier preparation has of course ensured this. She also has knowledge of what each group is doing and can thus direct discussion or research where problems are encountered, and possibly merge two or more groups when this would seem desirable. Individuals may be withdrawn from particular groups for various reasons, and from time to time all groups will be called together for a formal or semi-formal session.

A further important function concerns the keeping of records of the children's work and achievement. Freeman lists the following characteristics which are used as a basis for assessment in some English schools:

In the classroom: co-operation with the teacher; co-operation with other children; oral communication; written communication; standard of presenting work; interest; initiative; keenness to work; originality; ability to make decisions; sensitivity; self-understanding; academic potential; consistency; learning attainment – skill, knowledge, recall and understanding.

General: general bearing – speech, poise, confidence, appearance; reliability.

Social habits: exercises self-control; listens courteously; participates in group activities; demonstrates thoughtfulness for others; cares for materials and property; abides by school rules; and comes into school on time.

Work habits: has materials and is prepared for work; follows directions; does neat work; works independently and is not easily distracted; uses initiative in thinking; completes work on time; and does independent reading.

Finally, the teacher's task is also one of widening each individual's horizons. Starting with initial achievement, each child can be actively encouraged to take a step outside his specialization and interests.

As with other teaching styles, team-teaching has both advantages and disadvantages. The advantages as listed by Stephens[4] include: (1) new organizational patterns may emerge when teachers are prepared to work together; (2) the curriculum becomes less fragmented and less authoritarian in nature; (3) team-teaching reasserts the importance of people, and their relationships and reactions to one another within the school context; (4) it facilitates professional growth by providing teachers with opportunities to share ideas, plans and observations; it also allows for wider use of expertise; (5) it encourages children to develop broader ranges of interests; (6) it permits the organization of a larger group within which a child may find greater compatibility; (7) there are organizational benefits – it cuts down duplication of effort; allows for the freer use of audio-visual equipment; and results in less disruption when a teacher is absent; and (8) new and inexperienced teachers benefit in that they can take on a full teaching load gradually.

Some of the disadvantages may also be noted: (1) some children prefer a close relationship with one class teacher, and this is more difficult to achieve with team-teaching; (2) some equally find it difficult to accommodate to a large group; (3) different teachers will have different standards and this may confuse some pupils; (4) there may be differences among teachers themselves – clashes of personality, educational philosophy or differing attitudes, for example; (5) having more diffused responsibilities may result in a teacher's commitment to particular children suffering; and (6) team-teaching increases the power of the headteacher and this is seen by some as a disadvantage.

Pupil types

The large-scale observational study of primary classrooms reported by Galton and his fellow researchers[15] identified four broad pupil types. These were, first, the *attention seekers* who either sought attention or were the focus of most of the teacher's contacts with individuals, most of the interactions being concerned with routine or task work. Second, the *intermittent workers* who had the lowest levels of interaction of all four types, though the highest levels of contact with other pupils. Third, *solitary workers* who were considered the most interesting of the four types. They received very little attention from the teacher and made contact with her either as a member of her audience when she was talking to the whole class or when listening and watching while some other pupil received her attention. They showed great reluctance to interact with other pupils. And fourth, the *quiet collaborators*. The main feature of this type of pupil was that he usually interacted with the teacher not so much as an individual as when he was part of a group or class audience. Such interactions were usually about task work.

The role of the teacher in the open classroom

We have so far touched incidentally on the role of the teacher in the open classroom with regard to specific aspects like vertical grouping and team-teaching. At this point we should like to identify three general characteristics of the open teacher's role that may be seen to permeate many aspects of her work.

First, the role takes on a broader and more diffuse character than is the case with the traditional teacher. The open educator is not primarily a transmitter of knowledge. The terms used in Britain and the United States to describe her work give some idea of the range of tasks she may be called upon to perform – diagnostician, resources specialist, learning manager, counsellor, facilitator, interactor.

Second, because the philosophy underpinning the practice of open education is concerned with developing a child's inner potential, the teacher must primarily be *an observer* watching, as Dearden explains,[22] 'for signs of readiness, looking for spontaneous interests and activities, seeking to read the signs of the inner ripening that will give him his cue. For what he, the teacher, must do will depend very much on the lead which the growing child gives him to follow.'

Third, if, as Stephens explains,[4] the key word in the traditional classroom is *control*, then the corresponding key word in the open classroom is *trust*. This implies an optimistic view of human nature on the part of the teacher and a confidence that children, given opportunities, will develop self-discipline and will learn although they may travel by unorthodox routes.

Box 23 contains a description of an outstanding informal teacher at work. Notice in particular the versatility as she switches from one task to another, the managerial skill, the ways in which she communicates with the class and her role as observer.

Implications for student teachers

The alert reader will have already grasped many implications of the preceding review for his or her own teaching so there is little purpose in labouring the points here. However, there do seem to be a handful of key points that are worth rehearsing:

1 Have a good idea of what the key concepts *integrated day* and *integrated curriculum* mean; and tease out their practical implications for day-to-day operations.

2 Have some understanding of the way the open educator perceives the nature of the child and the assumptions he holds about knowledge and children's learning. What are the implications of these for the teacher's role?

3 Appreciate the need to create sufficient *time* for individuals and groups so that the potential problem of 'individual neglect' is anticipated.

4 The effective functioning of an unstructured or semi-structured day requires a tightly structured environment. This calls for efficient use of space, materials and equipment.

5 Two features that may figure more prominently in the open classroom compared with the traditional classroom are *noise* and *work avoidance*. What steps will you take to deal with them?

6 Remember the importance of record-keeping, even though you may only be in school for a few weeks.

Box 23

A teacher at work

'She had excellent eye-contact and vigilance. Some informal teachers operate head down, and fail to see that pupils at one end of the room have lost interest or are disrupting others. The teacher has the kindly, beady eye of many a successful practitioner, able to split her attention between the individual or group she is with and the rest of the class. Periodically she scans the class, and is mobile enough to intervene in any problem before it escalates.

'This vigilance is transmitted to the whole class in subtle ways. At intervals she publicly reviews the class's progress. "Now you two are still painting; Ian you're preparing assembly; Neil I think it's time you left that, isn't it?" It represents an alerting of the whole group to the fact that she is publicly aware of what is going on: but it is a light touch.

'Another message regularly transmitted is that of pupil independence. In many informal classrooms, pupils are so dependent on the teacher that she is overwhelmed with crowds of up to ten or twelve children gathered around her desk, or trailing her around the room. This teacher has no more than one or two soliciting her attention at any one time.

'"Have more faith in your own judgement," she says to one boy who has crossed out correct solutions to his sums, because he thought that two questions should not have the same answer. "Don't work together if you can do it on your own," she tells another small group; yet co-operative working is also permitted when each participant is making a contribution, and not just riding on the backs of others.

'Setting-up operations are conducted with great clarity. A small group of people is being introduced to some new number work. Explanations are crucial in informal teaching: otherwise children have no proper idea of what the task entails. Both subject matter and the way of handling the task are crystal clear after the teacher has explained them, largely by question and answer and a few intriguing mysteries: "I'm not going to say one word about number seven, but you just think carefully about it."'

Source: adapted from Wragg[23]

Notes and references

1 Bennett, N. (1976) *Teaching Styles and Pupil Progress*. London: Open Books.
2 Note: there is evidence to suggest that the term is increasingly being applied at the secondary level.

3 Note: we shall use terms like open classrooms, open education and open schools fairly interchangeably in this section.

4 Stephens, L.S. (1974) *The Teacher's Guide to Open Education*. New York: Holt, Rinehart and Winston.

5 Pluckrose, H. (1975) *Open Schools, Open Society*. London: Evans Brothers.

6 Note: for recent research on open plan schools, see Bennett, N., Andreae, J., Hegarty, P. and Wade, B. (1980) *Open Plan Schools*. Schools Council Project. Windsor: NFER.

7 Barth, R.S. (1975) Open education: assumptions about children, learning and knowledge. In Golby, M., Greenwald, J. and West, R. (eds) *Curriculum Design*. London: Croom Helm in association with the Open University Press.

8 Dearden, R.F. (1971) What is the integrated day? In Walton, J. (ed.) *The Integrated Day in Theory and Practice*. London: Ward Lock Educational.

9 Dearden, R.F. (1976) *Problems in Primary Education*. London: Routledge and Kegan Paul.

10 Allen, I., Dovet, K., Gaff, M., Gray, E., Griffiths, C., Ryall, N. and Toone, E. (1975) *Working an Integrated Day*. London: Ward Lock Educational.

11 Mycock, M.A. (1970) Vertical grouping in the primary school. In Rogers, V.R. (ed.) *Teaching in the British Primary School*. London: Macmillan.

12 Withal, R. (1956) An objective measurement of a teacher's classroom interactions. *Journal of Educational Psychology*, 47.
Resnick, L.B. (1972) Teacher behaviour in the informal classroom. *Journal of Curriculum Studies*, November.

13 Garner, J. and Byng, M. (1973) Inequalities of teacher–pupil contact. *British Journal of Educational Psychology*, 43, 234–43.

14 Boydell, D. (1975) Individual attention: the child's eye view. *Education 3–13*, 3 (April), 9–13.

15 Galton, M., Simon, B. and Croll, P. (1980) *Inside the Primary Classroom*. London: Routledge and Kegan Paul.

16 Adelman, C. and Walker, R. (1974) Open space – open classrooms. *Education 3–13*, 2 (October), 103–7.

17 Rance, P. (1968) *Teaching by Topics*. London: Ward Lock Educational.

18 Lane, S.M. and Kemp, M. (1973) *An Approach to Topic Work in the Primary School*. London: Blackie.

19 Haslam, K.R. (1971) *Learning in the Primary School*. London: George Allen and Unwin.

20 Warwick, D. (1971) *Team-Teaching*. London: University of London Press.

21 Freeman, J. (1969) *Team-Teaching in Britain*. London: Ward Lock Educational.

22 Dearden, R.F. (1972) Education as a process of growth. In Dearden, R.F., Hirst, P.H. and Peters, R.S. (eds) *A Critique of Current Educational Aims*, Part I of *Education and the Development of Reason*. London: Routledge and Kegan Paul.

23 Wragg, E.C. (1978) A suitable case for imitation. *The Times Educational Supplement*, 15 September.

RELATED ISSUES

Of the many educational issues that ought to be included in a course of teacher education we have chosen to discuss the three which, in our opinion, are of paramount importance to those entering the teaching profession during the 1980s. Each of the three issues has been the subject of a major Government Report. The first has to do with the multi-cultural nature of contemporary British society, and with the role of the school in promoting the rights, the interests and the aspirations of all of its pupils. At the time of writing the interim report of the Rampton Committee (1981) has been published and we await the deliberations of its successor under the chairmanship of Lord Swann. The second issue is concerned with that sizeable proportion of our school population which the Warnock Committee (1978) has chosen to designate as 'children with special educational needs'. Our third and final topic relates to the heightened awareness of human relationships that teachers can gain from the study of language and communication in the classroom. It arises directly from the influential Bullock Report (1975) and its recommendation that all teachers in initial training should follow a 'substantial course of language in education'.

MULTICULTURAL CLASSROOMS

Immigration to Britain over the past twenty years or so has brought about fundamental changes in our society. We are now an ethnically-mixed and a culturally-varied nation. One consequence of this is that our institutions are having to adapt in order to reflect and to cater for the many mixed communities that now exist throughout the country. Schools in particular are having to change to accommodate the needs of immigrant pupils in many areas. Whether or not schools are prepared to make sufficient changes and modifications in their organizational policies and practices to meet the needs and aspirations of all their members is a matter of current concern, for as one study[1] shows, many teachers appear to hold what can be described as an *assimilationist* viewpoint with respect to immigrants and their needs.

The term *assimilationist* refers to a point of view that dominated official and educational policy in the early days of immigration in the 1960s. This sought to help immigrants accommodate to the host society by giving them a working knowledge of the English language and of the indigenous culture, and was based on the belief that once English language proficiency had been acquired, all other problems would diminish. The National Foundation for Educational Research study to which we referred above shows that as far as many teachers are concerned, it is all right to impart information about the religions and homelands of minority groups but beyond this they are divided in their opinions about the extent to which they are prepared to make changes in their curriculum planning and teaching in light of the multicultural composition of contemporary British society. It is our firm belief that an *assimilationist* viewpoint is both patronizing and dismissive of other cultures and lifestyles. All over the world minority groups now actively assert their determination to maintain cultural continuity and to preserve their religious, linguistic and cultural differences. Increasingly, therefore, the host society is turning its attention to the concept of *cultural pluralism*. What exactly does this term imply? Simply that second generation British-born blacks, Sikhs, Hindus and Moslems, while sharing many of the same interests and aspirations of white pupils, are at the same time determined to retain their involvement in the richness of their own minority cultures. *Cultural pluralism*, then, implies a system that accepts that people's lifestyles and customs are different and operates so as to allow equality of opportunity for all to play a full part in society.

Our task in this section* is to discuss an outline for a *multicultural curriculum* that, according to its author, is a natural response to the altered nature of British society and which, from our point of view, exemplifies the practical consequences of a culturally pluralistic position.

A multicultural curriculum

Jeffcoate[2] defines a multicultural curriculum as one in which choice of content reflects the multicultural nature of British society and the world and draws significantly on the experiences of British racial minorities and cultures overseas. He justifies such a curriculum for the following reasons. First, there is what Jeffcoate calls a 'pathological' justification for developing a multicultural curriculum arising out of the pernicious and pervasive racism in British society. Schools, Jeffcoate believes, have a clear duty to make a concerted response to the evil of racism by promoting racial self-respect and interracial understanding. Second, a multicultural curriculum can be justified on the notion of minority group rights. That is to say, ethnic minorities are entitled to expect that their cultures will be positively and prominently represented in the

* We draw on material in Cohen, L. and Manion, L. (1982) *Multicultural Classrooms: Perspectives for Teachers*. London: Croom Helm. Chapter 8.

school curriculum. Third, if it is a fundamental task of the school to present an accurate picture of society to its pupils then it follows that other races and cultures are important elements in that picture. Fourth, a multicultural curriculum involves pupils in more interesting, stimulating and challenging experiences than one which is not.

Having set out a justification for a multicultural curriculum, how does one go about selecting learning experiences that might be incorporated within it? We summarize Jeffcoate's five criteria of selection in Box 24 below.

Box 24

Criteria for selecting learning experiences for a multiracial curriculum

1 A curriculum for the final quarter of the twentieth century needs to be international in its choice of content and in its perspective. An insular curriculum focusing on Britain and British values is unjustifiable and inappropriate.

2 Contemporary British society contains a variety of social and ethnic groups; this variety should be made evident in the visuals, stories and information offered to children.

3 Pupils should have access to accurate information about racial and cultural differences and similarities.

4 People from British minority groups and from other cultures overseas should be presented as individuals with every variety of human quality and attribute.

5 Other cultures and nations have their own validity and should be described in their own terms. Wherever possible they should be allowed to speak for themselves and not be judged exclusively against British or European norms.

Source: adapted from Jeffcoate[2]

Drawing on his experiences with the Schools Council, Jeffcoate identifies some limitations in the organization of materials and methods for multicultural classrooms.

There is not a lot to be said, he warns, for isolating topics on India, Africa or the Caribbean which are not part of a comprehensive multicultural policy. Indeed, where schools have poor relations, such efforts are likely to be counterproductive. A sounder approach is to construct a learning programme around regular themes drawing on a variety of cultures for source materials with which all pupils can identify. That said, there is still the need for some kind of overt, systematic study since themes of themselves cannot provide pupils with an appreciative understanding of the logic and integrity of a way of life different from their own. Jeffcoate argues that the humanities curriculum should divide its attention evenly between local and international studies, these serving to complement one another in the process whereby children make sense of their world. Having decided to incorporate minority cultures into their curricula, schools should avoid defining these cultures solely in terms of patterns of life and experience in countries and continents of origin. It may be far more pertinent for children to look at these minority cultures as they are currently evolving and taking shape here in Britain. Finally, Jeffcoate has something to say about development studies, that is to say, those types of investigation of the Third World that are particularly popular in secondary schools. Too often, it seems, they infringe the fifth criterion we identify in Box 24, by making European concepts and categories integral to their operations. The multicultural curriculum involves a change in perspective as well as a change in content, an end, in effect, to ethnocentrism which views other cultures in a disparaging or, at best, condescending way.

In Box 24, we list Jeffcoate's criteria for choosing learning experiences in the multicultural curriculum. In an earlier paper[3] he has outlined a *modus operandi* for curriculum planning in the multicultural school based on the traditional objectives model. His expressed intentions in the article are to establish the primacy of objectives in curriculum planning in multicultural education and to explore what factors might govern their selection. The latter we have included in Box 25 below. Jeffcoate justifies his preference for the objectives model because, as he explains:

> We share the basic assumption of the objectives school that the function of formal education is to bring about desired changes in children. We want them to have acquired certain identifiable knowledge and skills and developed certain identifiable attitudes and behaviours by the time they leave school. We must be prepared to make these knowledges, skills, attitudes and behaviours the starting point and focus for our curriculum planning.

While recognizing that the objectives model has certain weaknesses, Jeffcoate is careful to defend his own particular taxonomy. For him, multicultural education is *primarily affective*, being concerned with attitudes and only instrumentally cognitive. But, as he goes on to explain:

> It is a different sort of affectivity from the affectivity of creative work or aesthetic judgement. Even though the overriding objectives, respect for self and others, stipulated in the classification could hardly be called 'correct', they are ones we believe to be necessary for

children and for society, and we could go some way to justifying their selection; equally, they are not objectives that could be said to be open to negotiation. Many of the objectives in the classification are knowledge objectives, and I have called these 'instrumental'. In order to come to respect themselves and others, I am suggesting children must be in possession of certain facts. The first three specific knowledge objectives are, then, a necessary (but not, of course, a sufficient) condition of the overriding objective of respect for others. It is at this point that we find ourselves at odds with the dominant progressive ideology. We do not dissent from the importance they attach to skills but we also attach importance, in a way they would not, to specific items of knowledge which we feel to be predicated by our overall affective targets.

In stressing the need for the acquisition of distinctive knowledge Jeffcoate concedes that he may be adopting a somewhat unfashionable stance. He goes on to discuss factors governing the selection of objectives. In particular, he reviews the way in which they are significantly affected by a school's value system (its philosophy of education) and its definition and analysis of the situation (problems, needs and so on).

Each of these three models is sufficiently open-ended and contains sufficient principles to be used as a suitable starting point for the construction of a multicultural curriculum. Jeffcoate's classification of objectives is set out in Box 25 overleaf.

Clearly, Jeffcoate's approach is one of *moral persuasion*, concentrating as it does on how respect for self and for others should be the cornerstone of a non-prejudiced society (but *only* from the point of view of the dominant community, notes Gundara).[5] Gundara and others[5] have criticized Jeffcoate's work for its essentially neutral stance. They point to a lack of stress on socio-political aspects of multicultural education* and cite a typology for the multicultural curriculum suggested by Williams[6] which includes, *inter alia*, a socio-political perspective which asserts that what passes for knowledge is no more than the dominant ideology of a particular society. Williams calls for a multicultural curriculum which challenges the value consensus in British society and thereby leaves open the possibility of a diverse society consisting of relatively separate but equal groups. Such an approach might focus upon the history and the literature of this country, using historical experiences and literary responses as a key to understanding the effects of colonialism upon our

* Whether this particular criticism is justified in light of the contents of Box 25 we leave readers to judge.

Box 25

A classification of objectives in multiracial education

(A) *Respect for others:*
Cognitive (knowledge)
All pupils should *know*:
    the basic facts of race and racial difference;
    the customs, values and beliefs of the main cultures represented in Britain and, more particularly, of those forming the local community;
    why different groups have immigrated into Britain in the past and how the local community has come to acquire its present ethnic composition.

Cognitive (skills)
All pupils should *be able to*:
    detect stereotyping and scapegoating in what they see, hear and read;
    evaluate their own cultures objectively.

Affective (attitudes, values and emotional sets)
All pupils should *accept*:
    the uniqueness of each individual human being;
    the underlying humanity we share;
    the principles of equal rights and justice;
    and value the achievements of other cultures and nations;
    strangeness without feeling threatened;
    that Britain is, always has been and always will be a multicultural society;
    that no culture is ever static and that constant mutual accommodation will be required of all cultures making up an evolving multicultural society;
    that prejudice and discrimination are widespread in Britain and the historical and socio-economic causes which have given rise to them;
    the damaging effect of prejudice and discrimination on the rejected groups;
    the possibility of developing multiple loyalties.

(B) *Respect for self:*
Cognitive (knowledge)
All pupils should *know*:
    the history and achievements of their own culture and what is distinctive about it.

Cognitive (skills)
All pupils should *be able to*:
    communicate efficiently in English and, if it is not their mother tongue, in their own mother tongue;

master the other basic skills necessary for success at school.

Affective (attitudes, values and emotional sets)
All pupils should *have developed*:
   a positive self-image;
   confidence in their sense of their own identity.

Source: adapted from Jeffcoate[3]

society. Williams further suggests that a multicultural curriculum should teach about race relations and should explore the reasons for migration, government legislation and other controversial issues.

From this brief review it can be seen that there is as yet little agreement about the aims and objectives of multicultural education or about what ought to constitute a multicultural curriculum. In concluding with a look at some practical suggestions by Saunders[4] for ways of helping children explore the cultural diversity existing in multicultural classrooms we invite readers to consider to what extent Saunders' proposals reflect the thinking of Jeffcoate as we have tried to summarize the latter's viewpoint in this section of the book.

Box 26

Activities for exploring cultural diversity

Similarities and differences
1 Pair off the children either randomly or in friendship pairs. Each pupil takes a turn to list or call out a similarity between himself and his partner. Then each child of the pairs in turn is required to list or call out a difference between himself and his partner. This can be played competitively between pairs.
2 Divide the class into two groups using simple criteria, e.g. boys/girls; those with birthdays from September to February, those with birthdays from March to August. Each group will compete to draw up lists of similarities that are perceived within each group and lists of differences between the two groups.
3 The whole class draws up a list of characteristics common to the class and another list of differences between the class and other classes in school.
These three activities should lead in to a discussion of the ease with which people can be grouped and the advantages and disadvantages of grouping, as well as sensitizing pupils to human differences.

Individual differences
4 Illustrations can be cut from magazines to highlight individual differences in appearance. Illustrations of hair styles and clothes can also be collected and displayed.

These can be used to focus upon individual differences in discussion.

Identity

5 Collect examples of ways in which people can be identified or draw up lists if examples cannot be gathered. These can consist of birth certificates, NHS numbers, numbers on the school roll, passport photographs, fingerprints, footprints, names – fore and surnames.

Derivations of names

6 There are a number of ways in which names can be explored: derivations, significance of certain names, e.g. the Scottish 'Mac', the Sikh 'Kaur' and 'Singh'. These are better investigated by the pupils interviewing people of the relevant ethnic group.

The pupils can also be asked to discover names that have equivalents in other languages, e.g. John (English), Ian (Scottish), Sion (Welsh), Shane (Irish).

Culturally important categories

7 Every culture develops a rich vocabulary around objects and concepts that are important to it. Pupils in groups should first select categories which seem to be important within a culture and then compile lists of words associated with each category. For example:

Bread – white, brown, granary, French stick
Clothes (Western) – shirt, blouse, trousers, jeans
Clothes (Asian) – shallwah, sarree, turban
Curry – madras, keema, vindaloo

With older pupils it would be worthwhile to base a discussion on how language reveals our values; with suitable lists it would be possible to make cross-cultural comparisons.

Who is ideal?

8 With the pupils in pairs, ask each pair to draw up a profile of the kind of person they would consider ideal. Where there is doubt, more than one profile might be compiled.

After, say, half an hour a discussion should reveal that there is no universal ideal type, but rather that different situations make different demands and so call for different strengths.

Source: adapted from Saunders[4]

Notes and references

1 Brittan, E.M. (1976) Multiracial education II. *Educational Research*, 18 (2), 96–107.
2 Jeffcoate, R. (1979) A multicultural curriculum: beyond the orthodoxy. *Trends in Education*, 4, 8–12.

3 Jeffcoate, R. (1976) Curriculum planning in multiracial education. *Educational Research*, 18 (3), 192–200.
4 Saunders, M. (1981) *Multicultural Teaching: A Guide for the Classroom*. Maidenhead: McGraw-Hill.
5 Gundara, J. (1982) Approaches to multicultural education. In Tierney, J. (ed.) *Race, Migration and Schooling*. Eastbourne: Holt, Rinehart and Winston.
6 Williams, J. (1979) *The social science teacher*, 8 (4), cited in J. Gundara op. cit.
7 Dodgson, P. and Stewart, D. (1981) Multiculturalism or anti-racist teaching: a question of alternatives. *Multiracial Education*, 9 (3), 41–4.

CHILDREN WITH LEARNING DIFFICULTIES

Introduction

The idea is deeply ingrained in educational thinking that there are two types of children, the *handicapped* and the *non-handicapped*.... But the complexities of individual need are far greater than this dichotomy implies.... We wish to see a more positive approach and we have adopted the concept of *special educational* need.

These words are from the Warnock Report,[1] a comprehensive review of educational provision in England, Scotland and Wales for children and young people handicapped by disabilities of body or mind. Our task in this section of the book is to introduce student teachers to some implications of the Warnock Report, as they will undoubtedly impinge upon teachers' work in classrooms in ordinary schools during the 1980s.

One of the most startling statistics to emerge from the Warnock Committee's Report is that at some time during their school career *one in five children* will require some form of special educational provision.

Clearly, the Warnock Committee has widened the definition of special education to include children needing relatively mild remedial attention and it follows that special provision for this proportion of the school population means *provision in ordinary schools* as well as special schools. Research[2] surveyed by the Committee revealed that childhood disabilities giving rise to special educational needs are found in a much larger proportion of the school population than has commonly been assumed. One of the conclusions of the Report, therefore, is that the tendency to equate special education with special schooling is inappropriate, given the large number of children with special educational needs in ordinary schools.

What does this mean for the teacher? Simply this.

A teacher in a mixed ability class of thirty in an *ordinary school*, should be aware that as many as six pupils might require some form of special provision at some time, and about four or five children will need special provision at any given time. Such children (and those currently categorized as educationally sub-normal), the Warnock Report refers to as *children with learning difficulties*, a term it recommends should be employed to embrace children with emotional and behavioural difficulties and those receiving remedial education. While special schools will continue to be the main providers of special education for children with severe or complex physical, sensory or intellectual disabilities, those with behavioural or emotional disorders that are so extreme that they disrupt ordinary school classes, and those with less severe difficulties who even with special help do not perform well in ordinary schools, it follows that the task of recognizing early signs of possible special educational need and, where appropriate, coping with them in ordinary classrooms, will increasingly be the responsibility of teachers in ordinary schools.

Is this really feasible, readers may well ask. The answer suggested by the findings of a recent three-year study[3] is a resounding *yes*. To a far greater extent than is currently practised, the authors conclude, special educational needs can be met in ordinary schools providing, of course, that there is the requisite commitment and resources. Hegarty, Pocklington and Lucas[3] undertook a detailed examination of seventeen integration programmes in fourteen LEAs, the programmes themselves varying enormously in terms of the types of special needs that were catered for and in respect of the ages and the numbers of children involved. Box 27 shows the range and the scope of the investigation.

Teachers' reactions

In the space available to us we focus specifically on the attitudes and reactions of ordinary* teachers in the twenty-two schools involved in the research and on the problems of curriculum development in the integration of children with special educational needs into ordinary schools.

Two hundred and forty-seven teachers completed questionnaires revealing their knowledge of children with special needs and their competence in handling and teaching such pupils. The majority of them responded that they had relatively little or no knowledge when the various integration programmes were begun in their particular schools. At the end of the study, however, teachers were able to report a considerable increase in their understanding of specific handicaps, their greater knowledge being chiefly attributable to two sources: (1) direct

---

* 'Ordinary' teacher refers simply to any teacher who does not have a specialist role in relation to pupils with special needs.

experience of the pupils themselves, and (2) from interaction (largely on an informal basis) with more knowledgeable persons such as specialist teachers, educational psychologists and speech therapists.

Box 27

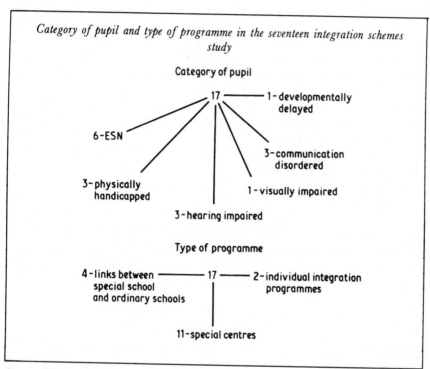

Category of pupil and type of programme in the seventeen integration schemes study

Category of pupil

17 ——— 1 - developmentally delayed

6 - ESN

3 - communication disordered

3 - physically handicapped

1 - visually impaired

3 - hearing impaired

Type of programme

4 - links between special school and ordinary schools ——— 17 ——— 2 - individual integration programmes

11 - special centres

Source: Hegarty, Pocklington and Lucas[3]

Although 'ordinary' teachers felt that they were fairly competent to deal with the pupils with special needs allocated to their classes, their comments showed that to no small extent their feelings of adequacy reflected the existence of specialist teacher facilities in their schools and the fact that their responsibilities for pupils with special needs were limited.

What the study clearly revealed was that integrating pupils with special needs into ordinary schools requires new ways of working on the part of the various professionals involved. There is, the researchers report, a need to collaborate with colleagues, share information, view pupils' problems in a comprehensive light, disseminate skills and generally move toward interdisciplinary working. This is very difficult to achieve in light of such obstacles as territoriality and traditions of isolated professionalism among teachers.

The curriculum and integration programmes

What of the curriculum in such programmes of integration? What is actually being offered to children with special needs in ordinary schools? The study revealed considerable diversity in practice. By way of example, Box 28 reports the type of provision made for pre-school and infant children with severe learning difficulties within a set of five special classes. Hegarty, Pocklington and Lucas[3] propose that the range of special educational provision can be conceived of as a continuum ranging from segregated special schooling to full attendance in a normal class, different forms of provision being seen as different points along the continuum. They outline the following range that is available to pupils with special needs:

1 Special curriculum

This is a curriculum that has little or no reference to work being done by age peers. Such curricula, they opine, are unlikely to find a place in integration programmes and are increasingly being called into question as providing a valid approach to special education.

2 Special curriculum plus

Special curricula have become less isolated from mainstream curricula as a result of the growing realization that all children are educable and that it is important to focus on similarities as well as differences. Thus a common curricular pattern, the researchers note, is 'basic skills plus general enrichment', a fair description of the curriculum in many special schools.

3 Normal curriculum, significant reductions

Here the emphasis is quite markedly on what pupils with special needs have in common with their peers. They follow a normal curriculum as far as is possible with modifications and omissions in order to meet their special needs. This approach is clearly different from one whose starting point is pupils' special needs even though such a programme may involve extensive withdrawal and the abandoning of several subjects.

Box 28

Provision for very young children with special educational needs

While there are considerable differences between the classes, the common aim underlying their curricular provision is to offer an enriched version of nursery and infant teaching practice: an abundance of learning resources; a stimulating learning environment; and individual attention – in relation both to children's general difficulties in learning and to specific difficulties (e.g. developing speech and language). A few children receive individual speech programmes prepared by a visiting speech therapist. Another aspect that is strongly emphasized is music and movement, provided by a peripatetic teacher. The classes are self-contained for teaching purposes, and the work children do owes little or nothing to the main school curriculum.

Each teacher will typically draw up termly aims for every child in each of the following areas: self-management; pre-number; pre-reading; speech and language; constructive and creative. Teachers aim to cover the basics – reading, writing, number and language – every day with each child. Other activities such as painting, shop and playing with large, wheeled toys take place twice weekly. Reading begins with the children's own names, progressing to matching words using flash cards. Children may produce their own books, the teacher or ancillary writing a sentence which the children has to copy and make a suitable drawing. Number work begins with counting objects, recognizing numbers, using songs and finger plays. Children also learn to sort, count and recognize numbers. Language work is particularly emphasized. It is strongly individualized, with children encouraged to name objects by pointing to them and saying the appropriate word. Teachers do not use specialized language schemes such as the Peabody Language Development Kit or Distar Language.

Given the severity of these children's difficulties, instruction must extend beyond the customary classroom activities and opportunities for teaching them must be sought throughout the day. For instance, toileting sessions can be capitalized upon for teaching the various parts of the body, lunchtime is an opportunity for teaching socially acceptable eating habits and so on. The close supervision which a generous staffing ratio permits is important since staff need to spend a good deal of time with these children. As one participant wrote, 'It is not enough to provide and encourage participation in (for example) play situations; the adults must be on hand to exploit with the individual child the first glimmer of a materializing association, be it visual, aural or kinaesthetic.'

Source: adapted from Hegarty, Pocklington and Lucas[3]

4 Normal curriculum, some modifications

Some pupils with special needs follow the same curriculum as their peers with some omissions and/or supplementary or alternative activities. Partially sighted children, for example, may be precluded from taking part in certain aspects of art and craft, concentrating instead on sculpture and such activities that are dependent on tactile senses.

5 Normal curriculum, little or no modification

Hegarty and his associates found many pupils with special needs following the same curriculum to all intents and purposes and in the same teaching groups as their peers. This was especially the case, they noted, in the case of the physically handicapped, but it also applied to others as well.

By way of conclusion, we report the comments of the researchers on pupils' social and emotional development. There was a broad consensus, they found, among teachers, parents and the pupils themselves that children with special needs benefit greatly from being placed in integration programmes. There were gains in self-confidence, independence and in the realistic acceptance of an individual's handicapping condition. Friendly relationships between pupils with special needs and their peers did occur but they tended to be limited and often involved outgroups in the school. Negative relationships such as teasing were reported to be comparatively rare. Particularly encouraging was the 'teachers' thoroughgoing endorsement of the integration programme in their schools'.

Notes and references

1 Great Britain: The Department of Education and Science (1978) *Special Educational Needs* (The Warnock Report). London: HMSO.

2 Pringle, M.L.K., Rutter, M. and Davie, E. (1966) *11,000 Seven Year Olds*. Harlow: Longman.
Fogelman, K. (1976) *Britain's Sixteen Year Olds*. London: National Children's Bureau.
Rutter, M., Tizard, J. and Whitmore, K. (1970) *Education, Health and Behaviour*. Harlow: Longman.

3 Hegarty, S., Pocklington, K. and Lucas, D. (1981) *Educating Pupils with Special Needs in the Ordinary School*. Windsor: NFER-Nelson.

LANGUAGE IN EDUCATION*

Introduction

The inclusion of a section concerning language in education expresses our support for the view of Wilkinson[1] who says that the study of language and communication is of value, not to give the teacher a body of information to teach, but to heighten his awareness of the nature of relationships between human beings, and between language, learning and thought. Barnes[2] goes further, observing that not only do teachers gain from a more sophisticated insight into the implications of their own use of language and into the part that language plays in their pupils' learning, but also that such insights can contribute dramatically to the effectiveness of teaching in schools.

Such views by these and other experts in the field are endorsed in the Bullock Report, *A Language for Life*,[3] which makes a strong recommendation that 'a substantial course of language in education... should be part of every primary and secondary teacher's initial training, whatever the teacher's subject or the age of the children with whom he or she will be working.'

Educationalists have long acknowledged the crucial role that language plays in the child's education though, as yet, there is no general agreement on the precise relationship between language and education. Indeed, so Olympian are the peaks of the problem that researchers have to begin modestly in the foothills. There they investigate a wide range of issues, four of which we have selected as being of direct concern to intending teachers. These are to do with (1) language and classroom interaction, (2) the characteristics of talk in the classroom, (3) the part played by specialist language in the classroom – so-called subject-specific language and (4) the consequences of language disadvantage and deprivation, with particular reference to ethnic minority pupils in multicultural classrooms.

Language and classroom interaction

The most important reason for observing and studying teacher–pupil dialogue in classrooms is that the dialogue taking place between

---

* In this section we draw on material contained in Cohen, L. and Manion, L. (1981) *Perspectives on Classrooms and Schools*. Eastbourne: Holt, Rinehart and Winston. Chapters 6 and 8.

teachers and pupils *is* the educational process, or the major part of it for most children. No matter how important other factors such as IQ, social class background, parental encouragement or children's individual language skills appear to be, they nevertheless remain external influences.[4] Such is the view of Stubbs, who goes on to observe that for all its importance, relatively little research has been undertaken on the *interactional aspects* of the teaching process in classroom settings.

Traditionally, much of the research to do with classrooms has been of a *normative* cast: this is to say that the process of education could best be understood by looking at *input variables* such as intelligence, motivation, social class background and personality, and comparing them with *output variables* – how well a child has done according to an agreed set of criteria. In other words, what happened between the input and output phases was largely ignored: few seemed to be interested in what was actually taking place *inside* classrooms. Stubbs argues that on commonsense grounds alone, it would seem that an understanding of teaching and learning would have to depend, at least in part, on observation of teachers and learners. Although an impressive body of information on learning theory has been built up this century, it has largely been derived from carefully controlled experimental situations. For this reason, it is extremely difficult to extrapolate the findings to 'real-life' contexts: in other words, we still know very little about *how* children learn in classrooms. Stubbs suggests that the only way to overcome this problem is to observe children in the classroom and, particularly, the way they interact with teachers and fellow pupils.

In thus pleading for a closer correspondence between what we say about education and detailed empirical investigation of what is actually *said* in the classroom, Stubbs identifies the kinds of specific questions to be asked. Given that many messages are conveyed by teachers to pupils, just how are they communicated? By *what* 'structure'? What *are* the rules of the verbal game? What specific behaviours? If they are specific, then they can be specified. We might easily continue the list. How are messages received by pupils? How are they assimilated, comprehended and acted upon? What part does the language of education, or of specialist subjects, play in promoting or hindering communication and learning? And how does a child's background, socially and linguistically, affect the transactions that take place?

Numerous reasons could be advanced, no doubt, to explain why there has been a shortage of naturalistic studies of classroom interaction. We refer to two of them. First, there is the enormous complexity of communicative behaviour, a complexity which can only be unravelled by on-the-spot observation and analysis. Earlier research methods have functioned more as a deterrent than an aid in this respect. The second reason is logically related to the first. Because there have been few naturalistic studies, we lack an appropriate terminology to talk about classroom interaction and the teaching process. As Stubbs[4] says in this regard:

> If one talks to teachers about their classroom experiences, one discovers immediately that there is simply no vocabulary of descriptive concepts for talking about teaching. Despite the vast complexity of second-by-second classroom dialogue, the discussion will be conceptually crude and oversimplified. It is time that teachers had an adequate descriptive language for talking about their own professional behaviour.

The descriptive language and body of concepts referred to by Stubbs, together with the theoretical framework to which these will relate, can only come from empirical studies of interactional processes at the centre of action, that is to say, the *classroom itself*. In this respect a beginning has been made and it is fitting to close this section with a brief review of some of the more important studies undertaken in this connection in the past ten years or so.[5] Most of them are case studies and are thus based on a detailed description of a group of lessons or even a single lesson.

A pioneering study in the field of classroom language is Barnes' *Language in the Secondary Classroom*.[2] His concern was to record the whole language environment of a first-year class during their first half-term in a comprehensive school with a view to investigating the ways in which a teacher's language might impede rather than facilitate learning because of the terminology or style used. He was thus interested in both spoken and written language, and also in the child as a producer and receiver of language. Being readily accessible and having many good examples of classroom exchanges, the book offers a very good introduction to the topic to student teachers.

In contending that many teachers when talking about their subject use a specialist language of instruction that might be a barrier to children's learning, Barnes identifies three categories: (1) specialist language perceived by the teacher as a potential barrier and therefore carefully 'presented' to them; (2) specialist language not so presented for various reasons; and (3) the language of secondary education which is made up of forms not specific to school subjects, nor likely to be used or heard by pupils in any other situation.

In a more recent study,[6] Barnes assumes that language is a major means of learning and that pupils' uses of language for learning are strongly influenced by the teacher's language which, he argues, prescribes them their roles as learners. This assumption thereby involves a shift of emphasis from the more traditional view of language as *a means of teaching*. In operational terms, therefore, this means that we learn not only by listening passively to the teacher, but by verbalizing, by talking, by discussing and arguing. By studying teacher–pupil interaction, one can begin to see how classroom language offers different possibilities of learning to pupils. Should pupils merely be passive listeners? Or should they be allowed to verbalize at some point? Or should active dialogue with the teacher be encouraged? Just three ways of pupils' participation in learning, but all under the control of the teacher's own speech behaviour.

Like Barnes' earlier study, Mishler's work[7] takes extracts of classroom dialogue and subjects them to perceptive analysis. Unlike Barnes, however, he is more concerned with showing how different cognitive strategies as well as different values and norms are carried in the language used, chiefly in the structure of teachers' statements and in the types of exchange developed between them and the children. By contrasting speech recordings of different first-grade teachers with each other, he sets out to extract different features in the language used and to show how these features reflect both different constructions of reality and different ways of learning about it: this is to say that what teachers say and how they say it creates a particular sort of world for the children.[4]

Mishler's main purpose, then, is to show how teachers' cognitive strategies are conveyed in the warp and weft of classroom dialogue. To this end, he is concerned with how attention is focused, with how teachers orient themselves and their pupils to the problem under discussion; the procedures for information search and evaluation; and the structure of alternatives, that is, the number of types of alternative answers to a question and their relationship to each other.

Writing of Mishler's work, Stubbs[4] says:

> Mishler's approach is one which could be of direct interest to teachers. By close study of transcribed lessons he shows how quite general teaching strategies are conveyed by the fine grain of a teacher's use of language. Such a study can therefore begin to throw a little light on how children learn what they do in school. Only by close observation of how teachers and pupils actually talk to each other can one discover how concepts are put across, how some lines of enquiry are opened up and others closed off, how pupils' responses are evaluated, and how their attention is directed to the areas of knowledge which the school regards as valuable.

In another comparatively recent study, Stubbs himself describes one way in which teachers in relatively traditional lessons control classroom exchanges.[8] A characteristic of much classroom talk is the extent of the teacher's *conversational control* over the topic, over the relevance or correctness of what pupils say, and over when and how much pupils may speak. In traditional lessons, children have few conversational rights. Whereas this has often been pointed out in general, the actual verbal strategies used by teachers to control classroom talk have yet to be systematically studied. What Stubbs shows is that a teacher is constantly monitoring the communication system in the classroom by such utterances as 'You see, we're really getting on to the topic now,' or 'OK, now listen all of you,' or 'Now, we don't want any silly remarks.' The teacher is thus able to check whether pupils are all on the same wavelength and whether at least some of them follow what is being said. Stubbs refers to such language as *meta-communication*.[4] 'It is,' he says, 'communication about communication: messages which refer back to the communication system itself, checking whether it is functioning properly.'

In conclusion, he adds:

> Such talk is characteristic of teachers' language: utterances which, as it were, stand outside the discourse and comment on it comprise a large percentage of what teachers say to their pupils, and comprise a major way of controlling classroom dialogue. Use of such language is also highly asymmetrical: one would not expect a pupil to say to a teacher: *That's an interesting point*. Such speech acts, in which the teacher monitors and controls the classroom dialogue are, at one level, the very stuff of teaching. They are basic to the activity of teaching, since they are the acts whereby a teacher *controls the flow of information* in the classroom and defines the relevance of what is said.

Characteristics of talk

It is only in the past ten years or so that the value of talk in the classroom has attracted the attention it deserves. This has been manifest in the steady flow of articles and books stressing the need for greater emphasis on spoken work in schools,[9] a need that has come about because, some believe, we have tended to devalue talk in the school and classroom. Whether this is true or not, one cannot deny that a considerable amount of talking does take place in schools; and this is so because our own culture depends to a very large extent on the spoken word as a means of transmitting knowledge. In reviewing the main characteristics of classroom talk, particularly that of older children, Edwards and Furlong[10] consider that not only is there so much of it, but that so much of what is said is both public and highly centralized. What they mean by being 'highly centralized' is that for much of the time in classrooms, there is a *single* verbal encounter in that whatever is being said demands the attention of all.

In pursuing the theme of centralized communication further, Edwards and Furlong explain that although it plays a very important part in classroom interaction, its role should not be overstated, for considerable amounts of incidental and unofficial talk take place amid official exchanges. The authors further point out that, notwithstanding the occasions when children talk privately to other members of the class, when they offer comments and pose questions when requested to do so, or when they talk 'unofficially', their main communicative role, as far as traditional classrooms are concerned, is *to listen*. This means that the communicative rights of teacher and pupils are very unequal. In effect, the authors point out, teachers usually tell pupils when to talk, what to talk about, when to stop talking and how well they talked. The normal conversation between two equals stands in marked contrast to classroom exchanges because of this very inequality. In the former, no one has overriding claim to speak first, or more than others, or to decide unilaterally on the subject. The difference between an everyday conversation and a classroom exchange is dramatically realized when each kind is recorded and transcribed. In the case of everyday exchanges, statements are often incomplete, they clash with the statements of others and they are interrupted. There are also frequent false starts, hesitations and repetitions.[10] Unless the transcript is edited, it is often difficult to make much sense of. By contrast, exchanges recorded in traditional classrooms are much more orderly and systematic. Indeed, Edwards and Furlong observe that they often look like a play script. As they comment, 'Most utterances are complete, and most speakers seem to know their lines and to recognize their turn to speak. Despite the large numbers, the talk appears more orderly.'[10] Thus it is that whereas in everyday informal conversations there is always the possibility that several speakers will perversely talk against one another or that one individual will eventually appropriate a disproportionate amount of the talking time, in classroom interaction contributors to a discussion must be carefully controlled. The authors point out that this is much more easily achieved if communication rights are *not* equally shared – 'if one participant can speak whenever he chooses to do so, can normally nominate the next speaker, and can resolve any cases of confusion.'[10]

The authors go on to explain that in so far as pupils are ready to be taught, they are likely to acknowledge that an able teacher has the right to talk first, last and most; to control the content of a lesson; and to organize that content by allocating speaking turns to the pupils. The teacher's right to decide who speaks, when, for how long and to whom, is mirrored in the small number of interactional possibilities in a typical lesson. Edwards and Furlong refer to such arrangements of speakers and listeners as *participant-structures* which they define as communicative networks linking those who are in contact with one another already, or can be if they choose.[10] Box 29 identifies common instances of such participant structures to be found in traditional classrooms.

Box 29

Participant-structures in traditional classrooms

In traditional classrooms, the participant-structures in order of decreasing frequency are as follows:

1 The teacher talking to a silent audience, and requiring everyone's attention.
2 The teacher talking to one pupil (asking a question, evaluating an answer, issuing reproof), but assuming that everyone else is taking notice.
3 A pupil talking to the teacher, with the rest of the class as audience.
4 The teacher talking to one or more pupils when the others are *not* expected to listen and may be allowed to talk themselves.
5 Pupils discussing among themselves with the teacher as chairman (neutral or otherwise).
6 Pupils discussing among themselves with the teacher absent.

Source: Edwards and Furlong[10]

Enlarging on the nature of them, Edwards and Furlong[10] say:

It is not difficult to link these structures intuitively to certain obvious stages in lessons – for example, to the teacher lecturing, checking on the reception of the lecture, inviting queries, sorting out problems, eliciting discussion, and trusting pupils to work on their own. . . . What even the simplest list brings out is the limited variety of interactional patterns characteristic of lessons, and how firmly most of them are centred on the teacher. There is usually a formalized allocation of speaking and listening roles. Teachers expect both a 'proper' silence *and* a 'proper' willingness to talk, and they manage the interaction so as to produce orderly and relevant pupil participation.

The authors go on to consider how this orderliness is achieved. In the well-ordered classroom, they explain, the teacher's turns at speaking are taken as and when he chooses, these being determined by the kinds of pupil he addresses and also the subject matter being taught. Thus teachers appear to talk less to younger pupils, to brighter pupils, and when they are teaching English or social studies, for example, as compared with science or modern languages.[10] However interesting these variations are, they are overshadowed by the difficulty most teachers seem to have in limiting themselves to much less than two-thirds of the time available for talking. Because much of the time appropriated by teachers is taken up by giving information and instructions, censuring pupils and evaluating them, Edwards and Furlong consider that most of their talking can be described as *telling*.

In seeing teacher talk in this context as *dominant performance*, Edwards and Furlong suggest that the teacher's message is made all the more effective because of his 'front of stage' location. The traditional classroom settings serve as a means of reinforcing the centrally controlled interaction.[10] As they say:

> The conventional groupings of desks or tables channel communication to and from the teacher, who is the obvious focus of attention. He can direct his talk to any part of the room, while the natural flow of pupil-talk is either to him or to other pupils through him. It is a setting which makes it difficult for the teacher to avoid talking *at* pupils, or to break up the interaction into more localized encounters. In classrooms which are physically more open, no single focus of attention may be visible at all. Symbolically and practically, there is a switch of emphasis from the teacher to the learner.

We shall return again to the use of space in classrooms when we consider aspects of nonverbal communication.

But the teacher cannot monopolize the talk totally. There has to be a certain amount of pupil participation; and this presents the teacher with significant managerial problems because of the numbers of children involved. Once a teacher stops talking, Edwards and Furlong ask, how are turns taken? How is the rule of one speaker at a time maintained? Who is to answer a particular question? Normally, it is the teacher's on-the-spot decisions that solve them – 'Turns are allocated, they are not seized, and pupils have to learn to bid appropriately for the right to speak.'[10]

We have been concerned in the section with some characteristics of talk in classrooms and have seen how most participant-structures focus on the teacher who either does the talking or who nominates others to do it. For further consideration of teacher dominance in this context we refer you to the work of Edwards and Furlong[10] who go on to examine further aspects of classroom interaction, including the shaping of meaning – the asking of questions, the management of answers, and the constraints imposed by the social nature of the setting.

Subject-specific language

An important aspect of language in the classroom is the part it plays in meeting the particular needs of individual subjects. By this we mean the creation or adoption of a specialist terminology and vocabulary to identify and label those features of a discipline that are peculiar to it and which help to distinguish it from other disciplines. Surprisingly, it is only comparatively recently that linguists, educationalists and researchers have started to look into this vitally important area of *subject-specific language*. Not only is it vitally important for communicative purposes, it is equally important for children's learning. One of the earliest writers to draw attention to the implications for learning of subject-specific language was Rosen. In an unpublished paper entitled 'The problems of impersonal language'[12] he writes:

> Much of the language encountered in school looks at pupils across a chasm. Some fluent children . . . adopt the jargon and parrot whole stretches of lingo. Personal intellectual struggle is made irrelevant and the personal view never asked for. Language and experience are torn asunder. Worse still, many children find impersonal language mere noise. It is alien in its posture, conventions and strategies. . . . These are extremes. Many children have areas of confidence and understanding but frequently have to resort to desperate mimicry to see them through.

Because the topic of subject-specific language, or language register,[13] is such a grossly under-researched area, we can at present only identify the sorts of questions that can be asked in this connection. Thus, we may ask, to what extent are subject-specific languages necessary across the curriculum? Does the use of subject-specific language facilitate learning? Or does it inhibit learning? Does its use affect a teacher's overall discourse? In other words, do the occasions when it is perhaps necessary to use subject-specific language influence those occasions when it is not necessary at all? To what extent do teachers 'colloquialize' a subject-specific language, or colloquialize when the use of a distinctively subject-specific language would be more advantageous? What proportion of a teacher's (or pupil's) spoken language is made up of subject-specific language as compared with normal, everyday language? What has the subject-specific language in one discipline in common with other disciplines? Is there any overlap? Finally, to what extent does a gulf exist between the teacher and pupil when it comes to using subject-specific language in the classroom?

More sophisticated questions have been posed by Edwards.[14] He asks:

If a subject register *is* apparent, are pupils expected to use it, or just understand it; is a receptive or a productive competence required? Do they learn it by imitation, or by coping with subject-specific tasks in which the form is determined by the function? How does the teacher 'mediate' between the language of his pupils, and that which he considers appropriate to his subject? When a teacher says something like this, is it a one-man performance which he does not yet expect his pupils to match, or does he expect an approximation to it, or does he 'translate' pupil contributions into the appropriate form while responding to the content of what they say?

'Put that into the distillation flask and then distil off, and then we get thermometer recording the correct temperature which is boiling point for acetone. Then we collect the acetone which came over as a distillate (Barnes[2])'.

Answers to questions of this nature must at present be speculative for, as Edwards points out, we know so little about the language that teachers use.

In their interesting analysis of 'subject language', Edwards and Furlong[10] observe that distinctive forms of speech associated with particular social groups may serve two main functions. First, they make it possible to transact business more efficiently by providing a language that is both brief and precise, and second, they symbolize membership of a group and loyalty to it. The special language of school subjects, they suggest, can be seen in this way – as a mixture of intellectual necessity and group solidarity. They go on to explain thus:

> The necessity arises from the development of special terms for objects and ideas of special, perhaps even unique, importance to that discipline. But many more esoteric terms are used than are strictly necessary. This additional usage has been called conventional rather than intellectual, though any implication that they are merely verbal habits would be misleading. Both necessary and conventional usage serve to mark off some special area of interest, and teachers' frequent preoccupation with the right terminology (even when it is hard for an observer to see what the fuss is about) is a way of indicating the separation of academic from everyday knowledge, or of one academic territory from another.

As pupils are inducted into the use of 'subject languages', not only are they thus in a position to begin to make the fine discriminations denied them by everyday language, their sense of belonging to a particular specialism and specialist group is reinforced.

Because their interests are sufficiently specialist to warrant it, some disciplines have a range of specialist terms so obviously different from their everyday meanings that there is little risk of confusion. One only has to think of subjects like physics or cybernetics. Yet subjects like history or sociology, each of which is concerned in its own way with reflections on human behaviour, draw upon a vocabulary part of which is appropriated from everyday language. It is words which overlap in this way, which have a special significance superimposed on their everyday meaning, which cause problems of communication. In instancing the 'special language' of socio-linguistics, which has its own esoteric terms as well as old words with new meanings, or nuances of meaning. Edwards[14] asks if the special language offers or facilitates new insights, new ways of observing, classifying and relating the phenomena. Or does it, he asks, seem to be a 'translation' which adds nothing to the commonsense knowledge, a new way of *talking* about language which mystifies but does not enlighten? Tantalizing questions which only more research can answer.

We have spoken of the dearth of research in this field, but what has been undertaken so far? One of the pioneering studies in this area is that of Barnes.[2] He investigated language interaction in twelve lessons in the first term of secondary education. In that part of the study which he called 'The language of instruction', Barnes dealt with the topic under three headings – specialist language presented; specialist language not presented; and the language of secondary education. Our principal concern here is with the first of these categories. Under 'specialist language presented', teachers were aware of certain of the technical terms they used and showed this by 'presenting' them, i.e. a term is supplied by the teacher and a definition asked for, or at other times the teacher explicitly gives a name, or asks pupils to give a name, to a concept which has been already established. For example, in one particular chemistry lesson in a grammar school, the words *chromatography, pestle and mortar, suspension, effluent* and *chlorophyll* were presented to the class. Examples were much less common in the lessons from non-selective schools with the sole exception of a history lesson which presented *city states, patriotic, enquiring mind, language, truce* and *pentathlon.* Neither in science nor maths lessons could a systematic policy be perceived, either in the selection of concepts to be taught or in the order of presentation of the concept and a term to represent it.

Box 30 contains an extract from an exchange between a teacher and pupils in a biology lesson. This example underlines an assumption which Barnes found was shared in some degree by six of the twelve teachers observed: that the teaching of terminology is seen as part of the task. As Barnes himself says:[2] 'It is clear from the substitution of "trachea" for "windpipe" that it is not merely the referential function of the word that is valued; the teacher is valuing that of the two synonyms which carries with it (for her, not the pupils, of course) the stronger suggestion of a strictly biological context.'

Box 30

The use of terminology in a biology lesson

Teacher	Where does it go then?
Pupil	To your lungs, Miss.
Teacher	Where does it go before it reaches your lungs? . . . Paul.
Pupil	Your windpipe, Miss.
Teacher	Down the windpipe. . . . Now can anyone remember the other word for windpipe?
Pupil	The trachea.
Teacher	The trachea . . . good. . . . After it has gone through the trachea where does it go to then? . . . There are a lot of little pipes going into the lungs . . . what are those called? . . . Ian?
Pupil	The bronchii.
Teacher	The bronchii . . . that's the plural. . . . What's the singular? What is one of these tubes called? . . . Ann.
Pupil	Bronchus.
Teacher	Bronchus . . . with 'us' at the end. . . . What does 'inspiration' mean . . .?

Source: Barnes[2]

Side by side with these and similar presentations, some teachers use specialist language without explicitly presenting it. Some of these, Barnes found, were technical terms of the subject which are well enough known to be unlikely to present difficulty: in an English lesson, *stress* and *rhyme*; in physics *diagram* and *pulley*; in mathematics, *point*; and in history, *a major city*.

Others were as much part of the teacher's idiolect as part of the subject register; one mathematics teacher used 'split' repeatedly, whereas another used 'sliced' and 'divided' in similar contexts.

All these examples came from non-selective schools; they were few and trivial enough for their effect upon the children's learning to be ignored. In the grammar schools, however, Barnes found that language of this kind bulked more large. The extract below illustrates the difficulty the teacher in question had in thinking of his subject without using its terminology:

If we did it using a different method actually . . . where we heat up the grass with acetone actually . . . heating it under, er . . . an enclosed system except . . . I'll have to show using a diagram on that . . . well er . . . under reflux conditions so that we didn't lose the acetone then we could actually finish up with the grass a white colour.

Of this extreme example, Barnes says that 'it can be surmised that this teacher's enthusiasm for his subject and his abundance of knowledge tended to stop him from perceiving his pupils' needs. Talk of this kind would certainly discourage many pupils; it is tempting to make guesses about which pupils would be best able to tolerate such language and to continue to attend to it until such times as they could begin to take part.'[2]

As part of his conclusion to the total study, Barnes[2] says:

The study so far provides a basis for arguing (a) that some teachers fail to perceive the pedagogical implications of many of their own uses of language, and (b) that a descriptive study such as this provides a potential method of helping teachers to become more aware. Whether they are able to carry over this insight into their own work has not been shown, however.

Another study looking at the problem of subject-specific language was undertaken by Richards.[15] It was concerned with identifying existing subject registers and describing their characteristics. Thus the investigation involved the analysis of the language of a selection of school subjects. The three hypotheses formulated at the outset of the study stated that:

1 There is no difference between the language a child encounters in school and his ordinary speech.
2 There is no significant difference in the demands made upon a child's language by the different subjects of the curriculum.
3 The linguistic features of the language used in the various subject lessons are not sufficiently differentiated as to suggest that they constitute different registers.

The first hypothesis was not upheld, the results indicating that people do encounter language forms which *are* different from their ordinary speech:

Characteristically such language shows increased formality of style, makes use of a specialized vocabulary and contains certain repetitive patterns of syntactic structure which are often more complex than would occur in the language normally employed by the pupil. In some cases the language is peculiar to the subject and appears to have a useful function in that it carries concepts and meanings that cannot be readily expressed in other forms.

Data collected and analysed in connection with the second hypothesis showed that distinctions with respect to language demands *do* exist among subjects. Examination of the subject histograms in Box 31 shows, for example, the proportion of factual to reasoning questions within a subject. Richards herself says:

> Maths makes nearly twice the reasoning demands of any of the arts subjects. Physics and chemistry also show considerably higher proportions of reasoning questions than the remaining subjects. In the same category, biology is slightly ahead of the arts subjects, its reasoning score being identical with its factual score. This factual score is second highest to geography and puts biology farther ahead of the remaining arts subjects in the category than these same arts subjects are ahead of physics and chemistry.

With regard to the third hypothesis, Richards found that there appear to be grounds for asserting that within schools language varieties exist which can be thought of as rudimentary registers that become increasingly differentiated and in evidence with the pupil's progress through the school. The degree to which a particular variety becomes more or less developed is dependent also on the level of course. When teaching O or A level courses, teachers tend to employ language that is closer to the subject norm depicted in supporting texts than they do when teaching CSE or remedial courses.

We conclude our review of verbal communication in the classroom with a brief examination of a topic which could have far-reaching implications – language deprivation and disadvantage.

Language deprivation and disadvantage

In touching upon the issue of language deprivation and disadvantage among children, we immediately find ourselves in the midst of controversy and hedged in by a welter of unresolved difficulties, not the least of which is the lack of unequivocal empirical evidence. The controversy appears to have a number of heads to it. First, there is the terminological debate – is 'disadvantaged' or 'deprived' the more fitting term? Second, there are competing viewpoints – is the problem best viewed psychologically or sociologically? And third, there are important philosophical considerations – what *is* the purpose of education? What is equality? In what sense can 'deprivation' be compensated for?

Further, much of the controversy stems directly from inadequately developed theories and the need for substantial research projects to answer such questions as: What environmental factors influence

Box 31

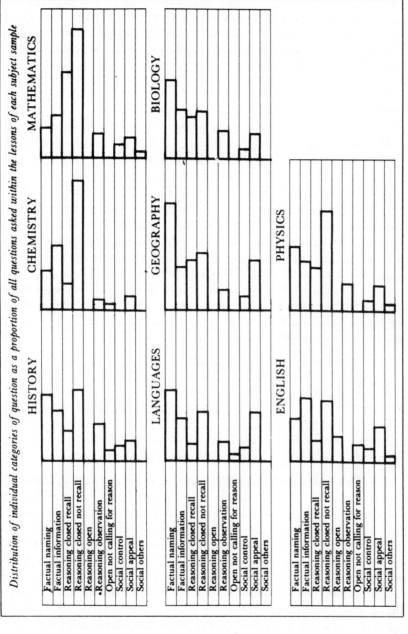

Distribution of individual categories of question as a proportion of all questions asked within the lessons of each subject sample

MATHEMATICS

BIOLOGY

CHEMISTRY

GEOGRAPHY

PHYSICS

HISTORY

LANGUAGES

ENGLISH

Factual naming
Factual information
Reasoning closed recall
Reasoning closed not recall
Reasoning open
Reasoning observation
Open not calling for reason
Social control
Social appeal
Social others

Source: Richards[15]

language performance? Is the language of the disadvantaged child deficient? Does language influence cognitive development? Should educationalists intervene to help the disadvantaged child develop his language skills? What are the best classroom techniques for dealing with language difficulties? What are the social class differences in language performance? And what can cross-cultural studies tell us in these respects?

The contentious issues of terminology reflect the particular perspectives adopted at different periods of the debate. To begin with, in the early 1960s, children who came from poor families were described as 'culturally deprived'. But this term was later regarded as both misleading and insulting because it ignored the fact that such children had a quite definite culture of their own, though it differed from the dominant one. The term 'culturally deprived' was therefore replaced by 'culturally disadvantaged', which duly recognized a culture, but one which, being different from the dominant one, was regarded as being at a disadvantage. This being the case, the school was seen as an important agent in compensating for this disadvantage.

Any consideration of the concept of social disadvantage must at some point touch upon the issue of *heredity* versus *environment*, whether intelligence is innately determined or whether it can be significantly influenced by the environment. As Moss says:[16]

> If one sees people as falling into different social classes because of differences in innate ability, then it makes little sense to try to change the 'laws of nature'. However, if one holds the view that a person's class membership (including education and occupational status) is a product of that person's opportunities and experiences, then a democratic society has an obligation to ensure that all its people have an equal access to such opportunities and experiences.

The concept of intelligence underwent an important change in the late 1950s and early 1960s. Before this period, it was generally felt that intelligence was something a person was endowed with at conception, that the 'amount' was fixed and unchanging, and that members of 'better families' were favoured in this respect. However, with such notions as the reversibility of the effects of deprivation, the role of the environment in promoting this, and the importance of educational challenge, this view of intelligence was greatly modified. With such ideas and this changing conception of intelligence came the idea of *compensatory education* – the development of school programmes designed to remedy the problems of schooling of children from impoverished backgrounds.[16] As Moss explains:

Such programmes have attempted to assist poor children by compensating for assumed deficits in their early experiences. The experiences in question are those which are thought to be necessary for further learning. These deficits have variously been described and include such things as short attention span, poor language development, deficiencies in visual and auditory perception, low levels of motivation towards learning in the school, unfamiliarity with school objects, and so forth.

Not everyone has welcomed this so-called attempt at compensation. Bernstein,[18] for instance, says that education cannot compensate for society. He attacks the labelling of children and suggests the problem lies in the schools. He criticizes the concept 'compensatory education' which he says 'serves to direct attention away from the internal organization and the educational context of the school' and that it 'implies that something is lacking in the family, and so in the child'. He stresses the need to provide an 'adequate educational environment' in general, and to stop thinking of it in terms of 'compensation'. Like Labov, another critic, he emphasizes the need to consider the child's own existing culture rather than regarding this as a 'deficit system' that needs to be filled out. The implications of these views for language education have yet to be fully drawn.

Most researchers into verbal behaviour in the classroom rely on words alone.[10] As Edwards and Furlong point out, such researchers assume that the verbal behaviour is a sufficient sample of the total behaviour – 'that any nonverbal communication necessary to generate and sustain classroom interaction is either subsumed in, or subordinate to, what is actually said.' In a sense, this assumption is forced on researchers because of the difficulty of obtaining nonverbal data. However, for the remainder of the chapter, we look at some features of nonverbal communication in general in the hope that they will stimulate readers to consider, perhaps more seriously than they might otherwise have done, their value as means of contact and communication in the classroom.

Language in the education of ethnic minority pupils

Derrick[17] observes that 'For native or immigrant children English is the key to their future in this country, thus the teacher has to see that they acquire language for the full range of communication within the school.' Clearly a child can neither learn specific skills nor develop his potential ability until he can learn to speak, understand, read and write the language that is used in school. In this section we concentrate upon some major aspects of language difficulties experienced by children from ethnic minority groups, giving particular attention to the problems facing children of West Indian origin.

The ideas of Bernstein[18] on the ways in which types of language (i.e. the *elaborated code* and the *restricted code*) affect modes of thinking were influential in the early and middle 1960s in the setting up of compensatory language programmes for children who were said to be culturally and linguistically deprived. Many of Bernstein's ideas are thought to be applicable to the education of immigrant children who, although born in Britain, do not speak standard English. What in particular are the linguistic limitations of these children said to be? Taylor[19] suggests the following:

1 *Total language deficiency*, where not only is a foreign language spoken, but the written script is alien.
2 *Partial language deficiency*, where some, but very little, English is spoken in the home or where the child has acquired some English from having lived in Britain for a longer period of time. The vernacular script may or may not be based upon the western alphabet.
3 *Dialect impediments*, where some children may speak English fluently, but dialect interposes, or a 'pidgin' English is spoken so that problems of listening, interpreting and later reading and writing are present. This is a particular problem for some West Indian children where Creole dialects are present. We have more to say about this specific difficulty later in the section.

The Schools Council Curriculum Development projects[20] for teaching English to immigrant children were a direct response to the urgent need voiced by teachers up and down the country to find ways of helping immigrant children attain linguistic proficiency in English. The specific objectives of the Schools Council Programmes were, first, to prepare materials and carefully graded schemes to meet the needs of teachers of non-English speaking children in order to help such pupils achieve an adequate command of English for school and society. Second, the programmes were intended to support the provision of in-service training in order to explain the purposes of the new materials to teachers and to give them opportunity both to use and criticize the materials and to offer positive suggestions for their improvement. In the absence of research evidence showing that there were distinctive problems attached to the teaching of particular ethnic minority groups, the Schools Council Project aimed, initially, to produce a general package of teaching materials for all non-English speaking children. Full details of each of the SCOPE programmes are available in Taylor[19] and Hill.[21] As time went on, specific language kits were developed for use with particular ethnic minority groups. We illustrate two.

Box 32

Concept building

Source: E.J. Arnold (Publishers)[22]

Box 32 shows part of the Activity Book used in Unit 2, *Concept Building*, indicating the type of material specifically developed for use with West Indian children. The intention is to help children develop skills in classifying data. Central to the construction of the unit is the idea of a matrix by means of which children are encouraged to sort objects into sets. Box 32 shows that the matrix sheets consist of pictures arranged in rows and columns according to the classes to which they belong. Each matrix is accompanied by a series of workcards which provide children with writing experiences. Unit 2 also includes activity books, matrix cards, matrix builders, missing picture books and magnet cards.

Box 33 illustrates the sort of material included in a language kit developed for use with older immigrant children (aged fourteen or over) recently arrived from the Indian sub-continent who have little or no command of English. The materials deal with daily activities in a fictitious town, Camley, and are intended to introduce children to simple terms to do with their immediate environment.

A guide to teaching practice

Box 33

SCOPE senior course: we live in England

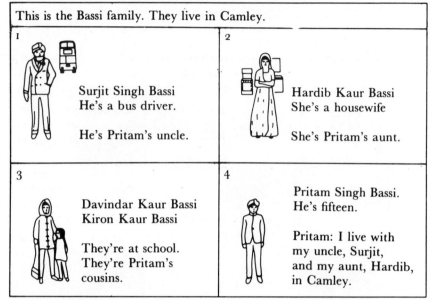

This is the Bassi family. They live in Camley.	
1 Surjit Singh Bassi He's a bus driver. He's Pritam's uncle.	**2** Hardib Kaur Bassi She's a housewife She's Pritam's aunt.
3 Davindar Kaur Bassi Kiron Kaur Bassi They're at school. They're Pritam's cousins.	**4** Pritam Singh Bassi. He's fifteen. Pritam: I live with my uncle, Surjit, and my aunt, Hardib, in Camley.

Source: adapted from Schools Council[20]

The Schools Council Curriculum Development projects were but one of a number of programmes of activity attempting to get to grips with the language problems of immigrant children. Space precludes discussion of pre-school language research, language teaching in multiracial infant classrooms, the work of the NFER in its five-year project for disadvantaged children, or the findings of the Educational Priority Area Action Research as they specifically relate to ethnic minority children.

Creole interference

In a recent book dealing with the West Indian language issue in British schools, Edwards[23] shows how *Creole interference* plays a crucial role in the underperformance of West Indian children. To understand Edwards' thesis we need to know a little about West Indian Creole. What follows is a summary of the major points set out in Chapters 2 and 3 of Edward's text.

  1 The linguistic situation in the West Indies is best seen in terms of a continuum with broad Creole at one end and standard English at the other, the social class and geographical location (rural/urban)

of the speaker, together with the particular social situation in which he finds himself, determining which part of the speech continuum will be drawn upon in conversing.

2 Although Creole shares a large part of the vocabulary of English, it is different both in its grammar and its sound system from standard English. Such are the differences that some would argue for Creole being treated as a separate language.

3 West Indians born in Britain are influenced by the Creole spoken by their parents and by older members of the West Indian community. Many use Creole widely in specific social interactions. There is, Edwards observes, great sensitivity as to when and to whom speech from the Creole end of the Creole – standard English continuum is used.

4 Despite the widely-held belief that all forms of non-standard speech are intrinsically inferior, there is nothing to suggest that Creole* or any other non-standard variety of speech is irregular, faulty or unstructured.

5 The commonly-held view of some teachers that West Indian children are inarticulate and nonverbal is challenged by the evidence that Edwards cites to show the impressive skills of West Indian children in the verbal games that constitute an integral part of their social activities.

6 Given the phonological†, morphological, syntactic and semantic differences of Creole as compared with standard English, we are in a better position to understand why Creole '*interferes*' with the production and comprehension of standard English. Edwards shows in detail how interference operates in speech, in comprehension, in writing, in grammar and in reading.

7 Edwards concludes that children influenced by Creole are often at a considerable disadvantage when educated through the medium of standard English, experiencing particular difficulties in comprehending and in producing standard English speech.

Attitudes towards language and educational achievement

As important as the differences that we have noted between Creole and standard English are the attitudes that people hold towards these

* Edwards[23] shows a section of a higher degree thesis written in Creole to illustrate the point that social acceptability rather than linguistic inadequacy determines the exclusion of non-standard varieties from writing.

† *Phonology* is concerned with sounds in a language, *morphology*, with the form of words and their functional relationships, *syntax*, with sentence construction, and *semantics* with the meaning of words.

differences. Teachers in particular should be sensitive to the special problems West Indian pupils face as a result of linguistic interference and should be made aware of the stereotypes that are held about West Indian Creole speech. Box 34 reports the results of an experiment[24] into stereotypic attitudes towards speech conducted with student teachers, West Indian children and their middle-class and working-class 'British' peers.

Box 34

Stereotyped attitudes to West Indian speech

The speech of four first-year secondary school children was tape recorded. The first was a Barbadian girl, born in Britain and completely bidialectical. She spoke once in the working-class Reading accent that she habitually used in school and later in a West Indian accent characterized by many phonological features of Creole, giving a speech sample that was recognizably West Indian but readily understandable to a speaker of British English. The other speakers were an English boy with a working-class Reading accent, a professor's son who spoke with 'received pronunciation', and a recently-arrived Jamaican girl whose Creole was barely recognizable to a British listener. All spoke fluently for half a minute about going to the dentist.

Attitudes towards these speech forms were recorded on questionnaire-type scales together with judgements about each speaker's behaviour, and his/her potential academic ability.

Among the child judges, both British and West Indians viewed West Indian speech negatively. Among the student teachers, no significant differences were found in their attitudes towards the two working-class speakers nor towards the West Indian girls. What did emerge, however, were highly significant differences in student teachers' attitudes and evaluations of the middle-class boy and the working-class speaker, and between the working-class children and the West Indian girls. There was an almost unanimous pecking order of preference:

middle-class speech, working-class speech, West Indian speech.

The same pattern was repeated with respect to judgements about the speakers' behaviour too.

Source: adapted from Edwards[24]

An interesting feature of Edwards' experiment was that it included West Indian children drawn from the same school as the working-class children described in Box 34. Clearly, West Indians' appraisal of their own speech is of fundamental importance to their linguistic and social behaviour.

Results showed that the West Indian judges tended to agree with both the student teachers and the 'British' child judges that the middle-class speech sample had highest status both in terms of speech and behaviour. However, Edwards detected a certain degree of ambivalence in their evaluations of West Indian and working-class speech samples. She reports:

Although they showed no marked preferences for either guise in their evaluations of speech, the working-class guise was rated favourably on behaviour. West Indian judgements of academic potential and desirability as a member of the school class corresponded most closely to those of the middle-class children. That is to say, they too assigned highest status to the middle-class boy whom they considered had the greatest academic potential and would be the most interesting member of the class. There was no evidence of any preference for the West Indian speakers, suggesting that feelings of group solidarity do not strongly influence their evaluations.

Edwards concludes that West Indian children have clearly internalized stereotypes of the dominant white society. Like all minority groups studied to date, she observes, they undervalue the speech and speakers of their own group.

We have here, have we not, all the makings of a self-fulfilling prophecy?

Teachers who do not or are not prepared to recognize the particular problems of Creole-speaking children in their classrooms may conclude that they are educationally backward when they give wrong responses or fail to respond to questions or commands. Features of Creole speech come to be associated with low academic ability and teachers are then led to behave differently towards Creole-speaking children. Low teacher expectations lead to low pupil performance. Looking at this process from the point of view of the child, Edwards notes how especially during the early stages the Creole-speaking pupil may feel threatened by the comprehension difficulties he is experiencing. These and the way in which the teacher behaves towards him produce what she describes as 'a state of linguistic insecurity' such that the child is very likely to appear inarticulate as a result. This, in turn, reinforces the teacher's preconceived ideas and the cycle is thus perpetuated.

Notes and references

1 Wilkinson, A. (1975) *Language and Education*. London: Oxford University Press.
2 Barnes, D. (1971) Language in the secondary classroom. In Barnes, D., Britton, J. and Rosen, H. *Language, the Learner and the School*. Harmondsworth: Penguin.

3 The Report of the Bullock Committee (1975) *A Language For Life*. London: HMSO.
4 Stubbs, M. (1976, 2nd ed. 1983) *Language, Schools and Classrooms*. London: Methuen.
5 Note: this short review draws on Stubbs (1976) op. cit.
6 Barnes, D. (1971) Language and learning in the classroom. *Journal of Curriculum Studies*, 3 (1), 27–38.
7 Mishler, E.G. (1972) Implications of teacher strategies for language and cognition: observations in first-grade classrooms. In Cazden, C.B., John, V.P. and Hymes, D. *Functions of Language in the Classroom*. Teachers College, Columbia University, New York: Teachers College Press.
8 Stubbs, M. (1976) Keeping in touch: some functions of teacher-talk. In Stubbs, M. and Delamont, S. (eds) *Explorations in Classroom Observation*. London: Wiley.
9 See, for example:
Jones, A. and Mulford, J. (eds) (1971) *Children Using Language*. London: Oxford University Press.
Rosen, C. and Rosen, H. (1973) *The Language of Primary School Children*. Harmondsworth: Penguin.
Lewis, R. (1973) Speaking in the primary school. *Speech and Drama*, 22, 2 (Summer).
10 Edwards, A.D. and Furlong, V.J. (1978) *The Language of Teaching*. London: Heinemann.
11 Stebbins, R. (1973) Physical context influences on behaviour: the case of classroom disorderliness. *Environment and Behaviour*, 5, 291–314.
12 Rosen, H. (1971) The problems of impersonal language. Quoted in Barnes, D., Language in the secondary classroom. In Barnes, D., Britton, J. and Rosen, H. *Language, the Learner and the School*. Harmondsworth: Penguin.
13 Note: 'Language register may be defined as a form of speech appropriate to certain circumstances or activities.'
14 Edwards, A.D. (1974) *Language in Culture and Class*. London: Heinemann.
15 Richards, J.W. The language of biology teaching. Unpublished M.Ed. thesis, University of Newcastle-upon-Tyne. Quoted in Richards, J.W. (1978) *Classroom Language: What Sort?* London: Unwin Educational Books.
16 Moss, M.H. (1973) *Deprivation or Disadvantage?* E202, Block 8, Educational Studies. A Second Level Course, Language and Learning. Milton Keynes: Open University Press.
17 Derrick, J. (1968) The work of the Schools Council project in English for immigrant children. *The Times Educational Supplement*, 25 October.
18 Bernstein, B. (1958) Some sociological determinants of perception. *British Journal of Sociology*, 9, 154–74.
Bernstein, B. (1960) Language and social class. *British Journal of Sociology*, 11, 271–6.
Bernstein, B. (1961) Social class and linguistic development: a theory of social learning. In Halsey, A.H., Floud, J. and Anderson, C.A. (eds) *Society, Economy and Education*. Glencoe, Ill.: Free Press.
Bernstein, B. (1965) A socio-linguistic approach to social learning. In Gould, J. (ed.) *Penguin Survey of the Social Sciences*. Harmondsworth: Penguin.

19 Taylor, F. (1974) *Race, School and Community: A Study of Research and Literature*. Windsor: NFER.

20 Schools Council, *English For Immigrant Children*. Curriculum Development Project. Leeds: E.J. Arnold.

(1969) *Scope 1: An introductory course for pupils 8–13 years*.

(1971) *Scope Handbook 2: Pronunciation for non-English speaking children from India, Pakistan, Cyprus and Italy*.

(1972) *Scope senior course for non-English speaking students 14 years and over*.

(1972) *Scope 2 for pupils 8–13 years at 2nd stage of English*. Harlow: Longman.

(1973) *Scope 3 Handbook 3: Language work with infant immigrant children*.

(1973) Taylor, J. and Ingleby, T. *Scope story book 5–12 years*.

(1973) Manley, D. *Scope supplementary plays and dialogues*.

21 Hill, D. (1976) *Teaching in Multiracial Schools*. London: Methuen.

22 Schools Council Project on Teaching English to West Indian Children (1972) *Concept 7–9*. Four units for multiracial classes. Leeds: E.J. Arnold.

Unit 1. Listening with Understanding.

Unit 2. Concept Building.

Unit 3. Communication.

Unit 4. The Dialect Kit.

23 Edwards, V.K. (1979) *The West Indian Language Issue in British Schools*. London: Routledge and Kegan Paul.

24 Edwards, V.K. (1978) Language attitudes and underperformance in West Indian children. *Educational Review*, 30 (1), 51–8.

Jeffcoate, R. (1979) A multicultural curriculum: beyond the orthodoxy. *Trends in Education*, 4, 8–12.

MANAGEMENT AND CONTROL IN THE CLASSROOM

Introduction

This section is concerned with management and control in the classroom. It does not pretend to offer a panacea for all the manifold challenges and difficulties that are potentially present in the modern classroom; nor does it attempt to deal with the more problematic aspects of behaviour like bad language, violence and truancy. To do so would be to swing the balance of the pages that follow in the direction of juvenile delinquency and so distort the overall picture of classroom behaviour. In any case, should these and comparable incidents arise in the course of a student teacher's school experience, they should be referred to a senior member of staff as soon as is practically possible. What we do aim to do in this section, however, is to offer the reader a framework for securing and maintaining the co-operation of pupils in classroom activities. To this end, it attempts to bring together a range of stimulating ideas, perspectives and concepts – some theoretical, others the result of recent research – that will provide the student teacher with an operational base for achieving a positive, humane and constructive approach to management and control in the classroom.

A word of caution, however. Important as it is for the reader to consider carefully the points raised in this section, particularly if he is concerned to achieve good standards of teaching, they cannot really be viewed in isolation. This is to say, they tie up with a whole range of contextual factors, some of which are touched upon elsewhere in the book, such as preparation and planning, suitability of material, teaching methods, teacher–pupil relationships and so on. If, for example, the work you give to your class tends consistently to be too difficult, or if your relations with the class are permanently abrasive, then no amount of reading or re-reading of this section will help you resolve the difficulties that will inevitably follow. The connections between the factors about to be discussed and the broader issues of pedagogy must be made by the reader.

It is useful up to a point to consider a teacher's management and control of his pupils in the classroom in terms of the key concepts of *power* and *authority*. Peters,[1] examining these concepts in the sphere of social control, stresses the importance of distinguishing between them. He says of *power* that it 'basically denotes ways in which an individual subjects others to his will by means of physical coercion (e.g. inflicting pain, restriction of movement), or by psychological coercion (e.g. withholding food, water, shelter, or access to means of attaining such necessities), or by the use of less dire forms of sanctions and rewards (e.g. by manipulating access to material resources and rewards, sexual satisfaction, etc.), or by personal influences such as hypnotism or sexual attraction. On the other hand, *authority* 'involves the appeal to an impersonal normative order or value system which regulates behaviour basically because of acceptance of it on the part of those who comply. It operates because of understanding of and concern for what is intimated within a rule-governed form of life, which those in authority help to create and sustain. Authority, of course, may be and usually is supported by various forms of power.'[1]

The classroom is a particular kind of social context and if the concepts are to be of value to us in our consideration of management and control in the classroom, they need to be interpreted in relation to this context. Take the teacher's *power*, for instance. Wadd[2] considers that this consists chiefly of four components: (1) charisma – the ability to attract and influence people with one's personality; (2) dominance – the ability to obtain control over a situation; (3) intellectual power – knowledge and mastery of one's subject(s); and (4) resources power – one's ability to organize all aspects of work in the classroom. He argues that the way in which these components function is an important determinant of the extent of the teacher's effectiveness. And further, the influence of each may vary with the particular teaching situation. Thus, resources power may contribute more significantly to the personal power of a teacher practising open education in an open plan school, whereas a teacher working in a difficult urban school may have to reply on dominance, implying a certain amount of physical or psychological coercion.

The teacher's authority[3] in the classroom will derive not only from his traditional role as a teacher, but also from the system of rules operating in the school at large and the classroom in particular. We shall shortly consider the importance of establishing a minimum list of rules (or at least revising existing ones) in order to define the classroom situation to the teacher's advantage and to indicate what is and what is not permitted. The value of arriving at such a list by discussion and consensus lies in the fact that they thus contribute to the 'impersonal normative order' to which both teacher and pupil can refer (or be referred). To enforce this order, however, it must be backed by rewards for those who conform and punishments for those who deviate.

Your control of pupil behaviour will therefore be through a subtle blending of personal *power* emanating from your personality and skills, and *authority* deriving from your status as teacher and from the established system of rules operating in the school and classroom. In the pages that follow, we outline a range of procedures that will assist you in implementing these two crucial concepts in the context of the classroom. We begin by taking a brief look at some of the contrasting views on how the task of classroom management should be approached.

Schools of thought on classroom management

Even the most casual study of teachers in classrooms would lead one to infer that between them they hold a range of viewpoints on the central issue of classroom management. Wragg[4] has identified a number of commonly-held views in this respect. In describing them, he warns the reader that the list is not exhaustive and that teachers should not necessarily be assigned to one category exclusively: they may change their view (and behaviour) according to the occasion. Briefly, they are as follows:

(1) Authoritarian

According to this view, teachers are held to be in charge and that it is their responsibility to establish and maintain order in the school. They make the decisions and give the orders within a well-defined and fairly rigid system of roles. The justification for a teacher assuming this stance resides in his greater knowledge and experience. Opponents of this view argue that it can become repressive and that it is not appropriate to an age in which children need to learn independence if society is to become really democratic.

(2) Permissive

Usually contrasted with the preceding view, the permissive school emphasizes individual freedom and choice. Traditional constraints on behaviour are thus kept to a minimum. The aim is to develop pupil autonomy so that pupils can make their own decisions and be responsible for their own behaviour. The critics of permissiveness contend that it all too often degenerates into a kind of *laissez-faire* situation having little or no real educational significance for those participating.

(3) Behaviour modification

This school holds to the views of behaviourist psychology which stresses the role of rewards and punishments in the control of behaviour. Thus the teacher's job is to encourage desirable behaviour and stamp out undesirable behaviour by administering or withholding suitable re-inforcements. It is objected to on the grounds that the treatment is mechanistic and that this implies that the people so treated are regarded as machines and not humans.

(4) Interpersonal relationships

The aim of this school of thought is to produce good, positive relationships between the teacher and pupils and among the pupils themselves. Emphasis on negotiation and suggestion will result in a healthy classroom climate in which learning will occur automatically. If the trick works, then problems of management will not arise. Critics of this view, however, contend that good personal relationships become an end in themselves and that the real purpose of the classroom enterprise, namely the acquisition of knowledge and skills, takes second place.

(5) Scientific

According to this view (which, incidentally, is one held by the present authors – though not exclusively), teaching is an activity which can be studied and analysed. It can be described as being scientific in the sense of being an objective and systematic analysis and later synthesis of the more important components of teaching and learning. It is also scientific in the sense that it draws on the findings of empirical studies as a means of establishing a body of theory on which practice can be based. Opponents of this perspective argue that teaching is *an art* and cannot therefore be subjected to such an analysis. For them, teaching – and this includes class management – is an intuitive thing.

Box 35

Folklore in the classroom

As part of the Teacher Education Project, Wragg[4] collected from student teachers the tips or 'tricks of the trade' given them that they had found most useful. The twenty-five most common are given below in descending order of frequency. Go through the list and consider their value.

1 Start by being firm with pupils: you can relax later.
2 Get silence before you start speaking to the class.
3 Control the pupils' entry to the classroom.
4 Know and use the pupils' names.
5 Prepare lessons thoroughly and structure them firmly.
6 Arrive at the classroom before the pupils.
7 Prepare furniture and apparatus before the pupils arrive.
8 Know how to use apparatus, and be familiar with experiments before you use them in class.
9 Be mobile: walk around the class.
10 Start the lesson with a 'bang' and sustain interest and curiosity.
11 Give clear instructions.
12 Learn voice control.
13 Have additional material prepared to cope with e.g. bright and slow pupils' needs.
14 Look at the class when speaking, and learn how to scan.
15 Make written work appropriate (e.g. to the age, ability, cultural background of pupils).
16 Develop an effective question technique.*
17 Develop the art of timing your lessons to fit the available period.
18 Vary your teaching techniques.
19 Anticipate discipline problems and act quickly.
20 Be firm and consistent in giving punishments.
21 Avoid confrontation.
22 Clarify and insist on YOUR standards.
23 Show yourself as a helper or facilitator to the pupils.
24 Do not patronize pupils, treat them as responsible beings.
25 Use humour constructively.

Source: Wragg[4]

* See Appendix 5 for a discussion of questions and questioning.

(6) Social systems

The 'social systems' view contends that the school and its inmates constitute a sub-system of a wider social system, influences from which affect the group's behaviour. These include political, social, financial and emotional emanations. The teacher thus needs to understand and be aware of these influences in order to work effectively in school, although learning is in essence an individual process. Many school problems thus need to be seen in relation to these wider contextual factors. Critics respond by arguing that teachers have little or no control over these factors and must, therefore, function within the framework of the school.

(7) Folklore

If the new teacher can assimilate the received wisdom of the profession, the 'tips for teachers' and 'tricks of the trade', then he will be suitably equipped to deal with most contingencies. As Wragg[4] explains, critics consider that tips are lacking in any theoretical basis, are random and unrelated to each other, and may suit the person who proffers them but not the recipient. Box 35 contains a number of common tips identified by Wragg in his project.

We shift our perspective now as we consider the kinds of things that pupils expect of their teachers in the matter of management and control.

Pupil expectations of teachers

Wragg[4] notes that pupils are only rarely brought into the act of thinking about classroom processes. For example, most rules are decided by adults, the content of lessons is frequently chosen by the teacher, and it is assumed that children must know how to learn on their own or in groups. Wragg then refers to examples of proposals that have been put forward for involving pupils more in this matter of classroom processes.

Glasser,[5] for example, has suggested that pupils should be involved in discussion about rules and procedures during lessons. He suggests that class time should be used for the teacher to explain about classroom rules and that discussion should take place about these during which they could be adjusted, new rules could be negotiated and problems discussed.

Wragg[4] also refers to ideas put forward by Gordon. He contends that to solve a problem one must decide who 'owns it': is it the teacher, the pupils or is it shared? He recommends a six-step approach: (1) define the problem; (2) generate possible solutions; (3) evaluate these solutions; (4) decide which solutions seem best; (5) decide how to implement the chosen solutions; and (6) assess the effectiveness of the solutions chosen. Both Glasser's and Gordon's approaches demand greater responsibility on the part of the pupils than is normally the case.

Another approach to involving pupils is to find out from them what they consider are the characteristics of good teachers, for it is generally known that good teachers are capable of maintaining good discipline. Nash,[7] for example, found that twelve-year-old pupils in a Scottish secondary school regarded favourably teachers who kept order, were strict and punished pupils; who actually taught them and kept them busy with work; who gave explanations, were helpful and could be understood; who were interesting, unusual and different; who were fair, consistent and had no favourites; and who were friendly, kind, talked gently and joked. A composite picture of the effective teacher is to be found in Box 36.

Box 36

The good teacher

Since as early as the 1960s researchers have endeavoured to ascertain pupils' definitions of the 'good' teacher. After studying the findings of the more important studies in this connection, Saunders constructed a composite picture which suggests that the good teacher:

is purposeful and in control of himself;

knows what he wants to teach and checks that the children are learning;

takes positive action when he discovers they are not making adequate progress;

is sensitive to the reactions of his pupils and responds by changing role smoothly and appropriately;

tries to understand the point of view of the learner;

shows respect for others;

is concerned for all his pupils.

Source: Saunders[8]

A more dynamic view of how pupils see effective teachers is to be found in Gannaway's study.[9] On the basis of interviews and observation, he constructed a dynamic model by proposing that teachers are progressively typified by pupils in a given sequence. The teachers are, in effect, subjected to a systematic series of tests by pupils, the first of which is *can the teacher keep order?* The next test is *can he 'have a laugh'?* And the final test to which the teacher is subjected is *does he understand pupils?*

Gannaway suggests that providing the answer to each of these is *yes*, and provided the teacher can put over something of interest in the lesson, then he 'has it made'. The implications of these questions are of particular interest. The first test, for instance, *can the teacher keep order?*, implies that the pupils expect him to do just that, to keep order. Of equal importance is the second challenge, *can he 'have a laugh'?* What is implied here is that in expecting the teacher to keep order, they do not expect him to be *too* strict, to impose a regime so harsh that the pupils will eventually rebel (we touch on this as a possible cause of misbehaviour in the next section). What is called for is a 'nice strictness' in preference to a 'nasty strictness'.[10] The final test, *does he understand pupils?*, is in some ways the most interesting of the three for it implies an understanding of the class, *as a class*, *as a group*, in contrast to understanding *individual* children, or a group of children on an individual basis. The difference is significant for it means that understanding a group is of a different order to understanding the individual: a different standpoint is required and different knowledge and skills.

The actual causes of misbehaviour in the classroom are manifold; we go on to identify at least some of them.

What makes pupils misbehave?

To answer this question comprehensively would require the wisdom of Solomon and more. Fortunately, our intentions in posing it are more modest. Briefly, they are designed to identify the broad types of disruptive behaviour so that the beginning teacher can know what to look for, have some idea of the cause(s), and decide what action (which may sometimes mean inaction) is called for on his part.

Saunders[8] has identified four main patterns of disruptive behaviour arising from social causes. These are:

(1) Antipathy to school

For such pupils, school is seen as having no place or purpose in their lives. It is an irrelevance for them and consequently they dismiss both school and teachers. This is by no means an uncommon cause of difficulties in the contemporary classroom. Indeed, as unemployment queues lengthen and jobs become more elusive, one could expect such antipathy to spread. The teacher's task in such circumstances is to know how to make schoolwork more relevant and meaningful. Related to this factor of antipathy is what has been termed *conflicts of interest*. This embraces differences in needs, values and goals between the pupil and the system as embodied in the teacher and usually results in a show of nonconformity by the pupil in question. (For a fascinating study of a small group of working-class boys who reject the norms and values put forward by their teachers, see Willis.[11]) Resolving conflicts of this kind involves *negotiation*. This will concern the pupil and teacher working out a mutually acceptable settlement, a model for which is set out in Box 37.

Box 37

Negotiating a settlement of a conflict of interest

Step 1: confronting the opposition

A direct expression of one's viewpoint and one's feelings is vital from the outset. Equally important is an invitation to the opposition to be as forthright themselves. Expressing feelings is often difficult but it must be undertaken and should be directed at the issues involved, *not* at the persons who are in conflict.

Step 2: jointly defining the conflict

Resolving a conflict necessitates defining it in a way that is acceptable to both sides. Therefore, focus on behaviour, not on individual characteristics; centre discussion on issues, not on personalities. Try to define the conflict as a problem to be solved, not as a battle to be won at all costs. Coercing pupils into doing what the teacher requires is a short-term strategy with poor long-term pay-offs. The smaller and more precise the conflict, the easier it will be to resolve.

Step 3: communicating co-operative intentions

A candid expression of one's intention to co-operate results in: (a) agreements being reached more quickly; (b) a reduction in an opponent's suspicion and defensiveness; (c) a greater comprehension by each protagonist of the other's point of view; and (d) more positive perceptions by both parties to the dispute of each other as understanding and accepting persons.

Step 4: negotiating and perspective taking

Successful negotiation requires sufficient detachment from one's original position to be capable of looking at an issue from alternative perspectives. Perspective-taking involves demonstrating to an opponent that one is capable of accurately perceiving his position and his feelings. This can be achieved by temporarily arguing an opponent's position.

A central aspect of successful negotiations, therefore, is taking the perspective of one's opponents and influencing them to do the same.

Source: Johnson[12]

(2) Social dominance

Saunders regards this as an extension of the antipathetic syndrome. He writes:

Some physically and socially mature pupils seem to have a need for frequent reinforcement in the form of attention from their peers. This is often achieved at school by challenging the authority of the teacher: if the challenge is not met it can be taken up by other pupils and the lesson ruined, and as a result the assertion of the teacher's authority becomes more difficult in future lessons.

How one counters the sort of machismo posturing that this particular problem often assumes is a perennial problem for teachers in present-day classrooms.

(3) Social isolation

Some pupils have strong acceptance needs and a strong yearning to be wanted by their peers. However, they tend to be on the periphery of the group instead of being fully integrated into it. To achieve a sort of affiliation, therefore, they adopt the group's behaviour though often in extreme form.

(4) Inconsequential behaviour

Saunders here refers to those children who seem unable or unwilling to anticipate the consequences of their actions. Such a child, Saunders explains, 'behaves impulsively instead of reflecting on the courses of action which are open to him and of the possible consequences of each; or he may be unable to inhibit the urge to meet a challenge'. Anticipating an action requires a degree of reflection that, judging from the frequency of this kind of problem in the classroom, many children are incapable of achieving.

    To these patterns of disruptive behaviour we can add the following causes of misbehaviour set out by Gnagey.[13] One or other of them will have been experienced already by the student teacher. Thus:

(5) Ignorance of the rules

Ignorance of the rules of classroom behaviour is a common cause of misbehaviour. This is particularly the case during a teacher's early contacts with a class. As we shall see in the next section, it takes time to implement a rule, for it has to be learned over a period of time by interpreting it in relation to specific concrete situations. In this respect, Gnagey distinguishes between *verbal* and *actual* rules, that is, rules that are acted upon and those that are not. As he says, 'Even if a pupil is presented with a neatly organized set of by-laws, he never really knows which statutes are operational and which are just on paper. As every seasoned teacher knows, classes have a very practical way of solving this problem. They simply proceed to try the teacher out, to see what they can get away with.'

(6) Conflicting rules

Difficulties can sometimes arise for the teacher when a child is presented with two sets of conflicting rules – those of the classroom and those of his home. What is permissible in one situation is frowned upon in the other. Invariably it is the home that is the more permissive environment in this respect. Alternatively, the clash may occur between classroom norms and those of the peer group culture outside school. Where the clash is a marked one, the teacher would be best advised to seek a negotiated settlement with the pupil in question if lasting peace is to be achieved.

Box 38

Home situations of badly behaved children

In a study conducted in the United States, the following factors appeared regularly in the home situations of children who constantly behaved badly in the classroom:

1 The discipline by the father is either lax, overtly strict or erratic.
2 The supervision by the mother is at best only fair, or it is downright inadequate.
3 The parents are either indifferent or even hostile toward the child.
4 The family members are scattered in diverse activities and operate only somewhat as a unit or perhaps not at all.
5 The parents find it difficult to talk things over regarding the child.
6 The husband–wife relationship lacks closeness and equality or partnership.
7 The parents find many things to disapprove of in their child.
8 The mothers are not happy with the communities in which they live.
9 The parents resort to angry physical punishment when the child does wrong. Temper control is a difficult problem for them at this time.
10 The parents believe they have little influence on the development of their child.
11 The parents believe that other children exert bad influences on their child.
12 The parents' leisure-time activities lack much of a constructive element.
13 The parents, particularly the father, report no church membership. Even if they are members, their attendance tends to be sporadic.

Source: Thurston, Feldhusen and Benning[14]

(7) Displacement

As we have just seen, inappropriate behaviour may occur in the classroom because it is perfectly acceptable in another context, like the home or neighbourhood. A similar situation may occur with respect to *feelings*: inappropriate feelings are often displaced on the people and objects in the school. Thus, a pupil's hatred for his father may be transferred to his male form teacher. In an age where there is increased social dislocation through divorce, separation and one-parent families, displacement as a cause of disruptive behaviour might be more widespread than ever before. In a study by Thurston, Feldhusen and Benning,[14] quoted in Gnagey, several factors appeared again and again in the home situations of children who regularly misbehaved at school. These we have listed in Box 38.

(8) Anxiety

A great deal of misbehaviour in the classroom is caused by anxious reactions to features in the educational environment – examinations, having to speak in class, being judged publicly, etc. Earlier research by Gnagey[15] disclosed that disruptive pupils tended to be more afraid than their well-behaved classmates.

(9) Leadership styles as causes of misbehaviour

Finally, Gnagey identifies a number of leadership styles on the part of teachers that can incite disciplinary problems rather than solve them. These include the *despot* and the *nonentity*. The despot, as he explains, embraces a *custodial* view of pupil control and his main concern is with keeping order. He tends to view pupils in negative and stereotypical terms. Pupil response to a lasting tyrannical style of this kind is invariably anger, which can manifest itself in a variety of ways, often indirectly as with vandalism or bullying or, in more extreme cases, arson. In a word, *displacement* is operating.

The nonentity, as the name suggests, is totally ineffectual. His generally over-permissive, non-interventionist approach, combined with an unwillingness to utilize such fundamental psychological principles as motivation and rewards, is likely to generate feelings of restlessness on the part of pupils and a tendency to be easily distracted.

One way of preventing behaviour problems arising in the first place is to have adequate rules as means of controlling pupil behaviour. It is to a consideration of this topic that we now address ourselves.

Rules in the classroom

Hargreaves[16] reminds us that rules specify acceptable forms of classroom conduct and that they are either laid down by the teacher or arrived at by agreement between him and the children. Rules play an important part in helping to define the classroom situation in terms of the teacher's dominance; and if this is not established early on, then the children will define the situation to their advantage and very much to the teacher's discomfort.*

Gnagey[17] likewise notes that the classroom teacher defines behaviour and misbehaviour by the number and kinds of rules he makes and enforces in his room. Indeed, reminders of 'expected' behaviour as defined by rules of this kind make up one of the most frequently-used techniques for controlling individuals and groups.[18] Although each teacher makes a somewhat different list, most rules are based on *moral, personal, legal, safety* and *educational* considerations.

Educational settings have traditionally featured too many rules, especially punitive ones,[19] and it is important that such a list be kept to a minimum for at least three reasons: (1) the number of disciplinary actions a teacher takes is kept to a minimum also; (2) rules contribute to stultifying the atmosphere of school and classroom;[19] and (3) there is some evidence from research[20] that rules *by themselves* exert little influence on classroom behaviour; in other words, they need to be seen in relation to other factors in the classroom situation. The criteria for helping to achieve such a minimum list are *relevance, meaningfulness* and *positiveness*. Thus:

Relevance

Making one's list relevant requires that a teacher has a clear idea of the objectives of a particular lesson or course of lessons. It follows that the list may be flexible and may vary from lesson to lesson, though not to the extent that would confuse children or give them the opportunity to justify misbehaviour.

Meaningfulness

Rules that are seen to derive logically from the nature of the task are more acceptable to children than ones that are imposed arbitrarily by the teacher and are not easily seen to relate to the task or context. What seems to be required here is a degree of negotiation between the teacher and his pupils. Wragg[4] found a striking difference between experienced teachers and student teachers in this matter of 'meaningful' rules.

* (See also Box 3, p. 19.)

Whereas the experienced teachers stressed the moral rules about 'right', 'proper' and 'sensible' behaviour, the student teachers never mentioned such rules (see Box 39).

Box 39

Rules

When, as part of the Teacher Education Project, *experienced* teachers were interviewed about their classroom rules, most were clear about them and were quick to enforce them. *Student* teachers, on the other hand, were much more vague and spoke of rules being established 'as the need arose'. Experienced teachers worked very hard in their first few lessons to put over their rules, student teachers often found pupils having to 'test the limits' to see what the rules were. Rules in school came from several sources. In addition to society's laws and conventions which apply during school hours, there are three further sources:

1 *Local authority*: such as country-wide rules about behaviour in the laboratory or gymnasium which may be written in official circulars.
2 *School*: for example, over uniform or running in the corridor, which may be contained in printed school rules or announced at assembly, having been agreed among the staff or decreed by the senior people in the school.
3 *Teacher*: such as 'no eating in class', 'must raise hand when answering', which will vary from teacher to teacher, as may the interpretation and enforcement of school and local authority rules. In the Teacher Education Project studies it was found that most rules were made by the teacher rather than discussed with pupils. Experienced teachers stressed the moral rules about 'right', 'proper' and 'sensible' behaviour, student teachers never mentioned such rules.

Rules are established in different ways. Some are announced amid considerable ceremony at an assembly or in a first lesson, often given out in printed form to emphasize the 'official' standing. Other rules or norms, especially at classroom level, are established by case law; for example, when someone calls out and the teacher asks him to raise his hand in future.

Source: Wragg[4]

Positiveness

Where possible, rules should be expressed positively since a positive statement offers a goal to work towards rather than something to avoid. Thus, 'work quietly' is preferable to 'do not talk'. A list of *don'ts* can have an inhibiting effect on classroom behaviour.

Hargreaves[16] suggests that the teacher should attempt to lay down his minimum list during the very first encounter with a class. These may cover such areas as entering the room, movement about the room, modes of address, when to talk and when not to talk, work and homework, attitudes, and the distribution and use of materials and equipment. He also recommends that these should be fairly comprehensive, though not so general as to offer little guidance in specific situations; and that during subsequent meetings with the class the teacher ensures that the rules are understood, learned and conformed to.

Defining the situation in terms acceptable to the teacher will take some weeks because, as Hargreaves explains:

> The rules must be often created and always clarified in relation to concrete incidents where the rules are applicable; because the pupils need time to learn the rules and how they apply in given situations; and because the teacher must be able to demonstrate his power to enforce the rules and gain conformity to them. The definition of the situation is, in short, a progressive and cumulative process. It is built up day by day, incident by incident, into a consistent whole.

As well as establishing rules, the student teacher should also make explicit to the children during his early contact with them just what they can take for granted, e.g. can they use the pencil sharpener without asking permission? Clarification of this kind serves a dual purpose – it keeps formal rules to a minimum and cuts out undue fussiness.

Other procedures (if not already established), though not strictly codifiable as rules, should likewise be made explicit early on, certainly during the first few contacts, e.g. do you require all the children's written work to be headed with the date? If so, make it clear to them when the first occasions for written work occurs and specify how you want it presented. A new line? On the left-hand side? Underlined? No abbreviations . . . or whatever.

In summary, good classroom management involves establishing clear rules where rules are needed, avoiding unnecessary ones, eliminating punitive ones, reviewing them periodically, and changing or dropping them when appropriate.

We continue by identifying some of the well-tried techniques used by experienced teachers for dealing with deviant behaviour in the classroom.

Suggestions for handling minor misbehaviour problems

The techniques reviewed below may be of some assistance to student teachers when dealing with minor misbehaviour problems of a passing kind such as inattention, distraction or mischievousness. When faced with infringements of this nature, the aim of the teacher should be *to cut short the incipient misbehaviour before it develops and spreads without interrupting the flow of the lesson or distracting other children unnecessarily.*

Constant monitoring of the class

Good and Brophy[21] have emphasized the need for monitoring or scanning as an important factor in successful classroom management. By this they mean keeping the class and its individual members constantly under observation. Kounin,[22] likewise, stresses the value of this technique, noting that teachers possessing it show *with-it-ness*, that is, an awareness of what is happening in class. And Peters[1] says, 'The good teacher is always, as it were, "out there" in the classroom, not wrapped up in his own involuted musings. He is aware of everything that is going on and the children sense vividly his perception of them as well as his grasp of his subject matter.' A teacher with this kind of awareness can respond immediately to a minor problem before it has time to develop into something more disruptive.

Brown[23] summarizes the main signals to look for when monitoring a class in this way. Briefly, these are:

1 *Posture*: Are the pupils turned towards or away from the object of the lesson?
2 *Head orientation*: Are the pupils looking at or away from the object of the lesson?
3 *Face*: Do the pupils look sleepy or awake? Do they look withdrawn or involved? Do they look interested or uninterested?
4 *Activities*: Are the pupils working on something related to the lesson, or are they attending to something else? Where they are talking to their fellow pupils are their discussions task-oriented or not?
5 *Responses*: Are the pupils making appropriate or inappropriate responses to your questions?

The vital need, then, is for the teacher constantly to scan his group in an active, alert and expectant manner. Not only is he thus in a position to check or deter incipient disturbances, he also shows the class that he is in the frame of mind to know what is going on. There are some classroom situations where the teacher is restricted in this respect – when he is writing on the blackboard, sitting at his desk or at a piano, or when dealing with an individual child or small group. On such occasions, not only must he be extra vigilant, he must be seen to be so.

On a more positive note, lively and interested classes, as Brown notes, usually sit with their heads slightly forward, their eyes wide open and a few eagerly waiting for a chance to speak.

Ignoring minor misbehaviour

Good and Brophy[21] consider that it is not necessary for a teacher to intervene in a direct way every time he or she notices a minor control problem. Indeed, research evidence[20] suggests that the combination of ignoring inappropriate behaviour and showing approval for desirable behaviour can sometimes be a more effective way of achieving better classroom behaviour. Further, the disruptive effect of the teacher's intervention, as Good and Brophy point out, can sometimes create a greater problem than the one the teacher is attempting to solve.

Having made the above recommendation, however, we need to file a caveat in the case of the student teacher experiencing his or her first teaching practice. The overlooking of a minor discipline problem by a *student* teacher, especially where the class knows the person teaching them is a student, could easily be misconstrued by pupils as either weakness or lack of awareness. They may even seize the opportunity to test the teacher out in his or her newness – 'We've got away with it once, let's go one better!' As the outcomes of a teacher's first few encounters with the children are vital to him in defining the situation and establishing the power structure he wants, it is advisable that all early challenges to his authority be checked and that he explores the more subtle technique of 'turning a blind eye' *later* in his practice, when he has the measure of the group.

Dealing with repeated minor misbehaviour

There are several techniques available to teachers for intervening in cases of *repeated* minor misbehaviour when it threatens to disrupt a lesson or spread to other children in the class. These should be used in preference to more dramatic procedures whenever the teacher wishes to check, for example, persistent inattentiveness or restlessness without distracting others. The more obviously useful of these techniques include the following:

Eye contact

One of the most effective ways of checking a minor infraction is simply to look at the offender and establish eye contact with him. A cold, glassy stare has an eloquence of its own. An accompanying nod or gesture will assist in re-focusing the child's attention on the task in hand.

Touch and gesture

A particularly useful technique in small group situations is the use of touch and gesture. A misbehaving child near at hand can easily be checked by touching his head or shoulder lightly, or by gesturing. The nonverbal nature of this approach ensures that others are not distracted, that is, Kounin's[22] notion of *smoothness* is preserved.

Physical closeness

Minor misbehaviour can also be eliminated or inhibited by moving towards the offender. This is especially useful with older children. If they know what they should be doing, the mere act of moving in their direction will assist in re-directing their attention to their work.

Inviting a response

Another effective means of summoning a child's wandering attention is to ask him a question. The utility of questioning for control purposes is often overlooked. It would seem reasonable to relate a question used for this end to the content of the lesson at the time of the incident, that is, to make it 'task-centred', not 'teacher-centred'. Thus, 'What would you have done in such a situation, John?' is preferable to 'What did I just say, John?'

Other nonverbal gestures

In addition to the ones noted above, there are other nonverbal means of expressing disapproval or checking an infraction. Common examples would include frowning, raising the eyebrows, wagging a finger or shaking the head negatively.

The advantages of these and similar techniques are that they enable the teacher to eliminate minor problems without disrupting the activity or calling attention to the misdeed. Eye contact, touch and gesture, physical propinquity and other nonverbal gestures are the simplest since no verbalization is involved.

Dealing with persistent disruptive misbehaviour

The techniques described so far will assist the student teacher in solving relatively minor problems of control and management. For more serious disruptions, we make the following additional suggestions.

Direct intervention

Good and Brophy[21] note that the direct intervention required for more serious misbehaviour may take two forms. First, a teacher can command an end to the behaviour and follow this up by indicating what alternative behaviour would be appropriate. In such a situation, intervention should be short, direct and to the point. It should thus *name the child, identify the misbehaviour* and *indicate what should be done instead.* When a child knows he is misbehaving, a brief directive indicating what he should be doing should be sufficient: 'Peter, finish the exercises I gave you.'

The second direct intervention technique which Good and Brophy suggest is simply to remind the children of relevant rules and expected behaviour. As suggested earlier, clear-cut rules defining acceptable classroom behaviour should be formulated early on in the practice (or revised if you take over the class teacher's existing rules), possibly after explanation and discussion with the pupils if they are old enough. Where this has been done, all the teacher has to do is to remind the class or child of them as soon as a problem manifests itself.

Another useful guide in this context is suggested by the work of O'Leary, Kaufman, Kass and Drabman[24] who studied the effects of loud and soft reprimands on the behaviour of disruptive pupils. Briefly, two children in each of five classes were selected for a four-month study because of their high rates of disruptive behaviour. In the first phase of the study, almost all reprimands were found to be of a loud nature and could be heard by many other children in the class. During the second phase, however, the teachers were asked to use mainly soft reprimands which were audible only to the children being reprimanded. With the institution of soft reprimands, the frequency of disruptive behaviour declined in most of the children. This sequence was repeated with the same results.

Here is a finding, then, which could play an important part in class management yet which is at variance with the more traditional approach that recommends addressing the culprit in a loud voice.

Interview techniques

In his discussion of management techniques in the classroom, Saunders[8] outlines two forms of interview that may be used for achieving workable arrangements with those pupils presenting lasting behaviour problems for the teacher. The *investigative interview* is a useful strategy where the more serious forms of misbehaviour are present and may be used where one or more pupils are involved. Saunders recommends that the interview should concern only the pupil or pupils involved in the incident for, as he explains, this reduces the possibility of 'acting up' and bias resulting from group pressures. Ideally, the pupil or pupils should be given time to 'cool off'. Where more than one is involved, each should be allowed to give his version of what took place, the teacher only interrupting to clarify questions of fact and to distinguish fact from opinion. Discrepancies in the story line should be resolved and a final account established that is acceptable to all. Saunders is of the opinion that defence mechanisms or strategies are often used by pupils when giving explanations in order to protect them from anxiety regarding the consequences of their behaviour. Those commonly used are *denial*, *projection* and *rationalization*. Where possible these should be identified and brought out into the open. The interview will eventually lead to appropriate action which may take the form of striking a deal with the pupils, punishment or referral to a higher authority. Box 40 summarizes the main points.

Box 40

Investigative interviews

Investigative interviews may be summarized as follows:

    try not to become emotionally involved;

    if possible exclude anyone not involved in the incident;

    each pupil should be required to give his own version of what happened;

    the teacher should clarify the facts and differentiate them from opinion;

    try to recognize the use of defence mechanisms;

    if possible, explain their use to the pupil;

    take further appropriate action;

    remember your actions may serve as models for other pupils.

Source: adapted from Saunders[8]

The second form of interview discussed by Saunders is the *reality interview*. This depends for its effectiveness on good personal relations between the teacher and pupil and on the knowledge that neither will be intimidated by each other. Given these conditions, the teacher should get the pupil to admit his misbehaviour. This achieved, the discussion should move on to an evaluation of the behaviour in question. Cause and effect links should be established. Finally, Saunders considers that the pupil should be encouraged to discuss a more effective course of action for the future, with the teacher impressing on him that he is responsible for his own behaviour and will subsequently be accountable for it. The main steps in this process are summarized in Box 41.

Box 41

Reality interviews

The principal guidelines to reality interviewing are:

discuss in private;
with no hint of intimidation from either side;
start from an existing relationship, if possible;
establish the need for frankness;
evaluate the misdeed;
link cause and effect;
establish other courses of action and their consequences;
discuss the most effective action for the future.

Source: Saunders[8]

Conflict-resolving strategies and techniques

Saunders[8] further discusses the strategies and techniques that teachers sometimes resort to in order to resolve conflict situations. These he considers in three broad categories – avoidance strategies, defusion strategies and confrontation strategies.

First, *avoidance strategies*. Saunders identifies strategies here which include high tolerance, feigned illness and engaging in banter. If a teacher can build up high tolerance, he will be in a position to ignore much of the conflict in which he is involved until a breakdown point is reached. Retreating from a conflict situation under the guise of illness is another technique sometimes employed. And engaging in banter with pupils is yet another means of side-stepping conflict. As Saunders says, 'Avoidance strategies may have some survival value, but they are maladaptive in so far as the individual teacher does not receive any measure of professional satisfaction and the conflict is not resolved.'[8]

Second, *defusion strategies*. These include delaying action, tangential responses, evasion and appeals to generalizability. Delaying action, as it suggests, involves putting off a decision to avoid precipitating a crisis. A tangential response is one that deals with peripheral issues, thus leaving the main source of conflict unresolved. Evasion is resorted to when a teacher is called on to justify his position and side-steps the issue. And an appeal to generalizability is resorted to when a teacher concedes that a demand is reasonable when it is made by one person, but not if others make a similar request. Like avoidance strategies, defusion strategies are generally unsatisfactory.

Finally, *confrontation strategies*. These include the use of power and negotiation strategies. A teacher resorts to power strategies when he uses the divide-and-rule approach; when he resorts to pseudo-power by threatening sanctions he knows he cannot implement; by manipulating rewards; and by resorting to school tradition – 'This isn't the way we do it here.' Negotiation strategies are invoked when there is the possibility of a rational solution to the difficulty. Saunders identifies three approaches in this respect – compromise, affiliative appeal and pseudo-compromise (see also Box 37).

In summary, then, whereas the conflict-avoidance strategies just noted may have a certain survival value to all teachers at some stage in their careers, as permanent features of one's professional behavioural repertoire they need to be regarded with suspicion because they offer neither long-term solutions nor personal satisfaction.

We next consider how a reprimand from a teacher can influence the response of the rest of the class.

The ripple effect

Research by Kounin,[22] who videotaped many hours of teaching in his study of indiscipline in the classroom, has revealed that a reprimand from a teacher to a child misbehaving in his class may influence the rest of the group although they are not actually party to the misdemeanour. Kounin labelled this *the ripple effect* and as such it may have either positive or negative influences from the teacher's point of view. When, for instance, a child being reprimanded is of high standing in the sociometric structure of the group, the ripple effect from an encounter with the teacher is usually strong. If the teacher succeeds in checking the misbehaviour, the effect on the rest of the class from the teacher's perspective is positive in that they will tend to accept the reprimand as fair and think of the teacher as an effective disciplinarian. In practical terms, it means that they will either improve their behaviour or be less likely to behave unsatisfactorily. If, however, the high prestige pupil rebels at the teacher's efforts to control him, this feeling may spread to his classmates, who may then consider the teacher's handling of the situation as unsatisfactory and consequently perceive him as weak and ineffectual. The practical consequences could be an escalation of the problem, with the rest of the class expressing resentment or generally creating an atmosphere not conducive to meaningful work.

Since it is therefore important to produce a positive ripple effect, that is, an improvement or inhibition of the behaviour of other pupils, certain characteristics of control need to be borne in mind. Gnagey[17] identified a number of such factors including *clarity, firmness, task-centred techniques, high-prestige pupils* and *roughness*. Each will be considered briefly.

Clarity

What Gnagey describes as a clear control technique, one embodying *clarity*, is one that specifies the deviant, the deviancy and the preferred alternative behaviour. Thus, 'John, stop talking and finish your essay' is preferable to 'Cut out the talking at the back there', for it is a clear command and therefore can be expected to have two beneficial effects on the rest of the class: *they will be less likely to talk themselves* and *less likely to be disrupted in their own work than would probably be the case with a command lacking clarity.*

Firmness

Firm control techniques prevent disruption more effectively than tentative ones. Gnagey recommends that they can best be implemented by moving towards the offender, issuing the command in an 'I-mean-it' tone, and following-through by seeing the command is obeyed before continuing with the lesson. Kounin and Gump[25] found that children responded to rules that were actually enforced ('followed-through') but ignored those lacking conviction and enforcement ('follow-through').

Task-centred techniques

A *task-centred approach* produces a more desirable ripple effect than one that is teacher-centred. By this is meant the need to stress the task in hand, or the effects of the deviancy on the task, rather than on the teacher or the teacher's relationship with the pupil. Thus, 'John, stop whispering and watch the demonstration, or else you won't understand when you have to do it yourself later' is better than 'Pay attention and listen to me'.

High-prestige pupils

Gnagey recommends that *high-prestige pupils* be identified and studied. He writes, 'As their responses to your influence have such a strong ripple effect on others, it will pay to find out which control techniques cause them to respond submissively with the least amount of belligerence.' In this connection, the reader is referred to the account of sociometric techniques in Oeser.[26]

Roughness

Gnagey explains that *roughness* refers to the use of threatening or violent control techniques on the part of the teacher that in turn are likely to produce negative ripples – anger, resentment, feelings of injustice or displacement. Kounin, Gump and Ryan[27] found that such techniques produced a considerable amount of disruptive behaviour among children who were not originally misbehaving themselves. A further consequence was that they also held the teacher in lower esteem because of his manner.

In summary, the beginning teacher should seek positive ripples through clarity, firmness, task-centred techniques, capitalizing on high-prestige pupils and the avoidance of roughness.

We continue by taking the important skill of giving orders and instructions a little further.

Issuing orders and instructions

Although some teachers are more effective at it than others, giving instructions to an individual, group or class is a skill that can be learned and improved with practice. Like other techniques, issuing instructions, orders and commands can be broken down into their basic components such as content, phrasing, manner of delivery and context.

The prevailing conditions play a part in the overall effectiveness of instructions; the class must be *still and silent*, ideally before an instruction is given. Thus, 'Stop whatever you are doing, please; no more talking, stop writing.' Then give your instruction.

The manner of delivery is also important. You have to avoid being too stern and imperious on the one hand, yet too diffident and unconvincing on the other. The one approach can induce fear (which is not desirable); the other, an ineffectualness on the teacher's part. A firm but pleasant manner is required. Marland's[28] advice in this connection is eminently practical: 'It is worth practising instructions on your own. Then listen to yourself as you give them in school and observe the response. *Develop a firm warmth, or a warm firmness.*'

Generally speaking, instructions tend to be more effective and to be accepted more gracefully when phrased in a positive, rather than a negative, manner. Accordingly, 'Be early for the practical lesson on Monday' in preference to 'Don't be late for Monday's lesson.' Or, 'Leave the room as tidy as you found it' rather than 'Don't leave the room in such a mess this week.'

Marland warns against framing an instruction in the form of a question. For example, the organizational and management problems encouraged by 'Anyone need paper?' will be minimized by expressing the point thus, 'Put your hands up if you're without paper.'

You should not give a second instruction until the first one has been obeyed. Take time to glance round the room and check that everyone has understood and carried out your order.

Finally, the following points may be useful to the reader in his consideration of the use of commands as a technique of control.

Task-oriented commands are often preferable to status-oriented ones. As Peters[1] observes, 'If commands are task-oriented rather than status-oriented they are a thoroughly rational device for controlling and directing situations where unambiguous directions or prohibitions are obviously necessary.'

Generally speaking, the reason for a command should not be given, as this introduces an element of doubt or suggests that it may not or need not be obeyed. In any case, if the system of rules operating in the classroom has been explained to the group at an earlier stage, there should be no need for elaboration.

A command should not be coupled with a statement of grievance, as this may arouse hostility towards, or induce disrespect for, the person issuing the command. For example, avoid this sort of utterance: 'Stop moving the chairs to the back of the room. I'm tired of telling you. You do it every time you come into the room.'

Similarly, a command couched in the language of a whine 'operates powerfully to bring about its own frustration'.[29]

Once you have got to know your class, requests – a more polite form of command – may be all that you need to structure the situation.

The voice issuing the command should be strong, decisive and warm.

The teacher's own expectations play a part, too. Children will tend to conform not so much to what he says in words but to what he actually *expects*. He must therefore *expect* more or less instant obedience to his commands as a matter of course.

The verbal context of the message is also important. It is vital that it stands out in relief from what the teacher has said immediately preceding its issue and, especially, from what he says subsequently. A directive can easily lose much of its force by becoming indistinguishable from its context in terms of timbre, tone, dynamics, manner and speed of delivery. Timing, the judicious use of pauses and silence, vocal dynamics, facial expressions and a touch of drama will all assist in achieving greater salience.

A teacher may further enhance the effectiveness of his commands by having the class come to associate them with certain additional nonverbal features such as clapping the hands, snapping the fingers, staring, gesturing or moving to a focal point in the room.

Rewards and punishments

Older books on the psychology of education make great play with the concepts of *extrinsic* and *intrinsic* rewards as aids to motivation and to a lesser extent classroom management and control. Indeed, their validity

202 A guide to teaching practice

and usefulness in these respects still holds good. Extrinsic rewards such as marks, grades, stars, prizes and public commendation are stock examples in this context and are there for the student teacher to exploit. Intrinsic rewards like the warm feeling from a job well done, or satisfying one's innate curiosity, or the kick one gets from solving a problem or achieving a standard one has set oneself, belong to an individual's subjective world and are as such beyond the teacher's direct control. But he can influence them *indirectly* through the use of extrinsic rewards. The connection between the two is often overlooked, for the skilful manipulation of extrinsic rewards over a period of time can lead to the more desirable intrinsic kind. Contrasting perspectives on rewards in the classroom by pupils and teachers respectively are indicated in Box 42.

Box 42

Pupil and teacher perspectives on rewards

In a study on the relative effectiveness of various incentives and deterrents as judged by pupils and teachers, it was found that:
  1 *Pupils preferred*:
     favourable home report
     to do well in a test
     to be given a prize
     to receive good marks for written work

  2 *Whereas the staff thought the most effective rewards were*:
     to be praised in the presence of others
     good marks for written work
     elected to leadership by fellow pupils
     teacher expressing quiet appreciation

Source: adapted from Burns[30]

Perhaps the most immediately accessible means of reward for the teacher is the *use of praise*, and its value in the classroom should not be overlooked. It has been demonstrated by Madsen, Becker and Thomas[20] that showing approval for appropriate behaviour is probably the key to effective classroom management. Much of this kind of approval will take the form of *verbal praise* so it is important for the teacher to understand both the constructive and damaging effects of its classroom use. Waller's[29] comments are apposite here:

The whole matter of control by praise is puzzling and a bit paradoxical. Where it is wisely carried on, it may result in the most happy relations between children and teachers. Where it is unwisely applied it is absurdly ineffective and ultimately very damaging to the child. Praise must always be merited, and it must always be discreet, else all standards disappear. Cheap praise both offends and disappoints, and it breaks down the distinction between good and bad performances. Praise must always be measured; it must not resort to superlatives, for superlatives gives the comfortable but deadening sense of a goal attained. Such praise as is used must open the way to development and not close it. Praise must always be sincere, for otherwise it is very difficult to make it sincere, and if it does not seem sincere it fails to hearten. Praise as a means of control must be adapted to particular children. It is a devise to be used frequently but only on a fitting occasion rather than an unvaried policy.

Everyone enjoys praise and you should try to direct it at both the individual and the class as a whole, as well as to a range of classroom behaviours – work, good behaviour, helpfulness, a quick answer. Nor should personal praise be overlooked – a girl's summer dress, a boy's new jeans. It is not always necessary to select the *best* work and behaviour, as one is not seeking absolute performance. Nor should you invariably praise only those who 'shine' naturally, as the idea is to get over to the child that praise is accessible to all and can be earned by them with striving. In some instances, especially where slower children are involved, it is more desirable to praise *effort* rather than the finished product.

There are two main ways of praising an individual child – either publicly or in private. Public praise in front of the rest of the class (or at morning assembly, in some circumstances) can be effective and appreciated providing it is not overdone or too effusive. The quiet private word of praise with a child is an approach which student teachers tend to overlook.

The persistent trouble-maker should be praised with care. Of him, Marland[28] writes:

If, as is often the case, he is seeking group status by his ostentatious behaviour, he will resent the public praise as an attack on his reputation, and as likely as not he will find some technique of expression or gesture that not only nullifies the praise but, worse than that, actually associates your praise with his scorn – thus devaluing it for others. . . . This does not, however, normally mean that he does not want the praise, merely that he doesn't want it openly. For such a pupil, the private word of praise is essential, and frequently effective.

There is a whole range of nonverbal signals that can be used to indicate approval; these can be used to reinforce verbal praise or else independently. For example, a smile, an affirmative nod of the head, a pat on the back or a hand on the shoulder all indicate acceptance of pupil behaviour. Similarly, the use and display of pupil ideas, like writing comments on the board, holding up a pupil's work for the class to see or displaying it on a display board, can also be regarded as nonverbal expressions of approval. And merely showing interest in pupil behaviour and presence by establishing and maintaining eye contact is yet another rewarding (from the pupil's point of view) use of nonverbal signals.[31]

Some American research findings[32] are worth mentioning in this context. Teachers use praise sparingly in standard classrooms. Further, teachers give more praise to high-achieving pupils; pupils to whom they feel more attached, or less indifferent; pupils whom they say they favour; and pupils for whom they have expectations of high future occupational status. The researches also indicate that boys receive more praise than girls and that praise varies with the social class status of the school's location.

We consider now the subject of punishment. We saw earlier how a teacher's control may be seen as stemming chiefly from a combination of personal power and authority. Discipline in a classroom is achieved by the successful exercising of this control to ensure conformity to the established rules. It is when there is a serious breach of the rules, a breakdown of discipline, that the need for punishment may arise.

Peters[1] points out that punishment is a much more specific notion than discipline and that at least three criteria must be met if we are to call something a case of punishment. These are (1) intentional infliction of pain or unpleasantness (2) by someone in authority (3) on a person as a consequence of a breach of rules on his part. Although some actions in the school situation are loosely referred to as cases of 'punishment' without meeting all these criteria, e.g. asking a child to do a piece of work again, they do nevertheless provide us with a useful frame of reference for our brief consideration of this important subject.

For some considerable time, the use of punishment as a means of assisting in the upbringing and education of children was discouraged not only on ethical grounds but also because of the possible harmful side effects. More recently, however, interest in the subject has revived and research undertaken latterly does seem to indicate that punishment may very well have a valuable part to play in the development and control of children.

Of course, a teacher who comes to rely heavily on punishment cannot hope to succeed except in a narrow and temporary sense. Whatever he achieves will be at the cost of undue negative emotional reactions such as anxiety and frustration and a permanent impairing of relationships.

Nevertheless, a teacher should not hesitate to resort to punishment when the occasion demands for, when properly used, it is a legitimate and helpful means of dealing with certain disciplinary problems.

We now consider the forms which punishment in the classroom might take, the occasions for punishment and ways of administering it.

Forms of punishment

Before deciding the forms of punishment you intend to use during your teaching practice, should the need for them arise, there are two points worth bearing in mind. First, you are not starting from square one: most schools will have an established system of punishment as part of their tradition and no doubt the forms it takes will be related to the rules that are operative in the school. You should thus find out what alternatives exist within the tradition so that you can use them when necessary (the case of corporal punishment presents something of a problem; even in those schools where it remains a legal alternative, it is inadvisable for you as a student teacher to resort to it). Second, it is better whenever possible to anticipate and thereby avoid incidents likely to culminate in the need for punishment. As Peters[1] says, 'Under normal conditions enthusiasm for the enterprise, combined with imaginative techniques of presentation and efficient class management will avert the need for punishment. Boredom is one of the most potent causes of disorder.'

Keeping a class in after school can be an effective deterrent and a particularly useful one for the student teacher, although this form of punishment does present the kind of dilemma to which Peters draws attention: 'There is also the problem of what to do with them when they are so detained. It becomes a farcical situation, and one that is very difficult to manage, if nothing constructive is done. Yet the conditions are scarcely ideal for doing much of educational value.' A further disadvantage with keeping children after school lies in the fact that some schools insist on giving children at least twenty-four hours' notice of the detention. Although sound practical reasons usually account for such a ruling, it can weaken the connection between the offence and the punishment.

A useful form of punishment for the individual offender is that of isolation. Its efficacy was noted by Waller[29] when he referred to it as 'a long lever that makes for conformity'. It is important for the student teacher to remember that it is not necessary to send a child out of the room to achieve isolation. Setting him apart from the rest of the class *within* the classroom can be just as effective and may be achieved by having him stand in a corner or, better still, sit on the floor or at a desk away from the others. This kind of psychological banishment can be especially effective providing it does not last too long. Offenders who have been particularly disruptive may be isolated with their work, but again the isolation should not last too long. Thompson[33] advises that no matter how naughty a child has been he should be given innumerable 'fresh starts', for children have a strong corporate feeling so that isolation counts as a severe punishment.

Negative utilitarian controls are frequently used by teachers. These may take the form of *behaviour restrictions* and *limitations of privilege* and may thus include missing part of a favourite lesson, a desired recreational activity, play time, or not being allowed to sit near the back of the class. Boys particularly dislike missing games. You will quickly discover additional means of controlling misbehaviour along similar lines.

Box 43

Forms of punishment

Reasonable punishment can take many forms, but some account must be taken of the forms customarily used in your school with the age range in question. Some common practices are:

keeping a child behind for a few minutes' discussion after the rest of the class have left, so that he is last in the queue for lunch, or it causes his friends to wait for him;

formal detention with some task to do that is not directly connected with the lesson so that his antipathy for the lesson is not increased by the punishment;

detention to finish work deliberately not completed in lesson time;

withdrawal of privileges, such as the use of a tuck-shop at break, or access to a common room or classroom other than when essential;

isolation or exclusion with work, either in a corner of the classroom or in another part of the school;

if property is damaged the pupil may be required to repair the article, if such action is appropriate, or to do a socially useful task such as tidying the classroom or picking up paper in the playground;

as a response to unacceptable language the pupil might be required to write out the offending words several times.

Source: Saunders[8]

Some kinds of punishments are better avoided and may be itemized as follows: (1) school work should not be used as a punishment. A child kept in from play or games, for instance, should not be given additional school work such as writing or mathematics. These should be associated with enjoyment. (2) Avoid collective punishments, such as keeping a whole class in, when only one or two individuals are culpable. Such action will provoke unnecessary resentment from the innocent members. (3) Forms of mental punishment such as severe personal criticism, ridicule, sarcasm and so on are not recommended. (4) Coercive sanctions, those involving a physical component such as caning, strapping, striking or shaking, should not be used; in any case, these forms of punishment are increasingly being outlawed by unions and authorities. (5) Only send a child to the headteacher as a last resort, or when you are confronted with a particularly serious case of misbehaviour. Such an action considerably weakens the teacher's authority. However, do not hesitate to seek advice privately from other members of staff when you need help. (6) Avoid banishing a child from the classroom. Where you feel isolation is warranted, let it be within the classroom.

The 'when' and the 'how' of punishment

Good and Brophy[21] in their analysis of punishment make a number of interesting points concerning *when* to resort to punishment. Generally speaking, punishment is appropriate only in dealing with *repeated* misbehaviour, not for single, isolated incidents, no matter how serious. It is a measure to be taken when a child persists in the same kinds of misbehaviour in spite of continued expressions of concern and disapproval from the teacher. Resorting to punishment is not a step to be taken lightly since it signifies that neither the teacher nor the child can handle the situation. One other point: punishment should not be administered if it is apparent that the child is trying to improve. He should be given the benefit of the doubt and, where possible, rewarded for attempts at improvement.

In considering the nature of punishment and the forms it may take in the classroom, we can easily lose sight of the way in which it should be administered. A moment's reflection tells us that we should at least be *systematic* in its application. So once again the efficacy of having agreed on a few basic classroom rules is brought home to us, for in providing us with an impartial frame of reference for teacher and pupils alike, not only do they ensure we will achieve the consistency we seek, they also guarantee that the recipients, in recognizing the logic and fairness of the punishment, will be less likely to respond emotionally.

Another factor in the punishing situation concerns the nature and extent of the talk the teacher engages in. Wright[34] explains that this can serve a number of functions, one of which helps the child 'to construe his actions in a certain way, to structure them cognitively and relate them to general rules'. In thus justifying the punishment to the child, the teacher's explanatory talk will clarify the nature of the offence, will provide reasons for judging it wrong, will explain its effects on others and will relate it to future occasions. A consistent *modus operandi* of this nature will give the child the necessary criteria for making his own judgements.

Box 44

Occasions for and nature of punishment ·

Good and Brophy[21] in their analysis of punishment offer several indicators and criteria for its use. These may be summarized as follows:

   when persistent misbehaviour leaves no alternative;

   as a stop-gap measure to suppress misbehaviour;

   it should follow closely from the offence;

   when used it should be done deliberately rather than emotionally and uncontrolledly;

   it should, ideally, be threatened before being used to give the pupil an opportunity of stopping his misconduct;

   it should be short and as mild as is consistent with indicating displeasure;

   ideally it should be combined with positive statements of expectations and rules, focusing more on what the culprit should be doing than on what he should not, explaining why there is no alternative to the punishment and what the other consequences of the misbehaviour might be.

Source: Saunders[8]

A third factor concerns the temporal relationship between the offence and the punishment. Wright[34] has pointed out that punishment placing restrictions on a child will be most effective if they are related to the offence, if they follow closely after it, and if removal of the restrictions is conditional upon improvement of behaviour. Punishment being thus logically related to the offence is more easily perceived as fair. A sanction should therefore be immediate and inevitable so that the cause and effect relationship is apparent. If it is prolonged to the point where the relationship becomes tenuous, the offender may become resentful.

Finally, we refer the reader to Box 45 which contrasts teachers' and pupils' views on punishment.

Box 45

Pupil and staff views on punishment

In the Teacher Education Project, it was found that:

1 *Pupils disliked*:
    corporal punishment;
    unfavourable report home;
    being made to look foolish in class sarcastically;
    being sent to the headmaster.
2 *Whereas the staff thought the most effective forms were*:
    good talking to in private;
    detention;
    extra work;
    being urged to make an effort.

Source: Wragg[4]

Behaviour modification

Psychologists have long been aware that most behaviour is affected by its consequences. These consequences may be seen as rewarding or reinforcing if, as a result, the behaviour persists or increases, and punishing if the behaviour ceases or decreases. In some circumstances behaviour may be extinguished if there is no consequence.

These principles lie at the heart of the recent approach to dealing with undesirable or maladaptive classroom behaviour which has come to be known as *behaviour modification*, the techniques of which are used to change specific patterns of inappropriate behaviour, e.g. hyperactivity in the classroom, excessive movement about the room, talking too much or disobedience. This method of handling behaviour problems is preferred by those who find the use of punishment in the classroom distasteful and who seek a non-punitive, positive approach as an alternative.

The behaviour modification approach in its most basic form consists of three components: (1) specification of the undesirable behaviour to be extinguished or minimized and the preferred desirable behaviour that is to replace it; (2) identification first of the rewards and reinforcements sustaining the unwanted behaviour so that they may be avoided, and second identification of the rewards and reinforcements that will increase the frequency of the preferred alternative behaviour; and (3) the consistent and systematic avoidance and application of these respective rewards and reinforcements over a period of time, together with a systematic record of changes in behaviour. A reinforcer in this context is defined by its ability to accelerate, or increase, the rate at which a behaviour will occur or, more simply, its effect on the learner.

There are a number of types of reinforcer that may be used in this context. The most natural and effective for teachers are *social reinforcers*. Thus, teacher attention, teacher praise, teacher approval and disapproval are powerful factors affecting children's behaviour, and they can be systematically varied to produce the sort of behaviour desired by the teacher. When employing these techniques, however, the teacher must be sure to reinforce the desirable behaviour as well as ignore the undesirable if he is to achieve his objective of creating the most favourable conditions for learning.

A particular instance of the application of behaviour modification techniques may concern some form of consistent anti-social behaviour on the part of a child in class. This kind of behaviour may often be sustained by reinforcements in the form of teacher attention and often by the approval or perhaps disapproval of the rest of the class. If this is the case, the behaviour modification approach would recommend ignoring the attention-seeking behaviour (e.g. a pupil constantly moving out of his seat) and making sure that the sought-after alternative behaviour (e.g. the pupil remaining in his place) is rewarded or reinforced with appropriate action (attention, praise or some kind of nonverbal approval like smiling) on the part of the teacher.

Such techniques may also be useful in the following situations providing they are employed systematically, consistently and over a period of time: failure to pay attention, day-dreaming, failure to show interest in work, not meeting work requirements, being uncommunicative and withdrawn, breaking class rules, overreacting to stressful conditions, insensitivity to other people, anti-social behaviours, hyperactivity, attention-seeking, disobedience and disrespect.

The results of experimental studies in behaviour modification are encouraging, though it will be some time before a more widespread adoption of the techniques is evidenced. A study by Thomas, Becker and Armstrong,[35] for example, demonstrates the possibilities of the approach. They showed that approving teacher responses served a positive reinforcing function in maintaining appropriate classroom behaviours. Disruptive behaviours increased each time approving teacher behaviour (praise, smiles, contacts, etc.) was withdrawn. When the teacher's disapproving behaviours (verbal reprimands, physical restraints, etc.) were tripled, there was much greater disruption, i.e. an increase in noise and movement about the room. The findings, therefore, emphasize the important role of the teacher in producing, maintaining and eliminating both desirable and disruptive classroom behaviour. Summaries of findings of similar studies in which the techniques of behaviour modification have been successfully applied to a range of maladaptive behaviours may be found in Hewett.[36]

Of course, from the student teacher's point of view, teaching practice is not the most ideal context for putting the techniques of behaviour modification to the test because of its length – a few weeks at most. Nevertheless, he may be in a position to select some consistently manifested behaviour problem and attempt to remedy it along the lines suggested above. He could then at least satisfy himself that the principles are sufficiently sound to warrant further investigation at a later date.

For further information on this subject we suggest you read Gropper and Kress[37] and Sloane.[38] The latter is particularly useful in that within the framework of behaviour modification it presents practical, positive procedures for solving and preventing problems of management and control. The concrete, practical suggestions throughout the text will help the reader to develop a systematic approach to all areas of classroom management. A similarly useful text is Clarizio's,[39] which offers a wealth of practical suggestions on rewards, extinction and punishment. Two introductory guides which outline the main principles of behaviour modification in the classroom are those by Givner and Graubard[40] and McAuley and McAuley.[41] Finally, a text dealing with the planning and implementation of behaviour modification programmes for severely handicapped children is Morris's.[42]

Anticipating management and control problems in the classroom

There are certain aspects and structural features of one's lesson that need handling with particular care and foresight because potentially they can be the cause of quite serious problems of management and control. The beginning of a lesson, for example, requires special thought because it sets the tone of the rest of the lesson. Similarly, transitions, that is occasions for a change of activity during the lesson, can also be vulnerable in their potential for disruption. As we have already considered these features of the lesson, it is sufficient for us at this point to suggest that you revise the appropriate sections.

Another important point for student teachers to bear in mind concerns *their first meeting with a new class*. As Wragg[4] has observed, the very first lesson with a class can go a long way towards establishing the kind of climate that will prevail for the rest of the practice or term. In the Teacher Education Project, he and his colleagues observed a hundred lessons given by thirteen experienced teachers at the beginning of the school year, and two hundred given by student teachers at the beginning of teaching practice. The differences between the two groups are listed in Box 46.

Box 46

Differences between experienced teachers and student teachers

Experienced teachers

were usually very clear about their classroom rules;

did not hesitate to describe what they thought was 'right' and 'proper';

were conscious of the massive effort needed to establish relationships with a new class;

used their eyes a great deal to scan the class or look at individuals;

were quick to deal publicly with any infraction of their rules;

were more 'formal' than usual;

were especially brisk and businesslike;

established their presence in the corridor before the class even entered the room;

introduced themselves formally, but, as if to temper the formality, gave incidental details of their personal background ('I've a son your age' or 'I was watching television the other night . . .').

Student teachers

were not so clear about classroom rules, either their own or those of other teachers in the school;

did not use terms such as 'right' and 'proper' when talking about rules;

were unaware of the massive collective effort the school and individual teachers had put into starting off the school year;

made less use of eye contact and were very conscious of themselves being looked at;

often neglected early infringements of classroom rules which then escalated into larger problems;

concentrated in their preparation on lesson *content* rather than rules and relationships ('Will I have enough material?' 'How can I find a topic which will make an impact?').

Source: Wragg[4]

The researchers also proposed a series of questions for student teachers to ask themselves prior to meeting a new class for the first time. These we have set out in Box 47.

Box 47

Self-questioning prior to first contact with a new class

1 What would you like to know about the class *in advance*, and why?
2 What sort of topic or theme will you choose for this first lesson, and why?
3 What will you be doing and thinking about:
    (a) an hour before the lesson?
    (b) five minutes before the lesson?
4 Do you plan to be present before the class arrives, if this is possible? If not, why not?
5 If you are present in the corridor before the lesson begins what will you be doing:
    (a) before entering the room?
    (b) as the children enter the room?
6 How will you begin the lesson:
    (a) if the class settles down quickly?
    (b) if the class is slow to settle?
7 How do you think the class will see you on first meeting you?
8 Are there any rules you will want to establish from the beginning? (And why are these your most pressing rules?)
9 What kind of relationship would you like to have with the class in the longer term, and how will you set about establishing it?
10 What teaching strategies, so far as you can see, will you employ during the first lesson (lecture? group work? individual assignments? question and answer? projects?) and why?

Source: Wragg[4]

Behavioural problems with some ethnic minority pupils

Although numerous studies have reported the incidence of behavioural difficulties among a proportion of ethnic minority pupils in British schools,[43] few have actually attempted to pinpoint the precise nature of the difficulties that confront teachers in some multicultural classrooms. One study that has, however, is Driver's.[44] The majority of problems he identified in classes containing a significant minority of children of West Indian origin were largely to do with classroom management and control. Many of the teachers' difficulties arose from interactional problems between the teacher and pupils, and between pupil and pupil. These concerned physical features, gestures and other codes of communication used by pupils.

First, in the important initial stage of getting to know a new class, many teachers regularly mistook and confused the identities of their West Indian pupils long after they had got to know the names and faces of English pupils in the class. The sureness of touch and certainty of judgement that follows from being able to identify an individual confidently was thus absent. Being able to name a person gives one some measure of control over that person.

Even where this was no longer a problem, Driver identified another range of potential difficulties. These were concerned with the basic expectations teachers had of nonverbal behaviour or of the correspondence between nonverbal and verbal behaviour. Thus individuals might look away from the teacher at those moments when social convention would not expect them to do so. There were also occasions when eye signals appeared to convey an imminent message (a verbal initiative or response) which did not materialize. As Driver notes, the expectations of individuals socialized in two cultural settings gave rise to misunderstandings and heightened ethnic awareness.

Second, on many occasions West Indian pupils averted their eyes from the teacher, a sign of deference towards and respect for him, yet it was received and interpreted by the teacher as an expression of guilt or bad manners. Such culture-bound, virtually involuntary gestures, learned in early childhood, can easily 'throw' a person from a different cultural background and upset the rhythm of exchange between the two. Again, it can generate uncertainty and insecurity in the teacher.

What it means in practice is that there is a code of classroom communication to which the teacher is denied access. Such a situation is rich in anxiety-potential for the teacher who, Driver considers, can respond in one of two ways. Either he can become increasingly dominant and strict, or he can adopt an easy-going posture. As he comments, each requires considerable emotional resources of courage and self-confidence on the teacher's part.

Third, quite apart from involuntary gestures and postures, there were a number of specific nonverbal signs used by some West Indian pupils to indicate specific meaning. Clicking the lips, or pouting them and plucking them with a finger were examples identified by Driver of derogatory expressions which many teachers failed to interpret even when they were directed at them. Again, the exclusive nature of such gestures can easily undermine a teacher's confidence even though some had only innocent connotations.

Fourth, there was the use of *patois* which few of the teachers understood. Most of the teachers, Driver observed, appeared to discourage its use, even with the threat of sanctions in some instances. It was clear to the researcher that a number of the teachers felt threatened by the regular use of a dialect that they could not understand, and that their concern showed itself in their attitudes and behaviour to those pupils using it.

So what practical suggestions can we make from Driver's case study?

The following seem to us to be particularly important:

1 Make a real effort from the very first moment of contact to get to know individual ethnic minority pupils by name and personality.
2 Study pupils' nonverbal behaviour, especially of the micro-reflexive kind like eye movements and facial expression,[31] and learn to distinguish their significance from similar gestures among English pupils.
3 Study other aspects of pupils' nonverbal behaviour that are deliberate, especially those that appear to have an exclusively ethnic meaning or significance, like pouting the lips.
4 School policy towards *patois* varies with the institution. Decide where you stand in relation to it. If you are sympathetic, learn the basics of its grammar and syntax;[45] if you feel it should be discouraged in the classroom, institute a weaning process, but be tolerant and patient.
5 Develop those subtle skills of observation so that you can discern pupils' moods and intentions even from the most fleeting of expressions or gestures.
6 Anticipate the kinds of difficulties identified by Driver so that you can maintain your classroom composure in the event of an expected or anticipated pupil response not materializing.

In conclusion, we quote from Driver himself:[44]

To be unskilled in these subtler managerial arts has consequences well known to teachers. Pupils who do not question the teacher's superior knowledge will nevertheless question and probe the authority and confidence used to manage the social situation. The process of negotiating the limits of acceptable behaviour beyond which punitive sanctions might be employed, is a real part of developing classroom relationships. If it becomes apparent to some pupils that the limits are imprecise or the teacher's negotiating skills are inadequate, it is highly likely that an attempt will be made to exploit these grey areas of the classroom régime.

The presence of West Indian children in the classroom implies an additional range of expressions and behaviours from the minority's cultural repertoire. While a confident teacher may be able to execute his management role in a 'normal' classroom situation, the same teacher may find he is less skilled in the presence of an ethnic minority with distinctive cultural behaviour unknown to him.

Notes and references

1 Peters, R.S. (1966) *Ethics and Education*. London: George Allen and Unwin.
2 Wadd, K. (1973) Classroom power. In Turner, B. (ed.) *Discipline in Schools*. London: Ward Lock Educational.

3 Note: the past few years have witnessed a considerable erosion of the teacher's authority. Some of the reasons for this change are rooted in the dramatic changes in society's beliefs and values that have taken place since the 1960s. For a brilliant account of these processes of change and the effects they have had on features of contemporary life such as the arts, popular culture and education, see Martin, B. (1981) *A Sociology of Contemporary Cultural Change*. Oxford: Basil Blackwell.

4 Wragg, E.C. (1981) *Class Management and Control: A Teaching Skills Workbook*. DES Teacher Education Project, Focus Books; Series Editor, Trevor Kerry. London: Macmillan.

5 Glasser, W. (1969) *Schools without Failure*. New York: Harper and Row.

6 See Brophy, J.E. and Putnam, N.P. (1979) Classroom management in the elementary grades. In Duke, D.L. (ed.) *Classroom Management*. NSSE Yearbook Volume 78, 2. Chicago: University of Chicago Press.

7 Nash, R. (1976) *Teacher Expectations and Pupil Learning*. London: Routledge and Kegan Paul.

8 Saunders, M. (1979) *Class Control and Behaviour Problems: A Guide for Teachers*. Maidenhead: McGraw-Hill.

9 Gannaway, H. (1976) Making sense of school. In Stubbs, M. and Delamont, S. (eds) *Explorations in Classroom Observation*. London: John Wiley.

10 Meighan, R. (1981) *A Sociology of Educating*. Eastbourne: Holt, Rinehart and Winston.

11 Willis, P. (1977) *Learning to Labour*. London: Saxon House.

12 Johnson, D.W. (1978) Conflict management in the school and classroom. In Bar-Tal, D. and Saxe, L. (eds) *Social Psychology of Education: Theory and Research*. New York: John Wiley and Sons.

13 Gnagey, W.J. (1981) *Motivating Classroom Discipline*. New York: Macmillan. London: Collier-Macmillan.

14 Thurston, J.E., Feldhusen, J.F. and Benning, J.J. (1973) A longitudinal study of delinquency and other aspects of children's behaviour. *International Journal of Criminology and Penology*, 1 (November), 341–51.

15 Gnagey, W.J. (1980) Locus of control, motives and crime prevention attitudes of classroom facilitators and inhibitors. Paper read at AERA, Boston.

16 Hargreaves, D.H. (1972) *Interpersonal Relations in Education*. London: Routledge and Kegan Paul.

17 Gnagey, W.J. (1968) *The Psychology of Classroom Discipline*. New York: Macmillan. London: Collier-Macmillan.

18 Goodlad, J.I., Klein, M.F. and associates (1974) *Looking behind the Classroom Door*. Worthington, Ohio: Charles A. Jones.

19 McIntyre, R.W. (1974) Guidelines for using behaviour modification in education. In Ulrich, R., Stachnik, T. and Mabry, J. (eds) *Control of Human Behaviour*, Volume III. Glenview, Illinois: Scott, Foresman.

20 Madsen, C.H. (Jnr), Becker, W.C. and Thomas, D.R. (1968) Rules, praise and ignoring: elements of elementary classroom control. *Journal of Applied Behaviour Analysis*, 1, 139–50.

21 Good, T.L. and Brophy, J.E. (1973) *Looking in Classrooms*. New York: Harper and Row.

22 Kounin, J.S. (1970) *Discipline and Group Management in Classrooms*. New York: Holt, Rinehart and Winston.

23 Brown, G.A. (1975) *Microteaching*. London: Methuen.

24 O'Leary, K.D., Kaufman, K.F., Kass, R.E. and Drabman, R.S. (1970) The effects of loud and soft reprimands on the behaviour of disruptive students. *Exceptional Children*, 37 (October), 145–55.

25 Kounin, J.S. and Gump, P.V. (1958) The ripple effect in discipline. *Elementary School Journal*, 35, 158–62.

26 Oeser, O.A. (1960) *Teacher, Pupil and Task*. London: Tavistock Publications.

27 Kounin, J.S., Gump, P.V. and Ryan, J.J. (1961) Explorations in classroom management. *Journal of Teacher Education*, 12, 235–47.

28 Marland, M. (1975) *The Craft of the Classroom*. London: Heinemann Educational.

29 Waller, W. (1932) *The Sociology of Teaching*. New York: John Wiley.

30 Burns, R.B. (1978) The relative effectiveness of various incentives and deterrents as judged by pupils and teachers. *Educational Studies*, 4 (3), 229–43.

31 Note: for a review of the main features of nonverbal behaviour and their relevance in the classroom, see Cohen, L. and Manion, L. (1981) *Perspectives on Classrooms and Schools*. Eastbourne: Holt, Rinehart and Winston.

32 Dunkin, M.J. and Biddle, B.J. (1974) *The Study of Teaching*. New York: Holt, Rinehart and Winston.

33 Thompson, B. (1973) *Learning to Teach*. London: Sidgwick and Jackson.

34 Wright, D. (1973) The punishment of children. In Turner, B. (ed.) *Discipline in Schools*. London: Ward Lock Educational.

35 Thomas, D.R., Becker, W.C. and Armstrong, M. (1968) Production and elimination of disruptive classroom behaviour by systematically varying the teacher's behaviour. *Journal of Applied Behaviour Analysis*, 1, 35–45.

36 Hewett, F.M. (1972) Educational programs for children with behaviour disorders. In Quay, H.C. and Querry, J.S. (eds) *Psychopathological Disorders of Childhood*. New York: John Wiley.

37 Gropper, G.L. and Kress, G.C. (1970) *Managing Problem Behaviour in the Classroom*. New York: New Century, Educational Division/Meredith Corporation.

38 Sloane, H.N. (1976) *Classroom Management: Remediation and Prevention*. New York: John Wiley.

39 Clarizio, H.F. (1976) *Toward Positive Classroom Discipline*. New York: John Wiley.

40 Givner, A. and Graubard, P.S. (1974) *A Handbook of Behaviour Modification for the Classroom*. New York: Holt, Rinehart and Winston.

41 McAuley, R. and McAuley, P. (1977) *Child Behaviour Problems*. London: Macmillan.

42 Morris, R.J. (1976) *Behaviour Modification with Children*. Cambridge, Mass.: Winthrop.

43 Rutter, M., Yule, W., Berger, M., Yule, B., Morton, J. and Bagley, C. (1974) Children of West Indian immigrants – I. Rates of behavioural deviance and of psychiatric disorder. Proceedings of the First International Conference on Special Education, London.

44 Driver, G. (1979) Classroom stress and school achievement. In Khan, V.S. (ed.) Minority Families in Britain. London: Macmillan.

45 Note: for a useful text in this respect, see Edwards, V.K. (1979) The West Indian Language Issue in British Schools. London: Routledge and Kegan Paul.

THE CLASSROOM ENVIRONMENT AND SITUATIONAL FACTORS

Introduction

So far in this section we have looked in detail at some of the more specifically pedagogical aspects of the teacher's work and how they affect the pupil – traditional and progressive approaches to teaching and learning, mixed ability teaching, management and control and so on. The rest of this section we devote to those features we described in our original model as 'classroom environment' and 'situational factors' (Box 2, page 16), the latter including extra-curricular activities. As regards situational factors in school learning, there are literally countless factors operating singly or interactively that impinge directly or indirectly on the teacher's and pupils' efforts throughout a lesson. Indeed, the lack of effort on the part of teacher or pupil could be seen as one such factor, and obviously a very important one at that. Even if, through some miracle, it were possible to identify all these factors, it would be quite impossible to discuss them all in a book of this nature. What we have done, therefore, is to select those that we feel the reader ought especially to be aware of. We begin with a review of *the physical environment*, and go on to consider successively *the emotional environment, teacher–pupil relationships*, the use of *modelling, teachers' attitudes and expectations*, and finally *extra-curricular activities*.

The physical environment

The physical environment is the framework for learning; and as it can contribute to either promoting or impeding learning, it must be under the teacher's control as far as possible. Indeed, the physical environment suitably ordered makes up part of the teacher's *resources power* that we spoke of earlier[1] as contributing to his *personal power*. We therefore recommend that the student teacher devotes meticulous care to the planning and organization of this aspect of his teaching, for his authority and power as a classroom performer derive in part from such preparation.

What does the ordering and controlling of one's physical environment entail? For both the traditional classroom and open plan areas, a multiplicity of factors are involved, but chiefly it entails arranging, organizing or utilizing satisfactorily such matters as seating and layout, teaching aids, equipment for practical lessons, audio-visual apparatus, activity corners and areas, notice boards, blackboards and display tables. Thoroughly organizing one's needs in this respect helps to establish an environment conducive to learning.

The importance of the classroom environment has been stressed by Marland[2] who writes, 'It would be fair to say that the physical impression of the classroom can be an ally or an enemy in teaching, and part of the art of the classroom is to *use* the room itself. Its arrangement can contribute to the control, the learning, the relationships and the pleasure of working together.'

The competent teacher must have the classroom environment, just as much as his children and the content of his lessons, well under control. We now consider three factors that are particularly relevant in this connection.

Preparation – equipment

It is especially important for the student teacher in an unfamiliar school to find out what equipment is available and where it is located. Most schools have the following: a radio, television, record player, tape recorder, cassette tape recorder, microphone, loudspeakers, movie projector, strip projector and an episcope. He should also find out where in the school these may be used. Particular items, like a cassette tape recorder, may be in great demand, so the student teacher should plan well ahead and book equipment he needs in good time.

Specialist teachers should get to know what is available in their subjects. Thus, a geographer may want to know what the school has in the way of atlases, wall maps and facilities for duplicating; the mathematics teacher may want to use calculators; the music teacher, the content of the school's record library, the range of musical instruments and sets of song books; and the PE specialist, what equipment, apparatus and facilities are available. Science teachers will want to know what equipment there is for experiments and practical lessons. It is particularly important where class practicals are involved to check that there is sufficient equipment and that it will be available when required. In schools where the laboratory technician is normally responsible for preparing equipment for teacher and pupil use, it is usually necessary to give him two or three days' notice of whatever will be required.

Primary teachers will want to know what basic materials are available for their use, and the range of additional material for free activities, for topic work and for maths. West[3] has compiled lists of equipment and material the primary teacher can expect to draw upon. For money transactions in maths, for example, he lists plastic money, paper money, real money, used stamps, PO counterfoils, used bus tickets, price lists from local shops, bill heads for shopping, charts of wrappers of priced goods and charts of coin values. Further information may be found from the same source, pages 43–7.

Notice boards

Notice boards and display boards are to be found in most classrooms and at various strategic points around the school. Apart from their basic function in communicating important information – timetables, class lists, fire regulations, etc. – they may also be used to display aids for learning, children's work and exhibitions arranged by the children or teacher – pictures, clippings, posters, etc.

A student teacher on arriving at his school can quickly discover the notice boards and assess the standards of presentation and maintenance by a quick tour of the school. If he is not very experienced in such matters, he can find ideas and inspiration for the upkeep of the boards he will be responsible for by studying those in the school that have been well kept. The important criteria are *freshness* and *relevance*.

We offer a few suggestions by way of a beginning:

1 Ask your class teacher to allocate you an area of board space for your exclusive use during the practice.
2 Divide it up so that a smallish part may be reserved for the children's personal interests and their own contributions. The larger part of the board space can be used for material relating to your own teaching – information, charts, diagrams for a project, for example. You can reserve another small part for a representative sample of the children's written work. This last section should be changed frequently – say once a week.
3 Take particular care with the labelling of the various exhibits. Bold, eye-catching lettering is desirable.
4 Information is not simply stuck on the board to be forgotten. Refer to and use whatever is displayed in the course of your lessons. Marland[2] suggests that the final minutes of a lesson can be given over to questions and answers in connection with work or information thus presented. Alternatively, a class can be sent in groups to do a worksheet based on a display.

5 Encourage the class to share in the maintenance of the boards.

You should remember that visitors to a classroom – and especially those of particular significance to you, like supervising tutors and external examiners – sometimes form their earliest and often lasting impressions of the student from the appearance of notice boards. And of course the same holds for those display tables for which the student is responsible. Bear in mind that notice boards and other means of display reflect something of the philosophy of education that prevails in the classroom.

Seating

It is the view of experienced teachers that careful attention to seating arrangements contributes as effectively as any other aspect of classroom management and control to overall success with a class subsequently. Although we fully realize that in most cases the student teacher must accept and use the classroom seating as he finds it, nevertheless we feel it important to establish one or two points of particular relevance.

First, the teacher's desk or table. In the past this was often positioned on a raised platform in the front centre position. As there is no longer the same need for it to occupy such a dominating location, teachers have experimented with different placings and many consider that for most purposes a front side position is probably the best. A desk so placed meets the criteria suggested by Marland:[2] (1) all the pupils can see the teacher when he or she is at the desk; and (2) the desk is clearly visible from the door. He further notes that he prefers to have his desk in a position which is easy for him to get at and round, which is adjacent to the best focal position for board work and questions, and which allows him to observe the class when he is helping an individual pupil.

The second point of relevance concerns the *pupils'* desks or tables. Arrangements here will largely be determined by the age and needs of the pupils. Formal rows will give fourteen-year-olds elbow room and privacy for individual work; four tables arranged as a rectangle will permit four to six eight-year-olds to work together. While recognizing that there is rarely an ideal layout, Marland suggests that an optimum one is worth striving for, yet at the same time preserving a reasonable amount of circulatory space.

Readers should remember not to attempt to teach or address as a class children arranged in groups without first ensuring that where necessary chairs have been turned to face the teacher. One often sees children uncomfortably screwing their necks round to attend to the teacher while their chairs continue to face away from him.

Box 48

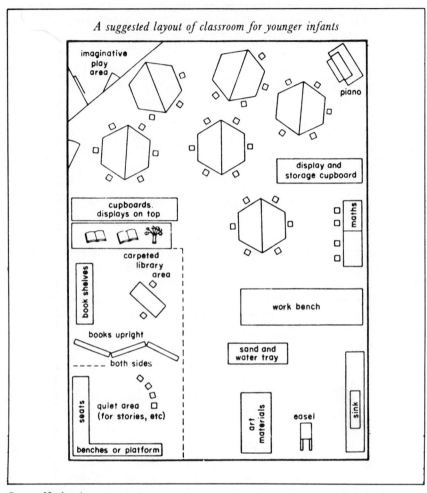

A suggested layout of classroom for younger infants

Source: Haslam[4]

Should children be allowed to sit where they like? Or should their seating be determined by the teacher? Although having a secondary or middle school classroom in mind, Marland strongly recommends that the initial seating of a class be done by the teacher and to a plan devised by him. He further suggests arranging a class alphabetically, a procedure which is simple, defensible, and which has practical advantages, one of which is apparent where mixed classes are involved. Since class misbehaviour sometimes results from interaction of pupils of the same sex, a single alphabetical ordering of the whole class will tend to lessen this possibility.

Box 49

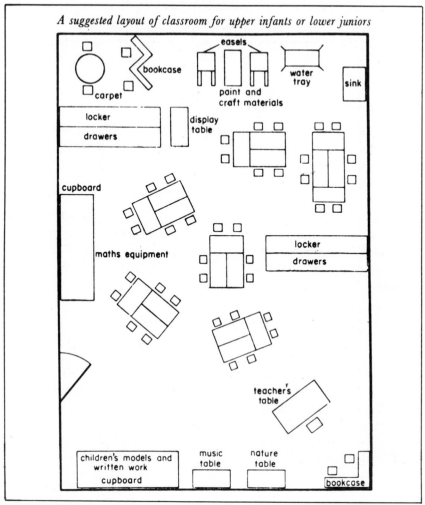

A suggested layout of classroom for upper infants or lower juniors

Source: Haslam[4]

Two additional points with regard to the importance of seating will be mentioned. The first concerns what to do with spare seats in a situation where there are more places than pupils. Marland advises:

I strongly recommend that you exploit the spare seats as buffers to improve the psychological separation of pupils or groups. . . . It might be wise with one class to keep the back row, the trouble-maker's instinctive chair-swinging row, empty. In another class you may distribute the empty chairs here and there, merely to thin the seating out. You may use your knowledge of the pupils in another class to decide that Gary or Elaine is best left sitting in isolation.

The second point arises from mixed ability classes in which the arranging of seating is even more important than in classes of like ability. Mixed ability grouping involves individual work, group work and sometimes class teaching. Whatever the need, planned seating can assist in achieving the appropriate learning situation and educational outcomes which the teacher seeks. As Marland says:

> The greater fluidity of mixed ability teaching implies the need for the control that comes from controlled seating. The seating plan, then, is a method of assisting the psychological insulation of crowded pupils, and can sometimes be subtly manipulated to separate certain individuals or leave others entirely on their own.

We hope that in the light of all this the reader will be a little more sensitive to the importance of seating arrangements and give it high priority in his consideration of the classroom environment. For those of you who will be working in primary classrooms, Boxes 48, 49 and 50 give suggested layouts.

The emotional environment

Important as the physical characteristics of the classroom are, the learning environment is more than just the sum of them. It also embraces such features as the teacher's voice, his attitudes and expectations, his belief system, humour, techniques of control, favoured leadership styles and the use of praise. These may be seen to contribute to what may be described as the *emotional environment*. This may be even more important than the physical environment, for not even the most desirable ordering and use of the physical environment can compensate for an impoverished emotional one.

We will now look briefly at some of these factors determining or contributing to a classroom's emotional tone.

Voice

The teacher's voice is of considerable importance in establishing emotional tone in a classroom. If it is relaxed, natural and mainly conversational in manner, it will assist in creating a relaxed, tension-free atmosphere favourable to interaction and learning. Further, the pupil's voice will in turn tend to reflect similar qualities. Conversely, the emotional tone will be adversely affected by an anxious, high-pitched voice which will tend to generate a correspondingly tense atmosphere.

Box 50

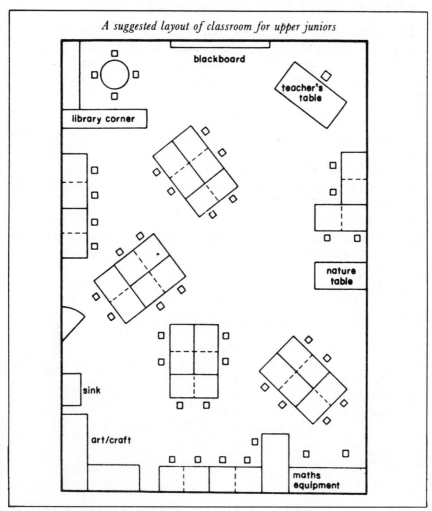

A suggested layout of classroom for upper juniors

Source: Haslam[4]

It is mainly the nonverbal aspects of speech – timbre, pitch, manner and speed of delivery, smoothness and flow – which contribute for good or ill to the classroom atmsophere.

Attitudes and expectations

The part played by a teacher's attitudes and expectations in the educational outcomes of a lesson is examined later in this section. It is important to note that they also assist in establishing the feeling tone of a classroom. A teacher who habitually maintains a cheerful, optimistic frame of mind, who expects the best from his pupils, and who is able to appraise the children's abilities and efforts realistically will be well rewarded, not least in the kind of atmosphere produced.

Teachers' beliefs, classroom atmosphere and children's behaviour

A further important determinant of a classroom's emotional tone concerns the teacher's professional orientation. A study by Harvey, Prather, White and Hoffmeister[5] replicating earlier studies found that teachers' belief systems determine the general tone or atmosphere of the classroom, and that this in turn affects the children in significant ways. Thus, teachers manifesting greater *abstractness* (i.e. those who were more resourceful, less dictatorial and less punitive) were associated with more educationally preferable behaviour in the children. By contrast, teachers having more *concrete* belief systems (i.e. less resourceful, more dictatorial and more punitive) affected children's performance less favourably.

Briefly then, the results show that the belief systems of teachers do affect their overt classroom behaviour and that this in turn is significantly related to the children's behaviour.

Humour

Another indispensable feature contributing to a favourable classroom atmosphere is humour. In the well-structured, purposeful organization of an effective classroom, there will be many opportunities for humour. Its manifold functions are more or less self-evident: it relaxes tension, helps establish natural relationships, facilitates learning and is of great value as a means of restoring sanity to a classroom after a disciplinary incident. Peters[6] remarks: 'Humour is a great catalyst in a classroom; for if people can laugh together they step out of the self-reference cast by age, sex and position.'

Marland's[2] advice on humour bears the stamp of experience:

> A joke goes a long way. Try to be light-hearted whenever you feel up to it. Try to chivvy recalcitrant pupils jokingly rather than by being indignant. . . . Be willing to make jokes at your own expense, and to laugh at your own foibles. Teachers' jokes don't have to be very good to be nevertheless highly acceptable.

He goes on to warn young teachers with high ideals and considerable theoretical understanding from taking themselves, their responsibilities and their pupils too seriously. Their 'humourless indignation' and 'sad intensity' may alienate their charges.

Techniques of control

In general terms, a teacher may use either positive or negative controls, or both. Positive ones may be either formal (marks, privileges, praise, encouraging competitiveness, fostering group approval) or informal (relaxing routines, using inducements like promising to read a story at the end of a lesson, using the children's Christian names). Negative controls may include punishments, deprivations, threats, censure, sarcasm, mockery or rejection.

The balance between the two types varies from school to school, class to class, and lesson to lesson. As one would predict, a more favourable classroom atmosphere and more effective learning result when positive controls predominate.

Leadership styles and teaching methods

The emotional ambience is very considerably affected by the kind of leadership style a teacher provides and the methods of teaching he adopts. One of the earliest attempts to observe and control objectively the climate variable in group life was White and Lippitt's.[7] Working with boys' clubs, they demonstrated the influence of leadership style on group life, its social-emotional climate, and productivity, findings which have strong implications for teachers and education.

Two of White and Lippitt's major conclusions were: (1) that different styles of leadership behaviour produce differing social climates and differing group and individual behaviours; and (2) that group members in a democratic social climate were more friendly to each other, showed more group-mindedness, were more work-minded, showed greater initiative and had a higher level of frustration tolerance than members in groups governed by autocratic and *laissez-faire* leadership styles.

More recent classroom research in America indicates that teachers who have an *indirect* influence on children (i.e. those who accept the feeling tone of the children in a non-threatening manner; who praise and encourage pupils' efforts; who accept and use pupils' ideas; and who ask questions) create a more favourable emotional tone than those having a *direct* influence (i.e. those who tend to lecture children; who act in an authoritarian manner; who give directions; and who are unduly critical).

Although *indirect* influences contribute to the 'warmth' of a classroom, research shows that most teachers adopt *direct*, traditional approaches, and that classrooms are neither 'warm' nor 'cold', but primarily neutral in tone.

Teacher–pupil relationships

Good relationships between a teacher and his pupils are vitally important in the give and take of classroom life: where they exist there is less likelihood of difficulties arising. Teacher–pupil relations is a fairly general term and, as Evans points out,[8] covers such topics as the influence of teachers on the immediate behaviour of their pupils and on their intellectual and social development, the contribution which teachers make to the mental health and adjustment of children, the children's likes and dislikes with regard to their teacher, and the effects on the teachers of daily contact with their pupils.

At the heart of effective teacher–pupil relations lies *respect for persons*. Dawney[10] considers that this involves 'treating children as individuals, recognizing and valuing their singular characteristics'. She goes on:

> For a child to develop and function as a person, he needs to be treated as someone who is important in his own right and not just as a member of a category. He needs help in developing the kind of self-concept that allows him to regard himself as of value. To treat children as persons in their own right involves regarding them as responsible for their own actions and therefore having some control over what they do.

She goes on to warn us, however, against showing an uninformed and uncritical respect towards children. This would be inappropriate, as she explains:

> It would be misguided for a teacher to let his respect for a child's point of view prevent him from showing his pupils what moral and intellectual standards imply. Constructive criticism of a pupil helps him to develop the sort of self-image and self-esteem that enable him to develop as an autonomous being, and thus has an important part to play in the judgements we make of him and to him.

Many of the factors contributing to effective teacher–pupil relationships, e.g. the personality of the teacher, are clearly beyond the control of the teacher and have therefore to be taken as 'given' when interactions occur. One factor, however, that does lie within the teacher's power to manipulate is what has been termed 'nonverbal immediacy behaviours'.[11] These signal that the initiator, namely the teacher, is approachable and available for communication. In that they can thus communicate interpersonal closeness and warmth, they can contribute positively to relationships. Indeed, research on immediacy constructs suggest that they can be a positive force in the classroom, particularly in bringing about better teacher–pupil relationships.

Box 51

Teacher–pupil relationships

Relationships can be established in many different ways. Teachers who have harmonious relationships with their classes often establish and cement these in a number of contexts by occasionally or regularly doing, among other things, some of the following:

Out of class

crossing the yard or walking down corridors talking to pupils;

chatting casually to groups or individuals during breaks or lunch hours;

looking out for quieter or more difficult pupils to talk to away from the classroom;

showing interest in extra-curricular activities such as clubs, sports, plays, music, etc.

meeting parents at parents' evenings or other school events;

knowing the school's catchment area and understanding the way of life of the people who work and live in it;

taking an interest, in a discreet way, in the social problems encountered by children;

being familiar with and understanding the leisure and recreational pursuits of the age group.

In class

talking to pupils in a friendly way as they enter the room;

monitoring children's work on an *individual* basis;

learning and using pupils' names;

sharing jokes and sharing good humour;

creating a sense of collective pride in what children do.

Source: Wragg[9]

The article by Andersen and Andersen[11] reviews a whole range of nonverbal immediacy behaviours in the context of the classroom. They include the following:

Proxemics or the use of interpersonal space and distance. There are two aspects here – physical distance and bodily orientation.

In the case of physical distance, many teachers fail to establish interpersonal closeness with a class because they remain physically remote in the sense that they stand at the front of the classroom or sit at a desk. Confident, effective teachers use the entire room and move among pupils.

As regards orientation of the speaker, more 'immediacy' is communicated when the teacher *faces* the class. As the authors say:

> Many teachers do not fully face their class when teaching. They hide behind desks, podiums, and tables, and often continuously write on the blackboard, with their backs to the class. Not only does this reduce the immediacy between teachers and their classes, it also removes any visual communication between them.

Kinesics or communication by body movement. Four aspects are relevant here – smiling, head nods, bodily relaxation and gestural behaviour.

One of the most effective immediacy cues is smiling. Research shows that smiling produces substantial positive therapeutic effects in relationships, including an increase in interpersonal acceptance. As the authors say, 'Teachers who frequently smile are communicating immediacy in one of the easiest and most powerful ways. Pupils at all levels are sensitive to smiles as a sign of positive affect and warmth.'

Head nods are another effective means of indicating immediacy, especially when used by a listener in response to a speaker. When used by a teacher to his class they provide reinforcement and indicate that the teacher is listening to and understanding what they say.

Bodily relaxation communicates immediacy by indicating freedom from stress and anxiety. It has been found that more 'immediate' teachers are more relaxed, whereas tense and anxious teachers communicate negative attitudes to their pupils who perceive them as cold and inaccessible.

Gestures, particularly hand and arm movements, communicate interest, warmth and involvement. In these respects they contribute positively to both interpersonal transactions and teaching.

Oculesics or the study of messages sent by the eyes. Eye contact is an invitation to communicate and a powerful immediacy cue.[11] As we saw earlier, teachers who use eye contact can more easily monitor the behaviour of their classes. They can also communicate more warmth and involvement to their pupils. The authors advise that teachers should position themselves so that they can and do establish eye contact with every pupil in the class, warning that immediacy cannot be successfully established by a teacher in the absence of eye contact.

In thus making himself more accessible by incorporating these skills into his classroom behaviour, the teacher is in a position to strengthen the relations he has with his pupils. Other practical ways of building up relationships are suggested in Box 51.

Modelling

Good and Brophy[12] have noted that many things may be learned in classrooms without deliberate instruction by the teacher or deliberate practice by the learner; and that such observations are supported by a growing body of experimental evidence. The learner only needs to see a particular behaviour demonstrated by another person before imitating it himself, sometimes consciously, sometimes not. The person who demonstrates the behaviour is called *the model* and the form of learning, *modelling*.

Modelling can be a most useful device for the teacher. Many skills, for example, can be learned more easily through observation and imitation than by trying to understand and respond to only verbal explanation and instruction. This is especially true for younger children whose abilities to follow detailed verbal instructions are limited. The process of modelling may thus be seen as a means of enabling a child to re-assemble components of behaviour he already possesses into new and alternative combinations.

The pervasiveness of modelling

Most teachers recognize the value of prepared demonstrations as teaching tools, especially in practical subjects. However, they are usually less aware of the more general modelling effects that may occur incidentally in the classroom, and are therefore less likely to take advantage of them through deliberate, planned modelling behaviour. There is thus a need for teachers to know that modelling effects can occur at any time.

In this connection, it is important to remember that if children detect discrepancies between what the teacher says and what he actually does, they will ignore what he says and be affected much more by what he does. Further, if they see discrepancies between what he says he expects and what he allows, they will tend to be influenced by what he allows. This aspect of modelling has important consequences for discipline, and especially so for the student teacher who, having once established a particular standard of behaviour, should insist that it is maintained.

What is learned from models

Good and Brophy suggest that exposure to a model can result in either or both of two responses by the learner: *imitation* and *incidental learning*. Imitation, perhaps the more obviously useful for the teacher, is the simpler; the learner observes the model's behaviour and then imitates it, making it his own. For example, a class will tend to respond to tactful and sympathetic treatment in the same vein; likewise, sarcasm or ridicule on the part of the teacher invariably produces a negative response from a class.

Incidental learning is a more subtle form of modelling than imitation. The learner observes the model's behaviour in specific situations and on the basis of these observations makes inferences about the model's beliefs, attitudes, values and personality. These inferences may subsequently affect a child's own behaviour.

Factors affecting what is learned from observing a model

The amount and kind of learning that results from observing others depends on a number of factors, one of the more important of which is *the situation*. Modelling effects are far more likely to occur in *new* situations where the expected behaviour of both the teacher and learner is unclear. When such ambiguous situations occur in the classroom, the potential for modelling will be considerable, especially at the beginning of a new academic year or, in the case of the student teacher, at the start of a teaching practice spell. As a result of such early contacts with his teacher, then, a child will make inferences about him and will decide whether he likes him, what kind of person he is and how he ought to respond to him. Further, the teacher's early behaviour will contribute to establishing the emotional and intellectual climate of the classroom.

It is thus vital for the student teacher to model appropriate behaviour from his first day in the school. Opportunities to teach through modelling will be greater at this time because many things will still be fluid and ambiguous. Later, when both teacher and class settle into predictable routines, it will be more difficult to bring about changes.

A second factor affecting what is learned from modelling is *the personality of the teacher*. A warm and enthuasistic teacher whom the children like will be imitated by them. There is the possibility that some of the pupils will adopt, or be influenced by, his attitudes and beliefs; and they may imitate his behaviour. However, children will be less likely to imitate a teacher whom they dislike or do not respect, particularly in the sense of adopting or conforming to his ideals.

Teaching through modelling

To illustrate the value of modelling as a teaching device, two areas of behaviour will be briefly described which exemplify the two kinds of response identified above, namely, imitation and incidental learning.

Imitation will be illustrated by the use of demonstrations in the classroom. These must be the most obvious means of using modelling as a teaching aid before a group. Many skills can be taught best by demonstration, especially with younger children. Some skills can be demonstrated with little or no verbalization. However, demonstrations tend to be more effective when accompanied by some verbalization. Demonstrations usually provide examples of more general principles that a teacher wants his children to learn. Thus, to maximize transfer value, a demonstration should not only show a child the physical movements involved in performing a task, it should also include explanations of the thinking that lies behind the movements.

Research shows that people tend to leave out important pieces of information when explaining or demonstrating something, assuming that the listener sees the situation in the same way they do. The expert instructor, however, breaks down a task into step-by-step operations, assuming little or no knowledge on the part of the learner. Each component or part of the task is identified and placed in context. The learner can thus master one step at a time.

Thinking aloud at each step in this way is crucial when the task is primarily cognitive and the physical movements involved are relatively less important or negligible. A task such as making an incision will require verbal commentary if the pupil is to understand fully. Where the processes are not verbalized, they will possibly be hidden from the learner.

Teachers not only educate through modelling, they also socialize children by influencing attitudes and values. In other words, they contribute to incidental learning. For example, good teachers model respect for others by treating children politely and pleasantly, and by avoiding behaviour that would cause them to suffer indignities. Many well-intentioned attempts to help children learn appropriate forms of social behaviour in this way are undermined by teachers not modelling the behaviours they would wish to promote. In this respect, Rutter and his colleagues[13] make the following observations:

Standards of behaviour in school are also set by the behaviour of the staff. There is an extensive research literature which shows that children have a strong tendency to copy the behaviour of other people – especially people in positions of authority whom they like and respect. Moreover, not only do they copy specific behaviours, but they also tend to identify in a more general way with the people whom they follow, and come to adopt what they perceive to be their values and attitudes. This means that pupils are likely to be influenced – either for good or ill – by the models of behaviour provided by teachers both in the classroom and elsewhere. These will not be restricted to the ways in which teachers treat the children, but may also include the ways staff interact with one another, and how they view the school.

In their own research, Rutter and his colleagues[13] systematically studied the school factors associated with educational attainment and pupil behaviour. The study identified particular features of school life which relate to pupils' academic achievement, their attendance records, and their behaviour both in and out of school, the principal concern being to find out why there are differences between schools in these respects. The researchers' findings on modelling processes may be found in Box 52.

Box 52

Modelling in the school

Our observations of good care of the buildings, and the willingness of teachers to see pupils about problems at any time, provide some examples of *positive* models. These actions convey the message that the school is valued and thought to be worth keeping clean and in good decorative condition; and that staff appreciate the needs of children sufficiently to give their own time to help them when they experience difficulties. *Negative* models would be provided by teachers starting lessons late and ending them early, and by their use of unofficial physical sanctions. If teachers react with violence to provocation and disruptiveness this may well encourage pupils to do the same. Similarly, if the teachers' own behaviour suggests that they disregard timekeeping, they can scarcely expect good timekeeping and attendance from the pupils.

Source: Rutter *et al.*[13]

Returning to the needs of the reader, we suggest he considers ways in which he can consciously use modelling processes in his own work. For example, at a cognitive level, helping children to develop skills in logical thinking and problem-solving; at an attitudinal level, encouraging them to develop an interest in learning for its own sake; at a social level, fostering a favourable group climate; and in a general way, adopting a humane and rational approach to life.

Teachers' attitudes and expectations and the influence they exert on classroom behaviour

It is apparent from a commonsense viewpoint that the attitudes and expectations a teacher holds with respect to the children he teaches considerably affect his behaviour towards them; and that this in turn influences *their* responses in a variety of ways. There is now a significant body of evidence illustrating the more negative aspects of these observations which is of particular interest to the student teacher.

Studies conducted in the United States, for instance, indicate that children of differing achievement levels were treated differently by their teachers; and that there were important differences in both the *frequency* and *quality* of the contacts between them.[14] Some of the consequences were that high achievers received more opportunity to respond than low achievers. They also tended to ask more questions. Further, teachers waited significantly longer for the more capable children to respond before giving an answer or calling on another child.

The findings disclosed, too, that teachers praised high achievers more than low achievers, the latter being more likely to be criticized for a wrong answer. Teachers also tended to 'give up' more readily with children who did not know, or who answered incorrectly, and this suggests that they expect and demand higher performance from high achievers. Related evidence from these same studies indicates that physically separating poor performers from the rest of the class by re-grouping them increases the likelihood of their being treated differently and inappropriately.

There have been a number of studies which reveal that in some situations differential teacher behaviour and expectations affect children's behaviour and achievement. Findings by Douglas[15] and Mackler,[16] for example, show that teachers' expectations about a child's achievement can be affected by factors having little or nothing to do with his ability; and that these expectations can determine the child's level of achievement by confining his learning opportunities to those available in a particular class. A child who is placed needlessly in a low grade is unlikely to realize his potential because his teachers do not expect much of him and consequently his achievement motivation will be affected accordingly.

Good and Brophy[17] suggest a model to demonstrate how teachers' expectations can function as self-fulfilling prophecies: this we illustrate in Box 53. It indicates that the teacher's expectations are not automatically self-fulfilling. To become so, they must be translated into consistent behaviour patterns.

The importance of these and similar findings for the student teacher is self-evident, for his success in the classroom is dependent in part on the adoption of suitable attitudes and expectations even though, as a student teacher, he may only be in school for relatively short periods of time. Because children are individuals, it is natural for teachers to form different attitudes and expectations concerning them, and as long as these are accurate and appropriate, they will be helpful in planning ways to meet the children's needs. However, they must be constantly reviewed and evaluated to ensure that they are modified in response to changes in the child's behaviour. Unless a teacher is prepared to monitor

Box 53

Teachers' expectations as self-fulfilling prophecies

1 The teacher expects specific behaviour and achievement from particular children.
2 Because of his different expectations, he behaves differently towards the different children.
3 The teacher's treatment tells each child what behaviours and achievements the teacher expects from him and this in turn affects his self-concept, achievement motivation and level of aspiration.
4 If the teacher's treatment is consistent over time, and if the child does not actively resist or change in some way, it will tend to shape his achievements and behaviour.
5 With time, the child's achievements and behaviour will conform more and more closely to what was originally expected of him.

Source: Good and Brophy[17]

his view of a pupil in this way, he may get caught in a 'vicious circle of failure'.

As Good and Brophy[17] observe, attitudes and expectations may be a teacher's allies if properly maintained and used. If, however, they are accepted without question and allowed to harden, they may become defence mechanisms enabling him to ignore or explain away problems instead of solving them.

In conclusion, one further point of interest may be added which again stresses the reciprocity of the relationship in this connection and it is this: a child will tend to fulfil the positive expectations *of a teacher whom he respects*. It is therefore incumbent upon the teacher to strive to earn such respect from the outset.

Notes and references

1 Wadd, K. (1973) Classroom power. In Turner, B. (ed.) *Discipline in Schools*. London: Ward Lock Educational.
2 Marland, M. (1975) *The Craft of the Classroom*. London: Heinemann Educational.
3 West, R.H. (1967) *Organization in the Classroom*. Oxford: Basil Blackwell.
4 Haslam, K.R. (1971) *Learning in the Primary School*, London: George Allen and Unwin.
5 Harvey, O.J., Prather, M., White, B.J. and Hoffmeister, J.K. (1968) Teachers' beliefs, classroom atmosphere and student behaviour. *American Educational Research Journal*, 5 (2), 151–66.
6 Peters, R.S. (1966) *Ethics and Education*. London: George Allen and Unwin.

7 White, R.K. and Lippitt, R. (1960) *Autocracy and Democracy: An Experimental Inquiry.* New York: Harper and Row.

8 Evans, K.M. (1958) The teacher–pupil relationship. *Educational Research,* 2, 3–8.

9 Wragg, E.C. (1981) *Class Management and Control: A Teaching Skills Workbook.* DES Teacher Education Project, Focus Books, Series Editor Trevor Kerry. London: Macmillan.

10 Dawney, M. (1977) *Interpersonal Judgements in Education.* London: Harper and Row.

11 Andersen, P. and Andersen, J. (1982) Nonverbal immediacy in instruction. In Barker, L.L. (ed.) *Communication in the Classroom.* Englewood Cliffs, New Jersey: Prentice-Hall.

12 Good, T.L. and Brophy, J.E. (1973) *Looking in Classrooms.* New York: Harper and Row.

13 Rutter, M., Maughan, B., Mortimore, P. and Ouston, J. (1979) *Fifteen Thousand Hours.* London: Open Books.

14 For example:
Good, T.L. (1970) Which pupils do teachers call on? *Elementary School Journal,* 70, 190–8.
Jones, V. (1971) The influence of teacher–student introversion, achievement and similarity on teacher–student dyadic classroom interactions. Doctoral dissertation, University of Texas at Austin.
Brophy, J.E. and Good, T.L. (1970) Teachers' communications of differential expectations for children's classroom performance: some behavioural data. *Journal of Educational Psychology,* 61, 365–74.

15 Douglas, J. (1964) *The Home and the School: A Study of Ability and Attainment in the Primary School.* London: McGibbon and Kee.

16 Mackler, B. (1969) Grouping in the ghetto. *Education and Urban Society,* 2, 80–95.

17 Good, T.L. and Brophy, J.E. (1974) The influence of teachers' attitudes and expectations on classroom behaviour. In Coop, R.H. and White, K. (eds) *Psychological Concepts in the Classroom.* New York: Harper and Row.

EXTRA-CURRICULAR ACTIVITIES

Introduction

Schools today are generally 'outward-looking' in their attitudes towards out-of-school activities and the part that they play in the overall educational programme. Most teachers acknowledge the importance of the well-prepared, well-organized visit for what it can do by way of widening children's understanding of the world in which they live. The *value* of out-of-school activities lies in their relevance to the pupils and to the school curriculum. That value is enhanced when some simple procedures are followed by the teacher:

Each visit should be preceded by meticulous preparation and planning.

The children involved should have a clear understanding of the purpose of the visit and the place that it has in the overall curriculum in which they are engaged.

An essential part of any out-of-school visit is the work that takes place *after* the visit has occurred. Teachers' preparation and planning should therefore consider the purpose that the collation, interpretation and discussion of observations and data collected and recorded during the visit will play in stimulating further interest and learning on the pupils' part.

Organizing out-of-school visits with safety in mind

Teachers bear considerable responsibility for the safety and well-being of their pupils. They are *in loco parentis* and their preparation and planning of out-of-school visits must always be made with this responsibility in mind.

The teacher is responsible to his employing authority, to his headteacher, to parents, and to the pupils in his charge. In planning out-of-school activities, he must, therefore:

Seek both the employing authority's and the headteacher's *approval* and *authorization* before embarking on any projected visit.

Be thoroughly conversant with the policies and regulations of his authority governing out-of-school activities.

Inform parents of any activity likely to involve risk or hazard.

Plan the visit with safety foremost in mind. This involves:

seeing that supervisory provision is appropriate to the age, sex and ability of the pupils involved;

making a preliminary visit, if possible, and by taking careful note of any possible hazards or risks that might be encountered, planning accordingly;

having worked out in advance clearly understood procedures for '*recall*', '*lost*', and '*accident*' situations.

Thoroughness of preparation is the keystone to a successful out-of-school visit. Anticipation of emergency situations that *could* arise is the most effective way of ensuring that they will not.

Travel arrangements and out-of-school visits*

Factors such as the nature of the visit, the distance from the school, the number of children in the party and the costs involved, determine the eventual choice of the method of travel. Whatever the final choice, whether walking, cycling, coach or rail, a number of commonsense considerations should be borne in mind:

Check that adequate third party insurance cover has been arranged for. The employing authority's public liability insurance policy generally covers the supervisory teacher but he is advised to be insured against any personal liability not covered by the authority's policy. The same applies to any other adults who may be accompanying the out-of-school trip.

Give the travel organization responsible, *well ahead of time and in writing*, all the necessary information they need to play their part in the organization of the visit, e.g. date and time of departure, destination, total numbers involved, estimated time of arrival, reservation of seats, required toilet and refreshment 'stops', etc. Obtain from the travel organization *confirmation of the agreed arrangements in writing*.

Inform parents *well ahead of time* about those aspects of the arrangements that directly concern them, *particularly* departure and return times, food, clothing and footwear requirements, etc.

Plan to contact a pre-arranged telephone number (e.g. the headteacher's, or the deputy head's) so that in the event of late return, waiting parents can be informed.

Day and half-day activities

The most commonly undertaken educational visits involve a whole or a half-day's absence from school. Teachers may find the following list of suggestions helpful in planning projected visits.

Consult with the headteacher and members of staff involved during the initial stages of planning.

Where possible, make a pre-visit in order to work out a realistic timetable for the range of activities occurring on location.

* For advice on general rules covering children's travel by rail, coach, underground, etc., see *Out and About* (1972) Schools Council, Evans/Methuen Educational.

Having done this, work out as accurately as possible, all the timetabling arrangements, particularly arrival and departure times at various stages of the visit.

Calculate the cost of the visit, not forgetting admission charges where appropriate, gratuities to drivers and guides, and all other such incurred charges.

Work out the supervisory arrangements required during the visit and discuss these with the school personnel involved well in advance of the projected visit.

Check that all insurance arrangements have been finalized on the part of the employing authority.

Submit a finalized, detailed plan of the visit and costs to the headteacher well in advance of the visit. This will allow time for internal arrangements to be made (e.g. reduction in school meals numbers; timetabling to accommodate absent staff; disruptions to such school activities as school teams, games, choir and similar activities).

Industrial and work visits

Impetus to industrial work-experience visits was given by the warm encouragement contained in the Newsom Report, which saw such activities as providing valuable opportunities for older pupils to gain first-hand experience of work conditions and the reality of the world beyond school. Some special considerations are involved in industrial visits:

It is particularly important that pupils should be well-briefed as to the exact purpose of the visit and the nature of the industrial environment they will experience. A preliminary visit on the teacher's part is therefore essential.

Industrial visits may bring pupils into close proximity with special hazards such as heavy, noisy machinery, dangerous industrial processes, etc. Pupils must therefore be thoroughly conversant with specific safety regulations *before* the actual visit. The teacher should ensure that any works-appointed guides know exactly what the purposes of the visit are and what their supervisory duties entail with respect to the pupils in their charge.

There are often legal restrictions involved in work-experience schemes which require specific insurance cover. This must be arranged in advance.

The specific approval of parents must be obtained in connection with any visit involving special hazard.

In the light of the above, the authorization and approval of the employing authority and the headteacher is imperative.

Professional responsibilities

There is no explicit statement of a teacher's duties and professional responsibilities apart from what is contained in schools regulations to the effect that 'the teacher shall be employed in full-time service, exclusively in the capacity of a teacher, and shall not be required to perform any duties except such as are connected with the work of the school, nor to abstain outside the school hours from any occupations which do not interfere with the due performance of his/her duties'.

Nevertheless, there are certain commonly-held expectations of the teacher as a member of a profession. First, he should at all times behave 'professionally' in his personal relationships with colleagues, pupils and parents. Second, he should be prepared to participate in the decision-making processes of the school, especially where he has particular knowledge and competence. Third, he should keep up with the job of teaching through his reading, his discussions with colleagues and, where necessary, by his attendance at in-service courses.

Most teachers experience trouble-free professional careers. There are, however, times when a teacher may require legal advice or assistance, as, for example, when a child is injured in his class, or when the legal responsibilities of a teacher taking a party of children abroad need to be defined. All professional associations of teachers have experienced legal executives in their full-time service who are able to provide advice in the event of difficulties arising out of the professional work of the teacher.

Accidents

Even after the most thoughtful preparation and planning, accidents can and do occur. What should you, the teacher, do?

First, immediately stop any activity on the part of the rest of the children which might cause danger during the time you attend to the injured child.

Make the injured pupil as comfortable as possible.

Seek medical help if you consider it necessary. In this respect, *always* err on the side of caution.

If the accident is serious:

arrange for an ambulance at once, giving the name of the pupil and the address at which his parents can be contacted;

report the accident to the headteacher or to a senior member of staff;

if at all possible, travel with the injured child and contact his parents.

Some pertinent additional advice is contained in the AMA booklet, *A Guide to Teachers*:

Equip yourself with useful telephone numbers in advance.

If a child suffers from a known malady (epilepsy or diabetes, for example) and the school has the information on accessible record, then it is your duty to acquaint yourself with the information and know what steps to take.

Do not accept responsibility for more pupils than you can realistically look after.

Never accept responsibility for a mixed party without the assistance of a member of the opposite sex.

PART IV
Evaluation, assessment and record-keeping

INTRODUCTION: WHY EVALUATE AND ASSESS?

In discussing the planning of individual lessons in Part II, we made reference to *three components of instruction* which we said serve as anchor points, helping to keep the lesson 'on target'. The third of those components, *evaluation procedures*, is the subject of this present section.

The question raised by Mager[1] which we equated with the process of evaluation, 'How will I know when I have arrived?', is of crucial importance to the student teacher. It is on the basis of the answers that he obtains to this question that his effective planning of on-going and future classroom activities depends.

Evaluation is centrally concerned with the making of judgements. In the setting of the school, for example, evaluation underpins (and precedes) the teacher's development of curriculum activities, his selection of specific objectives in his day-to-day lesson planning, and his choice of materials and methods by which to judge the progress of his pupils.

Evaluation in the classroom is inescapable. As a professional person, the teacher is charged with the responsibility of promoting the intellectual, social and emotional growth of his pupils. Such a task requires that he should plan the work and the activities of the classroom in the light of his knowledge of the progress and attainment of each of the pupils in his care. Such knowledge necessarily requires continuous acts of evaluation on the part of the teacher.

Definition of terms

Evaluation should be distinguished from measurement. While in one sense measurement is sometimes regarded as *quantitative* as opposed to *qualitative* evaluation, this particular connotation goes beyond the precise meaning of the term *measurement*. Measurement refers to ways of obtaining quantitative information; in no sense does the term imply the making of judgements. An arithmetic test, for example, measures the ability of individuals to comprehend certain mathematical concepts. The test, of itself, cannot determine who comprehends adequately or inadequately. It requires the teacher to interpret the test results and to make judgements about what constitutes an acceptable level of arithmetical comprehension. Making that judgement is part of the process of evaluation.

Evaluation and assessment in the curriculum: a model

TenBrink[2] has proposed that the process of evaluation may be conceived as consisting of three major *stages*, each stage containing a series of sequential *steps*. TenBrink's model is as follows:

STAGE 1

Step 1	The teacher must specify what judgements and decisions need to be made in the light of the underlying objectives that have guided his classroom activities.
Step 2	The teacher must describe the information that he will need to make particular judgements.
Step 3	The teacher must locate the information that he will need.
Step 4	The teacher must decide when and how to obtain the information.
Step 5	The teacher must select or construct the information-gathering instruments that he will need.

STAGE 2

Step 6	The teacher obtains the required information.
Step 7	The teacher analyses and records the information.

STAGE 3

Step 8	The teacher forms judgements.
Step 9	The teacher makes decisions.
Step 10	The teacher communicates those decisions to relevant sources.

By way of demonstrating the importance of the evaluation process in the student teacher's lesson preparation and presentation, the relevant steps of TenBrink's model have been superimposed upon the diagram of the teaching–learning process outlined initially on page 16.

Figure 3 below shows the primary purpose that evaluation serves. It enables the student teacher to make appropriate decisions about his on-going classroom activities and to plan future activities more purposefully and effectively in the light of his knowledge of the progress of his pupils.

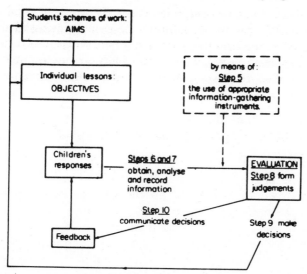

Figure 3 The evaluative process in lesson preparation and presentation

Appropriate decisions, however, depend upon correct judgements and these in turn can only derive from adequate *information-gathering instruments*. On the pages that follow, we turn our attention to Step 5 of TenBrink's model – the selection of information-gathering instruments.

In this section we outline a variety of information-gathering techniques that student teachers may find useful during teaching practice. Those readers who wish to pursue the range of tests and materials available to the educational assessor at greater length are referred to Lewis,[3] Chase[4] and Gronlund.[5]

Using questions*

Questioning is an obvious way in which the student teacher is able to gather information about his pupils' grasp of new material or their recall of previous work. *Asking* the 'right' questions in order to elicit required information is an art that the student teacher would do well to rehearse beforehand, rather than attempt to organize his questioning on the spur of the moment. *Writing* questions, too, is a skill that requires practice. The form and the content of the written question depends upon the purpose that the question is to serve.

* See also Appendix 5: Questions and questioning (p. 282).

Unstructured, structured and highly-structured questions. The degree to which a question allows only a limited number of ways of answering it or permits a wide variety of responses is a feature of its *structure*.

Open-ended or *unstructured questions* which invite a variety of responses are often employed by the teacher wishing to explore the wealth of ideas that his pupils have about a particular topic, or event. For example:

'Why do you think the robbers were content to wait?'

'What sorts of things were passing through his mind as he sat alone in the dark?'

The purpose of the open-ended question is to permit the respondent maximum freedom in making his thoughts and feelings explicit. In general open-ended questions are more appropriate information-gatherers in some subject areas than others. Most people, perhaps, would find it more acceptable to express the depth and range of their feelings about a poem, a picture or a piece of music by means of a series of open-ended questions rather than a set of highly-structured questions demanding one word answers. Highly-structured questions, however, might be more appropriate for evaluating pupils' grasp of a mathematical proof or knowledge of a chemical process.

Like all forms of questioning, open-ended questions need to be thought out carefully before being committed to paper. Above all else, the criterion of relevance is fundamental to the inclusion of any question in an evaluation procedure.

Sellitz *et al.*[6] provide a useful checklist of points to consider in formulating questions:

Is the question necessary? Just how will it be useful?

Are several questions needed on the subject matter of this question?

Do respondents have the information necessary to answer this question?

Does the question need to be more concrete, specific and closely related to the respondent's personal experience?

Is the question biased or loaded in one direction without accompanying questions to balance the emphasis?

Can the question be misunderstood? Does it contain difficult or unclear phraseology?

Can the question be better asked in a more direct or a more indirect form?

Is the answer to the question likely to be influenced by the content of preceding questions?

Is the question led up to in a natural way?

Does the question come too early or too late from the point of view of arousing interest and receiving sufficient attention, etc?

Structured questions are appropriate when the student teacher wishes to test pupils' understanding of specific subject matter, principles or concepts. Because they are 'structured', such questions permit a greater degree of objectivity in the assessment of answers, and because they generally elicit short answers, are easier to mark than open-ended questions. The typical format of the structured question is shown by Hudson[7] as follows:

Introductory statement and information
(a)   Initial sub-question
(b) ⎫
(c) ⎬ Successive (sequential) sub-questions
(d) ⎭
etc.

By way of example:

(a) *A bicycle pump is being used to pump up a tyre. Explain briefly the effect of each of the following changes:*
(b) the barrel of the pump is made much longer;
(c) the cross-section of the barrel is doubled;
(d) the connector joining the pump itself to the valve of the inner tube is made about four times as long.

    Source: Oxford Local Examinations. GCE Physics with Chemistry, 1973

The *introductory statement* is a crucial element in the construction of a structured question. It sets the tone by indicating exactly what the question is about. It need not necessarily be in written form; it could consist of a photograph, a diagram or a combination of any of the above. Hudson[7] suggests the following criteria to be used in choosing or constructing an introductory statement:

It should make it absolutely clear to the pupil what the question is about.

It should put the pupil at ease rather than provoke uncertainty as to the exact nature of the question.

It should employ language that is familiar to the pupil and should be written in the simplest phraseology.

The *sub-questions* that follow the introductory statement should be arranged as a series of specific enquiries, each of which relates to a different aspect of the main theme of the question. Each sub-question should require a unique and fairly short answer. Like the introductory statement, each sub-question should be immediately comprehensible, concise and accurate in its factual details. The sequential yet independent nature of the sub-questions should be carefully thought out by the question writer; their purpose, Hudson asserts, is to test just how far the pupil can follow the particular line of reasoning predetermined by the examiner.

Finally, it is essential that a *marking scheme* should be developed *at the same time* as the series of structured questions is being formulated. In this way, the student teacher can readily detect any ambiguities in wording and can spot unexpected flaws in his question construction.

Highly-structured questions. Where the range of correct answers to a question is strictly limited, as for example in the steps of a proof of a geometry theorem or the stages in a chemical process, a highly-structured form of question, consisting of pre-coded answers, may provide the most appropriate way of evaluating the knowledge of the test taker. Multiple-choice tests (see page 250 below) are often in this format. Highly-structured questions employing pre-coded answers are not necessarily limited in their use to evaluation in the physical sciences or mathematics.

For the student teacher who decides to use pre-coded answers to specific questions, *it is vital* that he should have thoroughly explored the subject matter of the test *beforehand* in order to ensure that the pre-coded answers he finally decides upon are *exhaustive* and *mutually-exclusive*. Thorough preparation in this respect can save a great deal of embarrassment at the hands of intelligent and inventive pupils.

Using objective tests

Objective tests are useful to the student teacher intent upon gathering information about his pupils' understanding of new material or their retention of previously taught concepts. Generally, objective tests are composed of a number of items – for example, missing words, incomplete sentences, true/false statements, multiple-choice answers, matching pairs of statements and responses, etc., accompanied by precise instructions to the testee on how he is to record his responses. They are called *objective* tests because the items that compose them 'must have a precisely predetermined correct response no matter what form it takes or what educational objective it assesses' (Hudson[7]). In other words, the term *objective* indicates objectivity in the marking or the scoring of the test.

Objective tests of recall, designed to assess pupils' recapitulation of factual knowledge, are simple in format, for example:

Type 1   The recall of an event, a name or a fact
To whom did Jesus address the following words?
'Is it not written, My house shall be called a house of prayer.'
'It is written, Man shall not live by bread alone.'
'Have ye not read even this, what David did when he was anhungred.'

Type 2   Sentence completion by insertion of a missing word
In the year ____ the treaty of Versailles was signed in the city of

_____

The President of the United States of America who succeeded John F. Kennedy was called _____

TenBrink[2] suggests the following guidelines in preparing sentence completion type items:

Do *not* take statements directly from text books.
Leave only important terms blank and keep items brief.
Limit the number of blanks per statement to one or two.
Try to keep the blank(s) near the end of the statement.
Make certain that only one answer fits each blank.

Type 3   Unlabelled maps, diagrams or processes
This type of objective test has wide application in geography, history, social studies and the physical sciences.

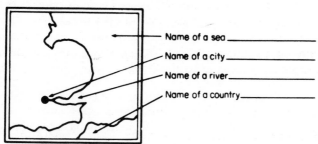

True–false items. The true–false test, like the recall items above, is best used by the student teacher to assess factual knowledge; it has little to recommend it as a means of evaluating pupils' understanding although when used in combination with other forms of testing it can provide the examiner with information beyond mere recall. The weakness of the true–false test – its encouragement of guessing – can be ameliorated somewhat by informing pupils that marks will be deducted for guesswork and then applying a simple formula in scoring the items. The interested reader is referred to Lewis,[3] pages 32–3, for further details.
An example of the true–false test item is as follows:

Henry VII succeeded Mary Queen of Scots   TRUE   FALSE
Elizabeth I reigned for thirty-six years   TRUE   FALSE

Matching pairs. This form of objective test is appropriate when the purpose is to test pupils' ability to make correct associations between two pieces of information, for example names and dates, English words and their foreign equivalents, structures and functions in biology etc. Matching pair items are popular with younger children. They are easy to score and to administer, the only required response of the pupil being to draw a line between correctly matched items.

By way of example:

Draw lines to link the capital city with the correct country

London	Australia
Copenhagen	France
Bonn	West Germany
Paris	Iceland
Reykjavik	Portugal
Lisbon	Denmark
	Norway
	Poland
	England

Several pitfalls in writing *matching tests* have been avoided in the above example. First, the lists are *uneven*. If six capitals had been listed against six countries, five correct responses would automatically ensure that the sixth connection was correct. Uneven lists avoid this possibility. Second, the lists are *short* and *homogeneous* (i.e. capitals and countries throughout). Long matching lists often lead to the inclusion of non-homogeneous elements. Third, pupils know exactly what is required of them through *simple instructions*. Avoid at all costs the following type of rubric:

> In the blank spaces to the left-hand side of each of the items ranked in Column A, write the corresponding letter appearing on the left-hand side of the items listed in Column B when you have decided which goes with which.

Multiple-choice. The multiple-choice item generally consists of a *stem* (a question or a statement), a small number of responses only one of which (the *key*) is correct, the others, although plausible, being incorrect and included to act as *distractors*.

For example:

Stem	What is the federal capital of Australia?	
Distractors	(a)	Sydney
	(b)	Perth
	(c)	Melbourne
	(d)	Adelaide
Key	(e)	Canberra

In other forms, the multiple-choice item may have several *key* (correct) responses. For example:

Put a tick next to each correct answer

In terms of world tonnage of ships built, Great Britain lost her leading position during the 1960s because of the following reasons:

The strong competition of Japan, Sweden and West Germany.

____

The slump in world demand for shipping in the late 1960s.

____

The difficulty of launching large vessels in the narrow, shallow estuaries of Great Britain.

____

The changeover from shipbuilding to oil-rig construction taking place in Britain in the 1960s.

____

The small number of British shipbuilding yards still in existence in the 1960s.

____

In constructing multiple-choice items, TenBrink[2] gives the following advice:

Carefully analyse the learning outcome to be measured.

Write the stem *and* the correct (key) response(s).

Write plausible distractors.

Arrange the distractors and the correct alternative(s).

Check for ambiguity and irrelevant clues.

Classification/matching pairs. Hudson[7] instances a modification of the usual multiple-choice presentation. It involves writing a series of multiple-choice items, each one having the same set of responses as the others in the series. This particular format has the advantage of making for substantial savings in testing time, printing materials and, not the least, the amount of reading required of the test taker. Hudson's example of the classification/matching pairs format is as follows:

This group of items consists of five lettered headings, followed by several numbered questions. For each question, choose the letter representing the heading which most appropriately answers it. Each heading may be used once, more than once or not at all.

A Aluminium
B Copper
C Phosphorus
D Sodium
E Zinc

1 Which one is non-metal? **(C)**
2 Which one is normally stored under water? **(C)**
3 Which one is the most electropositive? **(D)**
4 Which one forms a black oxide? **(B)**

Some techniques in designing objective items. Hudson[7] offers some general advice in connection with writing items for objective tests:

Choose the most appropriate item-type having in mind the purpose of the evaluation procedure.

Present the item as clearly as possible.

Ensure that the item is accurate in all respects.

Avoid giving clues to the correct (key) response.

Ensure that all options are grammatically consistent with the stem.

Ensure that all options are parallel in content and construction.

Keep the item as short as possible.

Ensure that the items are independent of each other.

Use negatives sparingly.

Set out the item clearly.

Using standardized tests

Although it is unlikely that student teachers will have recourse* to the use of standardized tests during teaching practice, it is important that they should be knowledgeable about these types of objective test. *A standardized test* is one that has been administered to a sample of individuals *representative of the population* for whom the particular test is intended. From the performance of those individuals sets of scores are calculated, for example, by age, by sex, or on the criterion of 'above average', 'average' and 'below average'. Since the individuals are representative of the wider population their scores can be generalized to that population. Thus any individual score can subsequently be evaluated by comparing it to these sets of scores or *norms*.

Organizations such as the National Foundation for Educational Research have developed numerous standardized tests for use with groups as diverse as nursery school pupils and university students. Standardized tests may be subdivided according to whether they are *individual* or *group* tests. They may also be grouped according to their

* Or indeed *access* to them. See Jackson, S. (1968) *A Teacher's Guide to Tests and Testing* (Harlow: Longman) for lists of standardized tests that are available to teachers, and for details of restricted test materials.

purpose. For example, *ability* tests are designed to measure the mental efficiency of the individual and have been employed in the selection and grouping of children for academic work. *Attainment* tests are specifically designed to measure achievement in certain areas of school work. Like attainment tests, *diagnostic* tests seek information about an individual's achievement in aspects of school work but are designed to pinpoint areas of weakness. Finally, *aptitude* tests are used in counselling older pupils about their relative skills in order to assist them in making appropriate employment choices.

Using essays

The figure below represents a *freedom of response continuum*, a term devised by Lewis[3] in relation to the relative 'openness' or 'closedness' of various types of test. It can be seen that essays are far removed from the multiple-choice item tests that we have discussed above.

'Open' essays
Essays
'Factual' and 'directed' essays
Short answer questions
Divergent thinking items
Completion items
Multiple-choice items

Figure 4 Freedom of response continuum (Lewis[3])

It is the freedom of response that is possible in the essay form of examination that is held to be its most important asset. Unlike the objective test, the essay allows the candidate to organize his thoughts and to communicate them in his own style; in short, it gives him freedom to be creative and imaginative in the communication of his ideas. There are disadvantages, however, in the essay as a gatherer of information. Essays are markedly more difficult to assess reliably. With only one assessor, a considerable degree of subjectivity can creep in to the assessment of essays. Even with analytical marking schemes (see below) the degree of agreement between markers may be low. Moreover, since only a limited number of essay titles can be given in any one examination, only a limited part of a syllabus of work can be sampled in a reasonable time. The individual who has the misfortune to choose a 'wrong' essay title may produce work which bears little relationship to his actual ability. Chase[4] has suggested some ways of overcoming these weaknesses in the essay form of test. First, all pupils might be asked to write on the same essay title(s), the principle being that individuals can only be compared to the extent that they have 'jumped the same hurdles'. Second, marking should be *analytic* rather than *impressionistic*. Analytic marking is based upon *prior decisions* about what exactly is being assessed in the essay – the content? the style? the grammar? the punctuation? the handwriting? On the question of the low degree of agreement between essay markers, Lewis[3] suggests the following ways of reducing the subjective element:

by marking for substantive content rather than style;

by fixing a maximum penalty for mistakes in grammar, syntax and spelling;

by multiple marking followed by a further close scrutiny of those essays placed near the pass–fail line.

In conclusion, in making decisions about the choice of either multiple-choice items or essay-type tests, the student teacher must ultimately be guided by one fundamental consideration. The appropriateness of any information-gathering technique rests upon the *purpose of the evaluation* and the *particular abilities* the student teacher is seeking to assess.

Forms of assessment

Continuous assessment in not unfamiliar to student teachers, many of whom follow college courses the evaluation of which involves the scrutiny of work that has been undertaken over a period of years.

During teaching practice students may encounter continuous assessment as a major form of evaluation employed in a wide range of curriculum activities. What are the particular advantages of continuous assessment? When should it be used? What responsibilities are placed upon the student teacher attached to a school where continuous assessment is practised?

Hudson's[7] definition of continuous assessment as a constant 'updating of teachers' judgements about their pupils which permits cumulative judgements about their performance to be made' is a useful starting point in considering the advantages of this form of evaluation and the circumstances in which it is best employed.

It is sometimes the case that in planning a particular class activity, the teacher's objectives include learning on the part of the pupils through their sharing and co-operating one with another in accomplishing the work to hand. Under such circumstances it may be more important for the teacher to monitor *how* pupils set about mastering certain tasks than to pass judgement upon the final produce of their efforts. It is on occasions such as this, where evaluation is dependent upon an accumulation of judgements on the progress or attainment of individual pupils that some form of continuous assessment may be most profitably undertaken. Similarly in certain areas of the curriculum, for example, in home economics, in geography fieldwork, or in the craft subjects, where the teacher's objective is to assess specific skills exhibited by pupils in carrying out their work, continuous assessment may be considered to be the most appropriate and effective method of evaluation.

At this point it is worthwhile reiterating an earlier observation: *the educational objectives that guide the initial planning of any activity should be the major determinants of the form of assessment by which that activity is eventually evaluated.*

Record-keeping

During teaching practice there is a clear obligation on the part of student teachers to continue the day-to-day running of their classes in line with the organization and methods employed by the regular class teachers. In certain forms of classroom and school organization, for example, where continuous assessment is practised, where vertical grouping and open plan schemes operate (see Part III, page 120), adequate record-keeping is essential to the success of the educational programmes. Similarly, in systems practising 'individualized learning' the need for individual records is crucial. It is the student teacher's responsibility to participate fully in the record-keeping system that is used in the school to which he is attached. What follows is an outline of the use of records and some suggestions for students who find themselves faced with the task of designing record systems for their own use.

Record-keeping is often considered an irksome chore by many teachers, although judging by the variations in the detailed requirements of a number of Local Education Authorities, the amount of time that teachers spend on official record cards must vary enormously. Official record cards with their spaces for name, address, date of birth, previous schooling, etc., are not the present subject of discussion; rather, our concern is with the personal record cards that the teacher keeps in connection with the ongoing work of his class and the progress of individual pupils within it. All teachers need to keep their own day-to-day records; more teachers, it would appear, maintain record books indicating the work that their classes are to accomplish during a particular period rather than accounts showing the progress and attainment of individual children. To some extent the form in which teachers maintain records is determined by the headteacher. It is probable, however, that the age of the children and the form of organization within the school are more important determinants. But why keep records at all?

In a recent study,[8] typical reasons given by teachers for keeping records were:

1 to chart pupil progress and achievement;
2 to communicate information to other teachers;
3 to ensure continuity of education throughout the school;
4 to ensure continuity of education on transfer to other schools;
5 to guide a replacement or a supply teacher;
6 for diagnostic purposes – to spot problems, identify underachievement and pupils needing extra help;
7 to provide teachers with information on the success (or failure) of teaching methods and materials;
8 as a statement of 'what has happened' – to inform interested parties (parents, educational psychologists, headteacher);
9 to give headteachers a general picture of achievement within the school.

What sort of records a teacher should keep depends, of course, upon what sort of records will best serve his particular purposes. Once a teacher has asked himself four fundamental questions[9] he is then in a position to determine his own specific record-keeping requirements:

1 What do I need to record?
2 Why do I consider these things worth recording?
3 What use am I going to make of the information?
4 How can it be collected efficiently?

Records, according to Foster,[9] can become straitjackets that imprison the teacher and lead to a rigidity in his teaching; equally, they can be his salvation, helping him to plan learning experiences more efficiently and to evaluate progress more purposefully. It all depends upon *the sorts of records* that the teacher devises for his particular purposes. Some general guidelines suggested by Rance[10] bear repetition:

Records must be easy to keep. They should require only the barest minimum of time to maintain them adequately.

They should be simple to understand and should be based upon knowledge that is common to all teachers.

They should provide enough detail about a subject to enable another teacher to make a balanced judgement.

Finally, it is interesting to note what teachers in general[8] say a school record should *not* be:

1 a waste of teacher time;
2 too jargonistic or too lengthy;
3 used to check up on the work of the teacher;
4 a substitute for, or an addition to, gossip in the staffroom, designed to transmit to a new teacher the opinions, impressions and prejudices of his/her predecessor;
5 used as a bureaucratic device to increase the school's control over the lives of its pupils.

Methods of record-keeping

Given the importance of the point made earlier about the individual nature of teacher-made records and the dangers that lie in the proliferation of elaborate, ready-made record systems, it would be invidious to attempt more than a brief comment about the general forms in which teacher-made and pupil-made records can be maintained, bearing in mind the criteria referred to above – ease of maintenance, simplicity and sufficiency of detail.

Record systems which contain a large element of visual display are often simple to maintain and easy to interpret both from the teacher's and the pupil's point of view. For an example of a very effective (and colourful) record chart of infant children's progress in the basic skills, made and maintained by infants, see Dean,[11] pages 54–5. Given the diversity of the activities of the modern, progressive classroom, the following examples of visual recording systems could prove useful to the student teacher faced with the necessity of devising some ways of monitoring his pupils' progress and achievement.

Histograms provide simple and easily-interpretable records of the attainment and progress of individual pupils. For example:

Names	Tables up to 10 X	T. U. + –	H. T. U. + –	T U x –	H. T. U x –	Fractions	Area	Volume
B. A.	█████████							
C B	█████████							
C. C.	█████████							
S. C.	████							

MATHEMATICS RECORD CHART   Form IX   Term ending March 29th

Figure 5 Mathematics record chart – histogram

Pie diagrams are particularly useful in recording information when the total amount to be recorded is known in advance. By way of example, Figure 6 overleaf is taken from Rance[10] and shows the amount of time that a child devotes to various aspects of work in an integrated day programme in a first school. The advantage of this form of visual display is that it allows the teacher to spot, at a glance, whether the children are spending the required minimum amount of time in each of the subject areas and activities during the course of a week or longer. The reader is referred to page 255 for a fuller discussion on the need for systematic records in programmes of 'individualized learning'.

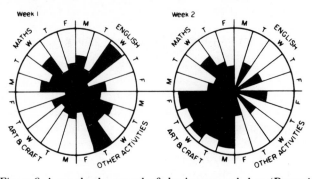

Figure 6 A teacher's record of the integrated day (Rance[10])

The 'tick-off' type of recording system, like the histogram described above, involves the listing of an exhaustive and/or sequential series of stages in, say, the development of mathematical concepts, reading skills or language development. These stages can be arranged down the left-hand side of a loose-leaf page with the children's names written in across the top. By way of example, a section of a reading skills evaluation programme detailed in Foster,[9] pages 36–50 has been set out in Figure 7 opposite in 'tick-off' format. It is worth consulting Foster's book for a full discussion of the development of record systems in connection with mathematical, reading, language and creative/humanities skills.

In another form, the 'tick-off' type recording system can be used with a response continuum similar to that employed in attitude scales. A check mark is then placed against the one comment that best indicates the frequency or the incidence of a skill, a behaviour or a personality trait. By way of example see Figure 8.

To conclude this section, what can be gleaned from the great variety of record-keeping systems employed in primary, and secondary schools that can serve as useful guidelines to student teachers? We return to the major recommendations of the recent study by Clift, Weiner and Wilson.[8]

Class............ *Date* .... *Sub-sections* Finding information; dictionary, encyclopedia and library skills.

Skills	*Names of pupils*							
	AB	*AC*	*DC*	*PD*	*EE*	*BK*	*JL*	*MN*
Finding information 1 Can select book by the title	√	√	√	√	√	√	√	√
2 Uses the table of contents	√	√	√	√	√	√	√	
3 Uses an index	√	√	√	√	√		√	
4 Uses a glossary		√			√		√	
5 Uses graphs and tables 6 Uses gazetteer and atlas		√ √			√ √			
Dictionary 1 Can arrange in simple alphabetical order	√	√	√		√		√	√
2 Can arrange in difficult alphabetical order		√			√			
3 Can use guide words in encyclopedia		√			√			
4 Uses encyclopedia to find information (a) with help		√	√		√·			
(b) alone		√			√			
5 Can select relevant information from articles		√			√			
6 Understands and can use library system		√			√			
7 Uses public library		√			√	√	√	

Figure 7 Reading skills evaluation (Foster[9])

Name . .J.G. . .

Aspect of behaviour	Always	Most of the time	Frequently	Occasionally	Hardly ever	Never
1 Plays well with other children			√			
2 Can keep himself/herself amused				√		
3 Can concentrate for a short time					√	
4 Can fasten own shoe laces		√				
5 Can go to toilet by himself/herself	√					

Figure 8 'Tick-off' type of recording system

The design of the record

The record should have:

1 a clear layout;
2 clear, stable printing that will not fade;
3 clear section headings;
4 the pupil's name in a prominent position;
5 sufficient space provided for comments;
6 a prominently placed key to explain the use of abbreviations, symbols and criteria for the assessment of pupils.

The content of the record

The record content should:

1 be relevant to the purpose of the record;
2 be clearly sequenced;
3 give direct indications rather than implications for future teaching;
4 give a clear distinction between entries concerned with pupils' school experiences and those which are assessments of attainment;
5 clearly present assessment information by stating:
    (a) the derivation of norms used when grading or rating;
    (b) the criteria used when deciding on pupils' competence;
    (c) details of standardized tests used as a basis for grading or rating;

(d) details of other testing techniques used;

(e) teacher-made test marks *in a standardized form.*

One final point. *Three golden rules of record-keeping* suggested by Rance[10] are:

keep as few records as possible;

always be on the lookout for ways of reducing those records already in existence;

regularly revise those records that are in constant use.

Oral assessment

While oral assessment is most commonly employed in testing the foreign language skills of older pupils, this is by no means its only application. Oral assessment can be used to advantage in examining pupils' abilities in spoken English where it is considered important that children should be able to participate in a discussion, to follow precise instructions, to sustain a logical argument on a chosen theme, etc. There may be a place for some form of oral assessment in the physical sciences, where, for example, the objectives of a course of work include accurate reporting of experimental observations, or developing logical explanations of physical phenomena. There are, however, particular difficulties in connection with oral assessment techniques. They are often time-consuming to conduct; moreover oral tests that are *reliable* and *valid* are very difficult to construct. In questioning the reliability of a test, the test-constructor is asking, 'If one were to re-test the same group of individuals again at a later date with the same instrument, how consistent would their scores be?' By validity, the test constructor is concerned with the degree to which scores obtained on one test would match those obtained on another test which purported to measure the same attribute, skills or characteristic. These limitations in connection with the use of oral tests suggest that the student teacher would do well to treat them with caution in any evaluation procedures he plans to undertake during teaching practice.

Assessing pupils' practical work

Some form of practical assessment is often a part of the overall evaluation procedure in such areas of the curriculum as biology, physics, chemistry, geography fieldwork, the art and craft subjects, and home economics. For student teachers intending to assess pupils' practical work during the teaching practice period, it is vital that decisions about *what* exactly is to be assessed and *how* it is to be assessed should be made at the *same time* as the work itself is being planned.

To illustrate one way in which a plan for the assessment of practical activities can be developed, an example is taken from Hudson[7] (see Figure 9). The plan is used later, in Figure 11 on page 264, as the basis for a method of evaluation of project-type work.

Hudson's example shows how each of the major categories of assessment selected in an evaluation scheme for a Joint Matriculation Board 'O' level surveying course are subdivided into three further sections, each of which, again, is graded on a five-point scale (see Figure 11).

Project work and its assessment

It is in first and middle schools that student teachers are more likely to encounter project work during teaching practice and where they themselves may be asked to initiate work of the *project* or *topic* variety. What principles should guide the student's planning of projects and how should work be assessed?

At the risk of repetition, the point must be made again that *only after the objectives of a particular project or topic have been thought through and made explicit can the most appropriate criteria for its assessment be determined.* Planning and assessment are not separate elements; they go hand-in-hand.

With the age, ability and background of the pupils foremost in mind, the student teacher should give careful thought to the choice of a project or topic. (See page 128 for further discussion of topic work.)

It is generally the case that the *degree of generality* by which a project is identified will determine the way in which it is tackled by the children. If the too-common practice of copying out of chunks of reference material is to be avoided, then the student teacher must so define the topic of interest as to permit pupils other ways of identifying, assessing and recording information relevant to their purposes. The initial identification and naming of a project is usually done at too general a level to be of use in defining exactly what children will do and how they will set about the task. What is required is a series of further refinings of the topic; a breaking down into its component parts in order to identify its possibilities. By way of example, Foster,[9] pages 82–9, shows how a project entitled 'Peoples of the World' was eventually broken down into a series of topics centred around the theme, 'The Clothes People Wear'. A flow chart was employed to identify some of the possible avenues of interest that the upper junior school children might wish to explore (see Figure 10).

Similar to the plan outlined below in connection with the assessment of practical work (Figure 9) we suggest the following scheme as *one* possible way of identifying relevant criteria in the assessment of project work and quantifying their presence or absence in the work of individual or groups of children (see Figure 11).

Major categories of assessment	Sub-sections of each category	Criteria for grading
(a) *Approach to task*	1 Consideration of local conditions 2 Initiative 3 Ability to give and to receive instructions	Award 4 marks to the pupil who is considered *outstanding* in his approach to, or performance in, the activity concerned.
(b) *Handling of equipment*	1 Overcoming difficulties 2 Thoroughness 3 Accuracy	Award 3 marks to the pupil who is considered to be *above average* in his approach to, or performance in, the activity concerned.
(c) *Recording of observations*	1 Legibility of bookings 2 Checking en route 3 Reducing and correcting	Award 2 marks to the pupil who is considered to be *average* in his approach to, or performance in, the activity concerned.
(d) *Translation of data*	1 Calculations 2 Preparation of plans 3 Use of scales	Award 1 mark to the pupil who is considered to be *below* average in his approach to, or performance in, the activity concerned.
(e) *Overall assessment of technical competence as a surveyor*	Award marks as follows: 10+ outstanding ability 8–10 above average 5–7 average ability 1–4 below average 0 no ability	Award 0 marks to the pupil who is considered to be unsatisfactory in his approach to, or performance in, the activity concerned.

Figure 9 An example of the development of an assessment scheme for the evaluation of a practical subject (surveying) (Hudson,[7])

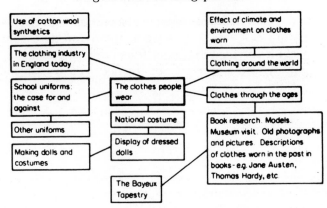

Figure 10 A flow chart development of a topic entitled 'The Clothes People Wear'

Major categories of assessment	Sub-sections of each category	Criteria for grading
(a) *Strategical considerations*	1 The suitability of the overall plan 2 The use of source materials 3 Ways of obtaining information	Award 5 marks for *outstanding* quality Award 4 marks for *above average* quality Award 3 marks for *average* quality
(b) *Selection criteria*	1 Basis for inclusion/exclusion of materials. 2 Organization and selection of materials, criteria employed 3 The 'balance' of the various sections of the project	Award 2 marks for *below average* quality Award 1 mark for *very poor* quality
(c) *Presentation*	1 Overall quality 2 General neatness 3 Aptness of illustrative materials	Award 0 marks for *unacceptable* quality
(d) *Attitudinal considerations*	1 Enterprise 2 Perseverance 3 Co-operation one with another	

Figure 11 A suggested scheme for the assessment of project work

Some problems of assessment

There is sufficient research evidence to show that both *test-takers* and *test-givers* mutually influence one another during evaluation sessions such as conventional examinations, oral assessments and the like (Rosenthal and Jacobson,[12] Good and Brophy[13]). It is important, therefore, that student teachers have some passing acquaintance with these research findings and their import.

Teacher expectations

A considerable and growing body of research in the general area of *teacher expectancies* suggests that children respond to the *teacher–evaluator* in terms of their perceptions of what he expects of them (Nash[14]). It follows, then, that the calm, well-organized student teacher embarking purposefully upon some aspect of evaluation probably induces different attitudes (and *responses*) among his class of children than an anxious, ill-organized colleague.

Children's responses to the examiner

During the test situation, children respond to such characteristics of the evaluator as the person's sex, age and personality. Although the student teacher can do little about his/her sex and age, it is important (and may indeed at times be comforting) to realize that these latent identities do exert potent influence. It could well be, for example, that the problems experienced by a female student conducting a test with older secondary school boys have little if anything to do with the quality of the test material or the amount of prior preparation she has put into the testing programme.

Motivation

Clearly, pupils need to be motivated if they are going to make a serious attempt at any test that they are required to undertake. The results of a test completed in a desultory fashion by resentful pupils are hardly likely to supply the student teacher with reliable information about the children's capabilities. Research suggests that motivation to participate in test-taking sessions is strongest when pupils have been helped to see the purpose of the evaluation, and where the examiner maintains a warm, purposeful attitude toward them during the testing session (Hudson[7]).

Anxiety

At some time or another most pupils experience anxiety when taking internal school tests or external public examinations. Wherever a child is put in a position of possible failure there is likely to be some degree of anxiety present. It is the examiner's responsibility to ensure that any evaluation session be conducted with as little tension as possible. To a large extent, it is the examiner's own demeanour that sets the tone in the examination room. Research shows that children differ considerably in the degree to which they experience *test-anxiety* (Sarason *et al.*,[15] Barker-Lunn[16]). Examiners who 'urge the children to do their very best' can make the highly-anxious child even more anxious. The best strategy appears to be to adopt as neutral an attitude as possible during the evaluation period.

The test-room

The advice generally given in connection with the location of a test or examination is that the test-room should be well-lit, quiet and adequately ventilated. To this we would add that, wherever possible, children should take tests in familiar settings, preferably in their own form rooms under normal school conditions. Research suggests that distractions in the form of extraneous noise, walking about the room by the examiner, and intrusions into the room, all have significant impact upon the scores of the test-takers, particularly when they are younger pupils (Lewis[3]).

Giving instructions

An important factor in reducing pupils' anxiety and tension during an examination is the extent to which they are quite clear about what exactly they are required to do. Simple instructions, clearly and calmly given by the examiner, can significantly lower the general level of tension in the test-room. Student teachers who intend to conduct testing sessions may find it beneficial in this respect to rehearse the instructions they wish to give to pupils *before* the actual testing session. Ideally, test instructions should be simple, direct and as brief as possible.

By way of conclusion, students may wish to consult a recent text by Black and Broadfoot,[17] *Keeping Track of Teaching*, which illustrates a range of diagnostic assessment schedules used in primary and secondary schools and deals with the wider issue of *school self-evaluation* which falls outside of the brief of this particular section.

Notes and references

1 Mager, R.F. (1968) *Developing Attitudes Towards Learning*. Belmont, California: Lear/Siegler/Fearon.

2 TenBrink, T.D. (1974) *Evaluation: A Practical Guide for Teachers*. New York: McGraw-Hill.

3 Lewis, D.G. (1974) *Assessment in Education*. London: University of London Press.

4 Chase, C.I. (1974) *Measurement for Educational Evaluation*. Reading, Mass.: Addison-Wesley.

5 Gronlund, N.E. (1981) *Measurement and Evaluation in Teaching*. London: Collier-Macmillan.
Gronlund, N.E. (1982) *Constructing Achievement Tests*. Englewood Cliffs, New Jersey: Prentice-Hall.

6 Sellitz, C., Jahoda, M., Deutsch, M. and Cook, S.W. (1965) *Research Methods in Social Relations*. London: Methuen.

7 Hudson, B. (1973) *Assessment Techniques: An Introduction*. London: Methuen.

8 Clift, P., Weiner, G. and Wilson, E. (1981) *Record-keeping in Primary Schools*. Schools Council Research Studies. London: Macmillan.

9 Foster, J. (1971) *Recording Individual Progress*. London: Macmillan.

10 Rance, P. (1971) *Record-keeping in the Progressive Primary School*. London: Ward Lock Educational.

11 Dean, J. (1971) *Recording Children's Progress*. London: Macmillan.

12 Rosenthal, R. and Jacobson, L. (1968) *Pygmalion in the Classroom: Teacher Expectation and Pupils' Intellectual Ability*. New York: Holt, Rinehart and Winston.

13 Good, T.L. and Brophy, J.E. (1974) The influence of teachers' attitudes and expectations on classroom behaviour. In Coop, R.H. and White, K. *Psychological Concepts in the Classroom*. New York: Harper and Row.

14 Nash, R. (1974) Pupils' expectations for their teachers. *Research in Education*, 12, 47–61.

15 Sarason, S.B., Davidson, K.S., Lighthall, F.F. and Britton, K.R. (1960) *Anxiety in Elementary School Children*. New York: John Wiley.

16 Barker-Lunn, J. (1970) *Streaming in the Primary School*. Windsor: NFER

17 Black, H. and Broadfoot, P. (1982) *Keeping Track of Teaching*. London: Routledge and Kegan Paul.

POSTSCRIPT

We began in Part I by presenting some perspectives on teaching and learning, and by relating teaching practice to the wider framework of teacher education. The second part of the book was devoted to preparing and planning for teaching practice. We looked at the purpose of the preliminary visit and the kinds of information that may be obtained. Aims and objectives were examined in some detail and after a brief reference to planning schemes of work, we concluded with an extended review of the lesson note.

Part III was concerned with the practice of teaching and embraced teaching strategies, the classroom environment, situation factors, control and discipline, and out-of-school activities. The final part looked at the techniques of evaluation, assessment and record-keeping.

We have introduced a wide range of concepts and drawn upon a considerable amount of research evidence in the hope that you will be all the more able to understand and come to grips with the exciting challenges offered to you by teaching practice.

It only remains for us to wish you every success and satisfaction in the venture.

APPENDICES

APPENDIX I. RESOURCE MATERIALS AND TECHNICAL AIDS

The rapidity of developments in educational technology in recent years
has left many teachers bedazzled by the range and sophistication of
audio, visual, audio-visual and reprographic equipment currently
available on the educational market. According to one expert
(Hanson[1]) our schools are facing a log jam of information and materials
as a result of a resources explosion. Another commentator (Edwards[2])
talks of an industrial jungle with a super-abundance of hardware
currently exceeding demand from schools, and a conspicuous lack of
standardization among the products available. There is danger in this
situation. A preoccupation on the part of teachers with the technical
details of this or that piece of equipment, or the desire of the headteacher
to keep up with the educational Joneses can frustrate the correct choice
of resources to meet specific objectives. Certain principles should guide
the decisions that school staff make in respect of materials and technical
equipment. We turn now to a discussion of those principles.

Selecting materials and technical aids

At a general level, factors that should be considered in the selection of
materials and aids are shown graphically by Romiszowski.[3] His analysis
of the task of media selection is presented in similar 'flow chart' form to
the model of the teaching–learning process outlined on page 16. His
model serves to emphasize the careful consideration that must be given
to situational factors before deciding upon appropriate media and
materials.

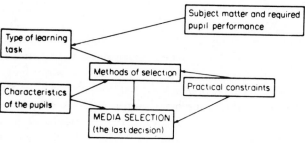

Source: Romiszowski[3]

Edwards[2] suggests that irrespective of function, there are certain criteria that should govern the selection of all resource materials. While these might seem too obvious to need listing, it is surprising how often, in practice, they are ignored. The prospective user or purchaser should ask himself the following questions:

Do the materials or aids meet the need they are meant to?

Are they too small, or too large, for the work they will be required to do?

Will there be sufficiently expert staff to work them, and sufficient staff time?

Will there be suitable accommodation?

Will there be sufficient money to maintain and operate them?

The resources of the school

In Part II we made a number of suggestions in connection with the student's visit to schools before teaching practice begins. In the present section, some additional discussion focuses upon the educational resources of schools on which students may draw during their teaching practice.

Almost anything that the teacher uses to meet an educational need is a *resource*. Often, however, when referring to resources in schools, student teachers may encounter the terms *software* – used in connection with materials such as filmstrips, transparencies, records, tapes, etc. – and *hardware* – generally meant to refer to the technical means employed in transmitting or projecting those materials. Such pieces of equipment as the overhead and the slide projector, and the record player are, in common convention, *hardware*.

It is in the student teacher's own interests to find out exactly what the educational resources are of the school in which his teaching practice is to take place. Often as not, the range of such provision is more dependent upon the educational philosophy of the headteacher and senior staff than upon the size of the school or the health of its financial budget. Where learning is seen as an active, individual process, provision of resources is likely to be generous; where learning is viewed as a passive, receptive procedure, provision may be more frugal.

Either the deputy headmaster or the school librarian or a member of staff designated as resource-co-ordinator is likely to possess detailed information of the educational resources of the school and their locations throughout the school building(s). Some schools have developed sophisticated retrieval systems in connection with their resources. The would-be user can, within a matter of minutes, obtain exact information about a particular resource, its location and its pattern of usage (for example, the demands made on a set of Jackdaw history packs throughout first forms in a comprehensive school).

Using school resources inevitably involved the student teacher in close co-operation with regular members of the school's staff. Planning well ahead, booking equipment in adequate time, returning it promptly and in good condition, are matters of commonsense and common courtesy.

Finally, using resource items to best advantage involves considerable thought on the part of the student teacher. Some advice given by Hanson[1] is germane. In connection with the resource item:

Who is going to handle it, teacher or pupil?

Is the idea being pitched at the right pupil level?

Is the most effective method being employed?

Have alternative methods been sufficiently explored?

Is original material, or the real thing, available?

Which medium best meets the particular need?

Is the vocabulary at the right ability level?

Are the sentence structures too complex?

Is additional material needed for the most and the least able?

Are we asking the right questions? Are we allowing the pupils to ask their own questions?

Should questions and problems be separated from the material to be studied?

Student teachers are strongly encouraged to give this degree of consideration to the selection and use of resources during teaching practice. Highly successful lessons don't just happen – they are purposely planned for.

Still visual media

The term *still visual media* refers to a wide range of materials and equipment that can be used in the classroom – for example, the blackboard, diagrams, wall charts, photographs, posters, flannel boards, magnetic boards, flip charts, opaque, strip and overhead projectors. It is not intended here to give any detailed account of the use of such media. Rather, the reader is referred to four texts, whose various contents are now discussed.

Coppen[4] contains an account of 'still pictures for classroom teaching'.

The section is thorough and is clearly written and illustrated. It is particularly useful in connection with the organization of blackboard work, the preparation of wall charts, and the various ways in which flannel boards and magnetic boards can be used in the classroom.

Romiszowski[3] gives a detailed account of still visual media. The student may find the discussion of algorithms – charts describing procedures and processes through the techniques of task analysis – particularly useful. Romiszowski's account of the problems of screening when using overhead projectors in classrooms is thorough. The section ends with a comprehensive, sectionalized list of addresses of the manufacturers of software and hardware visual media.

Hearnshaw and Kitching's[5] small pamphlet was specifically produced to introduce university lecturers to the range of equipment available within their own institution. Its utility goes beyond this modest brief. It is clearly presented, succinctly written and particularly useful in the ways in which potential users are led, by means of flow charts, to make appropriate decisions about the use of equipment.

Edwards[2] gives a comprehensive account (accompanied by photographs) of specific pieces of visual apparatus commonly used in schools. Student teachers should find Edwards' account useful because of the detailed discussion of the advantages and the disadvantages experienced by teachers in the use of these various items of visual equipment.

Some fundamentals of visual communication

While detailed instructions on the use of specific visual media may be left to the specialist texts referred to above, it may be useful to the student teacher to have at hand a number of general comments and suggestions in connection with the use of visual communication media.

The blackboard

Write clearly and large enough for all pupils in the classroom to see. Stand to one side of the board when writing in order that the children may follow what is being written and you can easily maintain eye contact with the class. Coloured chalks help sustain interest in blackboard work and add contrast. If you do not find freehand drawing on the blackboard easy, there are a number of ways in which you can get round the problem. See Coppen.[4]

There is a wealth of useful information on the use of the blackboard in an older text, Davies and Shepherd.[6]

Selecting pictures, charts, diagrams, etc.

Selecting visual materials for their suitability involves decisions not only about the age, ability and aptitude of the class, the content, the size and the amount of detail in the visual material itself, but also requires careful thought about *how* the material is going to be used. It is not enough simply to display appropriate visual materials in the hope that children will abstract from them the information that you would like them to assimilate. The teacher must know *how* the material is to be employed, *how* it is to be integrated into the on-going work of the class, *how* the children are to be directed to use the material to best advantage (by means of questions? by workcard assignments? as individuals? as members of small groups?, etc.).

Displaying pictures, charts, diagrams, etc.

Displaying visual materials in the classroom is often a problem because of the lack of adequate pin-up space. Avoid using sellotape on walls. Instead, try one of the proprietory brands of adhesive such as *Plastitak* or *Blutack*. Coppen[4] recommends the use of 'klemboy clips', which can be glued on walls some 3 ft apart; the attachment of a thin steel strip to a blackboard surface and the use of small magnets to support display material; a 'washline' of thin nylon cord stretched across the classroom, the visual materials being suspended by means of spring-clip clothes pegs. Students may wish to follow the further suggestions contained in the pamphlet *A Guide to the Production of Wall Charts*, obtainable from the National Committee for Audio Visual Aids in Education, 33 Queen Anne Street, London W1M 9LD.

Flannel boards, magnetic boards, plastic boards

Flannel, magnetic and plastic boards have an important communication advantage over the conventional blackboard in that they allow the teacher to 'build up', step-by-step, the visual illustration of a story, an account of a process, or the labelling of a diagram. They are most effectively used when the teacher has worked out *beforehand* the sequencing and co-ordination of the aural and visual elements in the presentation.

Filmstrips

Filmstrips take the sequencing and co-ordinating process referred to above one stage further in that they are constructed as a *close-step series* of visual presentations generally accompanied by a set of paragraphs to be read in conjunction with particular frames of the filmstrip. An added advantage of the filmstrip, of course, is that the teacher is able to skip frames or return to specific frames to reiterate important points. A fuller discussion of the use of filmstrips is contained in Coppen.[4]

Films

The film is now well-established as an audio-visual aid and many schools possess some type of cine projector. In this section, it is intended to raise a number of issues in connection with the selection and use of films in the classroom. The format of presentation follows Hearnshaw and Kitching.[5]

Searching and selection. The list of sources of film materials contained in Appendix 3 should enable the teacher to locate the film which best *seems* to suit his particular purposes.

Preview. The *actual* suitability of the film can only be determined by preview. Is it educationally suitable? Is it technically suitable?

Planning and preparation. Having selected an appropriate film, how is it to be used? When is it to be shown? What prior preparation will the children require in order to maximize the learning experience? What internal school arrangements need to be made?

Presentation. How can the film be shown to best advantage? What arrangements (both physical and technical) need to be made on the actual day in order to ensure smooth and efficient presentation?

Follow-up. What kinds of activities have been planned by way of following up the presentation to assist the children in consolidating the learning experience?

Evaluation. To what extent did the film achieve the purposes intended by the teacher? In what ways could its use have been better planned and prepared for? How suitable were the follow-up exercises in retrospect?

For a description of film equipment and its use, the reader is referred to Romiszowski.[3]

Sound media

The term sound media is often used to refer both to the audio equipment such as the radio, the tape recorder and to combinations of sound and visual media (audio-visual) such as the synchronized slide-tape recorder. In this section, it is intended to direct the student to useful parts of specialist texts rather than embark upon any detailed discussion of the wide range of audio-visual equipment currently available.

Trowbridge:[7] pages 5–31 of this text are recommended reading to student teachers for the clear way in which practical questions are raised in connection with the use of audio equipment. Why tape recorders? Why battery powered? Why cassette loading? What model to choose? At the same time, the author discusses important educational considerations in Chapter 3, 'Children at work with small tape recorders', and Chapter 4, 'Organizing tape recorder accessories'.

Romiszowski:[3] pages 159–90 deal briefly with the advantages and the disadvantages involved in the use of radio and gramophone records in the classroom but discuss at length and in some detail the use of sound media in language laboratories.

Edwards:[2] pages 31–40 contain detailed information on a number of illustrated pieces of sound equipment and also give tips on many aspects of their use and maintenance.

Cable:[8] this text contains useful sections on aural aids and on audio-visual materials and techniques. There is also a comprehensive section of practical suggestions in connection with recording, and with the rudimentary electrical knowledge necessary to deal with shorts, overloading, earthing equipment, etc.

Oates:[9] this comprehensive text is recommended to the student who seeks a course of self-instruction in the use of a wide variety of audio-visual equipment.

Television

The television set is now commonplace in most British schools and much of the television material developed by the BBC and IBA for school use has been allocated a permanent place in the weekly timetable. The generally high quality of the content and the presentation of this material far exceeds what even the most able and assiduous teacher could achieve within the course of one lesson.

It is absolutely essential that the teacher should carefully scan the publications of the BBC and IBA on broadcast materials to schools in order to select, *weeks in advance*, those programmes which might usefully complement or supplement his planned syllabus of work. Such forward planning necessarily takes into consideration internal school requirements such as advanced booking of the TV set, the TV room, the arrangements for the movement of children or the supervision of specific groups of viewers.

Physical arrangements for television viewing

A number of useful suggestions for the optimum physical arrangements for television viewing are contained in Coppen.[4]

Wherever possible, the TV set should be placed in front of the window so that light does not fall directly upon the screen.

Obtrusive light from other sources should be excluded by blinds or curtains.

The centre of the screen should be 5 ft or $5\frac{1}{2}$ ft from the floor with an upward viewing angle of less than 30 degrees.

The class should be seated in a fan-shaped pattern with no child nearer than one-third of the screen expressed in feet, that is to say, with a 23 in. screen television, the nearest child should be 8 ft away. No child should be more than 20 ft away from the screen.

To achieve these conditions, it is often most convenient to place the TV set in a front corner of the classroom with the screen facing diagonally across the room.

The 27 in. TV set is generally large enough for a class of about 35 children to be able to view comfortably and to read words without difficulty.

Follow-up to television broadcasts

Research has shown that without follow-up as much as 80 per cent of the content of the TV programme can be quickly lost. Adequate follow-up is therefore essential. To be fully effective it must be planned for *well in advance*. The Schools Broadcasting Council puts it this way:

> The responsibility of using the broadcasts so that they make the maximum contribution to the children's needs lies fairly and squarely on the teacher, and rightly so. It is for teachers to select what they require, by being able to foresee the relation of the broadcast with the work going forward in the class, to guide children's anticipations and reactions so that they reap as much benefit as they can from it, and to provide and co-operate in work which may flow from it. (The teacher's) foresight and preparation are essential if the children's interest is to be stimulated, guided and nurtured to full educational use.

APPENDIX 2. USEFUL INFORMATION AND SOURCES

Societies and associations

Even in the best-provided school, where supplementary materials and technical aids are readily available to assist the teacher in his classroom work, there can never be enough to fully cover all requirements. There are, however, a number of sources outside of the school upon which teachers can draw.

Many societies and associations both in this country and abroad provide services for teachers and schools either free or at a nominal subscription charge. They publish materials such as newsheets, posters, wallcharts, illustrated discussion sheets and reference books. They provide audio-visual materials such as sets of photographs, slides, films and filmstrips. They arrange school visits, lecture programmes and in-service seminars for teachers. Some have local specialist advisers where services are available to the teacher in planning project work or out-of-school visits, etc. Most have an information and advisory service generally provided free to members, who also have access to library facilities where available. An up-to-date list of societies and associations is published by The Schoolmaster Publishing Co. Ltd entitled *Treasure Chest For Teachers*.

Materials and services

The embassies, legations and high commissions of many countries offer a range of materials and services by way of promoting good relations, travel and, not the least, trade. The teacher can draw upon these sources to advantage. Because the production and postage of their educational materials is expensive, written requests for such materials should come from teachers, *not* from pupils.

A great deal of material such as reading lists, information booklets, maps, picture folders and newsheets is available *free of charge*. Other materials such as coloured filmstrips, coloured transparencies and records, are often made available on *free loan* to schools. Films are generally loaned at a *small charge*, or the borrower is required to pay *return postage*. Almost all embassies and legations have reference library facilities containing specialist material on the literature, history, art, music, geography and resources of their country. Librarians are extremely helpful in dealing with enquiries and requests for help. In making requests for library (and other) services, it is courtesy to include with an unambiguous statement of minimum requirements, a self-addressed label for reply.

The *Treasure Chest For Teachers* should be consulted for details.

Commercial, industrial and nationalized concerns

The world of commerce and industry provides another valuable source of supplementary materials for the teacher. While, in some cases, the material available is chiefly designed to promote a particular product, much more, especially that supplied by nationalized concerns, has a primary educational and instructional purpose.

An abundance of well-produced and often highly-sophisticated material is available from industrial and commercial sources. For example, *teaching kits* (with teachers' notes) and *wall charts* can be obtained which show basic information on the manufacture, use and application of materials and products. *Overhead projector transparencies* (again with teachers' notes) are widely available as well as *samples of materials* (sugar, fibreglass, flour, plastics, etc.) and films, slides and filmstrips. Two points are worth noting.

In general, the commercial and industrial suppliers of educational material are more likely than societies or embassies to make a *charge* for the matter they supply. Some kits are quite expensive (£20–£30); some films cost £10 or £20 to hire. The teacher should make sure that he knows exactly what costs he will incur *before* placing an order for materials.

The student teacher is advised to check with his college of education librarian or his education tutor that the material in which he is interested is not already available in college.

Community resources – museums and art galleries

Museums and art galleries are a further invaluable source of educational assistance to teachers. The scope of their various services and activities is detailed in the *Treasure Chest For Teachers*, and in two pamphlets, *Museum School Services* and *Handlist of Museum Education Services in Great Britain*, both obtainable from The Museums Association, 87 Charlotte Street, London W1P 2BX.

Most museums, from the nationally and internationally known to the local ones specializing in industrial archaeology, transport or agriculture, will arrange guided tours, lectures and film shows. In planning visits, the teacher should:

Notify authorities well in advance of party visits.

Prepare the children *well beforehand* (e.g. worksheets, questionnaires, etc.).

Time the visit with the age and ability of the children in mind.

Pay particular attention to the length of the stay, the periods of rest and refreshment, etc.

Ensure adequate supervision and control of the party at all times.

Most well-known galleries such as the *National* and the *Tate* in London provide guides and lecture tours to school parties. Often, city and local galleries, in addition to guided tours and intramural teaching, run a schools art loan service which includes paintings, sculptures and ceramics.

As with museum visits, the teacher should give ample advance notice of party numbers and should clear the finalized arrangements with the schools officer at the gallery.

Publishers of educational literature

There is a wide range of literature available to the teacher including newspapers, magazines, journals and books – all directly concerned with educational matters. It is only possible here to refer to some of the more widely-known of these materials and to point to some special publications which contain exhaustive lists of titles, names and addresses of educational publishers, educational journals, and suppliers of materials and equipment.

The major professional associations of teachers produce their own weekly newspapers – *The Teacher* (NUT) and *The Schoolmaster* (NAS). Likewise the newspapers, *The Times Educational Supplement* and *The Teachers' World*, contain educational commentary, articles and book reviews. In addition, the latter two publications carry classified advertisements of appointments vacant.

Educational Research is a well-known journal produced by the National Foundation for Educational Research and contains reports of research and experimentation carried out in various educational fields. Some universities publish their own educational journals, for example, *Educational Review* (Birmingham) and *Research in Education* (Manchester). Some journals are published by publishers with a strong interest in education, for example, *The Journal of Education for Teaching* (Methuen).

Sources of educational publications, journals, equipment and materials

The Education Committees Year Book is published each year by Councils and Education Press Ltd, 10 Queen Anne Street, London W1 M 9LD. It is a mine of useful information to the teacher. In addition to over 1,000 pages of information on schools, colleges, polytechnics and universities, the Committees Year Book lists:

> titles and addresses of some 190 educational periodicals and journals published in Great Britain;
>
> names and addresses of some 100 educational publishers in Great Britain;

names and addresses of some 164 members of the Educational Equipment Association.

By sending his own name and address or the address of his school, the teacher will receive up-to-date brochures of educational publications and equipment already on the market or about to be introduced. Publishers and suppliers of equipment generally include in their literature prepaid business reply envelopes to enable the teacher to secure inspection copies or more detailed information on materials and aids.

Teachers' unions

Three out of four teachers in Great Britain belong to one of the major teacher unions. School teachers, it would appear, are among the most highly organized of British workers.

The largest and most influential union, the National Union of Teachers has a membership in excess of 230,000. It is serviced by a large, permanent headquarters staff and publishes its own weekly newspaper. Its members are organized into some 1,100 local associations.

Smaller than the NUT, the National Association of Schoolmasters has some 56,000 members. The NAS has a history of greater militancy than the NUT and is comprised solely of men, most of whom teach in secondary schools. Smaller still are a number of teacher unions serving the interests of particular sections of the teaching profession, for example, the Union of Women Teachers, the Assistant Masters Association and the recently-formed Professional Association of Teachers.

Two functions can be identified in the work of teachers' unions. First, they act as highly-influential pressure groups aiming to shape public opinion on educational matters and to guide policy-making over a wide range of educational issues. Second, they aim to advance the professional working conditions, career prospects and remunerations of their workers.

APPENDIX 3. SOME REFERENCES AND ADDRESSES IN CONNECTION WITH AUDIO-VISUAL AIDS AND MATERIALS

School resource centres

See: Schools Council (1972) *School Resource Centres: Working Paper 43.* London: Evans/Methuen. Garnett, E. (1972) *Area Resource Centre.* London: Arnold.

Preparing visual aids

See: Coppen, H. (1971) *Wallsheets: Choosing, Using and Making.* NCAVAE, 33 Queen Anne Street, London W1M 9LD.

Slides and filmstrips

See: Judd, R.S. (1963) *Teaching by Projector.* London: Focal Press.

Overhead projectors

See: King, A. and Shelley, W. (1971) *Learning with the Overhead Projector.* London: Chandler Publications.

Tape recorders

See: Weston, J. (1973) *The Tape Recorder in the Classroom.* NCAVAE, 33 Queen Anne Street, London W1M 9LD.

Television

See: Diamond, R.M. (1965) *A Guide to Instructional Television in Great Britain.* Maidenhead: McGraw Hill.

Videotapes

See: *Higher Education Learning Programmes Information Service,* Councils and Education Press, Queen Anne Street, London W1M 9LD.

Films

See: *Classified Guide to Sources of Educational Film Materials,* Educational Foundation for Audio-Visual Aids in Education (EFVA), 254–256 Belsize Road, London NW6.

APPENDIX 4. SOME ADDRESSES OF PUBLISHERS OF CHILDREN'S LITERATURE

Abelard-Schuman, Furnival House, 14–18 High Holborn, London WC1V 6BX
Angus and Robertson, 16 Golden Square, London W1R 4BN
Ernest Benn, Sovereign Way, Tonbridge, Kent TN9 1RW
A. & C. Black, 35 Bedford Row, London WC1R 4JH
Blackie & Son, Bishopbriggs, Glasgow G64 2NZ
W. & R. Chambers, 11 Thistle Street, Edinburgh EH2 1DG
Chatto, Bodley Head & Cape Services, 35 Bow Street, London WC2E 7AN

William Collins, Sons & Co., 8 Grafton Street, London W1X 3LA

J.M. Dent and Sons, Aldine House, 33 Welbeck Street, London W1M 8LX

André Deutsch, 105 Great Russell Street, London WC1B 3LJ

Evans Brothers, Montague House, Russell Square, London WC1B 5BX

Faber & Faber, 3 Queen Square, London WC1N 3AU

Victor Gollancz, 14 Henrietta Street, London WC2E 8QJ

Hamish Hamilton, Garden House, 57–9 Long Acre, London WC2E 9JZ

William Heinemann, 10 Upper Grosvenor Street, London W1X 9PA

Heinemann Educational Books, 22 Bedford Square, London WC1B 3HH

Hodder & Stoughton, 47 Bedford Square, London WC1B 3DP

Hutchinson Publishing Group, 17–21 Conway Street, London W1P 5HL

Kaye & Ward, Windmill Press, Kingswood, Tadworth, Surrey KT20 6TG

Ladybird Books, PO Box 12, Beeches Road, Loughborough, Leics. LE11 2NQ

Macdonald Phoebus, Maxwell House, 74 Worship Street, London EC2A 2EN

Macmillan Children's Books, Little Essex Street, London WC2R 3LF

Methuen Children's Books, 11 New Fetter Lane, London EC4P 4EE

Oxford University Press, Walton Street, Oxford OX2 6DP

Pan Books (Piccolo), 18–21 Cavaye Place, London SW10 9PG

Pelham Books, 44 Bedford Square, London WC1B 3DU

Penguin Books (Puffin, Kestrel, Peacock), Bath Road, Harmondsworth, Middx UB7 0DA

Sidgwick & Jackson, 1 Tavistock Chambers, Bloomsbury Way, London WC1A 2SG

Ward Lock Educational, 47 Marylebone Lane, London W1M 6AX

Frederick Warne, 40 Bedford Square, London WC1B 3HE

World's Work, Windmill Press, Kingswood, Tadworth, Surrey KT20 6TG

APPENDIX 5. QUESTIONS AND QUESTIONING

The skilful questioning of a class performs a number of important functions. Socially, it helps to establish relationships and integrate groups through face-to-face interaction. Psychologically, it assists in creating, developing and maintaining a healthy emotional and intellectual climate as well as establishing appropriate levels of motivation.

Educationally, one function of questioning is to elicit information.

Thus, it may probe the extent of children's prior learning before a new subject or area of learning is introduced; or it may help to revise earlier learning; or consolidate recent teaching and learning. More than this, however, questions should have teaching value, that is, in asking the question a teacher is helping the pupil 'to focus and clarify, and thus have thoughts and perceptions that he would not have had otherwise' (Marland[10]).

Framing the question

The value to the student teacher of preparing questions beforehand as part of, or to accompany, a lesson plan cannot be over-emphasized.

Box 54

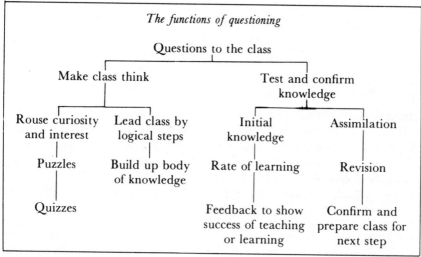

The functions of questioning

Questions to the class

Make class think — Test and confirm knowledge

Rouse curiosity and interest — Lead class by logical steps — Initial knowledge — Assimilation

Puzzles — Build up body of knowledge — Rate of learning — Revision

Quizzes — Feedback to show success of teaching or learning — Confirm and prepare class for next step

Source: Mills[11]

There are at least three reasons for this need. First, questions should be precisely and unambiguously worded so that they elicit the answer the teacher intends. The likelihood of misunderstandings and wrong answers is greater with unprepared, impromptu questions. Second, where a connected series of questions is required, it is difficult to organize them sequentially and logically on the spur of the moment. And third, a teacher is better prepared to deal with the unexpected if he possesses a body of well-thought-out questions.

A related issue is the desirability to prepare some questions with particular children in mind. An apt question, for example, worded especially for a slow or timid child can help develop his/her confidence and sense of achievement.

It is particularly useful when framing questions to distinguish two broad kinds – questions which test knowledge and questions which create knowledge. The former are referred to as lower order cognitive questions and the latter as higher order cognitive questions (you may find it easier initially to think of them as 'fact' questions and 'thought' questions respectively to distinguish the two categories, as these are terms of approximate equivalence).

Lower order cognitive questions embrace chiefly *recall, comprehension* and *application*; higher order questions, by contrast, involve *analysis, synthesis* and *evaluation*. Brown[12] elucidates the categories thus.

Lower order cognitive questions

Recall: Does the pupil recall what he has seen or read?

Comprehension: Does the pupil understand what he recalls?

Application: Can the pupil apply the rules and techniques to solve problems that have single correct answers?

Higher order cognitive questions

Analysis: Can the pupil identify motives and causes, make inferences and give examples to support his statements?

Synthesis: Can the pupil make predictions, solve problems or produce interesting juxtapositions of ideas and images?

Evaluation: Can the pupil judge the quality of ideas, or problem solutions, or works of art? Can he give rationally based opinions on issues or controversies?

We give particular examples of these kinds of question in Boxes 55 and 56. For additional information, the reader is referred to Bloom[13] and Brown.[12]

Studies conducted in the United States indicate that many teachers' questions fall into the recall category and that higher order cognitive questions are rarely used (Gall[14]). Although recall questions are especially useful in testing learning and focusing attention, questioning sessions made up exclusively of them may become boring and place undue emphasis on rote-learning. Ideally, lower order cognitive questions should be coupled with carefully selected higher order cognitive ones so that children are led to consider the implications of the facts or the circumstances that give rise to them. It must be remembered, however, that the latter do require the skill of being able to judge the extent to which children are able to respond appropriately to the more

Box 55

Categories of teacher questions

Lower order cognitive questions

Recall: What were the two kinds of objective identified in Part II?

Comprehension: What are the differences between an aim and an objective?

Application: Would you formulate a behavioural objective using the action verb 'list'?

Higher order cognitive questions

Analysis: Why did Mr Smith have discipline problems in the lesson you were observing yesterday afternoon?

Synthesis: What do you think would have happened had Mr Smith adopted a less authoritarian approach?

Evaluation: Which seems to be the best way to handle his class in that kind of lesson?

---

difficult and complex examples; and such judgement must be based on knowledge of the children's intellectual capabilities. Once a student has this knowledge, he should try to get a judicious balance of both types organized in carefully planned sequences.

Some questions need to be handled carefully or, in certain circumstances, avoided altogether. These may be briefly identified as follows.

Questions inviting a *yes* or *no* answer should not be used excessively, for a child has as much chance of being right as of being wrong if he guesses. *Yes* and *no* answers follow from binary questions of the recall type, and where such answers are unavoidable, another question, such as *how?* or *why?* should follow in order to provide explanatory or supportive evidence for the *yes* or *no*. Occasionally, a *yes* or *no* answer can be of disciplinary assistance when attentions are wandering: 'Do you understand, John?'

Questions having several equally good answers should be avoided if the teacher has only one answer in mind ('What should a driver have with him?' A map? his licence? a torch? a tool-kit? a first-aid box?). Formulations of this nature invite guessing. Questions having several equally good answers are permissible, however, when a teacher is building up a composite answer, e.g. when introducing a topic or project.

Composite questions – those involving a number of interrogatives – present difficulties even with brighter children and should be avoided.

Box 56

Lower order and higher order cognitive questions

The examples below from Brown[12] illustrate how lower order and higher order cognitive questions may be formed on the same topic. Item (a) questions exemplify lower order cognitive questions; and item (b) ones, higher order cognitive questions.

1 (a) What is the largest city in Holland?
   (b) Why is Amsterdam the largest city in Holland? (Analysis)
2 (a) Who is the author of *Catcher in the Rye*?
   (b) Which aspects of *Catcher in the Rye* suggest that the author is a young man? (Analysis)
3 (a) What does the theorem of Pythagoras tell us?
   (b) Why is the theorem of Pythagoras so important in geometry? (Evaluation)
4 (a) Who wrote *Hamlet*?
   (b) Describe the feelings of Hamlet for his mother as portrayed in the play of Shakespeare. (Analysis)
5 (a) What happened in *A Christmas Carol*?
   (b) What kind of relationship did Scrooge have with his employee in *A Christmas Carol*? (Analysis)
6 (a) What is the most common element found in the earth's crust?
   (b) Why is oxygen the most common element found in the earth's crust? (Analysis)
7 (a) What is the most widely spoken indigenous language in Africa?
   (b) Account for the distribution of two of the most widely spoken languages in Africa. (Analysis)
8 (a) Where is Stonehenge?
   (b) Discuss the recent theories of the stone formation at Stonehenge. (Evaluation)
9 (a) How many independent countries have been established in Africa during the past twenty years?
   (b) Why has there been a sudden increase in the number of independent countries in Africa during the past twenty years? (Evaluation)
10 (a) What are the two main levels of questions?
   (b) Which type of question do you consider the most important? (Evaluation)

Source: Brown[12]

Do not use questions beginning 'Who can tell me . . .?' or 'Does anyone know . . .?', as these may lead to various members of the class shouting out answers.

Questions testing powers of expression should be treated with care.

Similarly, those seeking definitions of words or concepts, especially abstract ones, should be handled carefully.

General questions that are vague and aimless should not be used ('What do you know about the French Revolution?'). Precision and clarity should be sought from the outset.

Guessing questions are sometimes useful for stimulating a child's imagination and actively involving him in discussion. If used too often, however, they encourage thoughtless responses.

Leading questions (those framed in such a way as to suggest or imply the desired answer – 'Wordsworth was the author of the first sonnet we read, wasn't he?') and rhetorical questions (those to which the pupil is not expected to reply – 'Do you want me to send you outside?') should be avoided because the former tend to reinforce a child's dependence on the teacher and undermine independent thought, whereas the latter may provoke unwanted or facetious replies. Questions should be asked only if the teacher wants a real answer.

Elliptical questions – those worded so that a child supplies a missing word or missing words – are of value when used to encourage slow or diffident children. Provided they are not used too often, they can give variety to a questioning session.

Box 57 indicates how questions may be related to the orthodox class lesson plan suggested earlier.

Asking the question and receiving the answer

Questions should be asked in simple, conversational language and in a friendly and challenging manner. A useful procedure is as follows: put the question to the class, pause briefly, then name the child you wish to answer. A sequence of this kind encourages everyone to listen and prepare an answer in anticipation of being asked. Respondents should be named at random rather than in a predetermined and systematic way, thus avoiding selective listening. As suggested earlier, it is to the teacher's advantage at this point to have prepared questions with particular children in mind. The more difficult questions for brighter children and easier ones for duller children help to sustain different motivational levels and maintain the flow of the lesson. It is especially important in this respect to try to draw out the more shy members of the class. The teacher should also counter the tendency to overlook children sitting at the back or sides of the classroom when distributing questions. Similarly, student teachers should resist the temptation to ignore those children who happen to be sitting near a supervising tutor.

Once a question has been put to a child, it should be left with him long enough for an answer to emerge. Lack of preparation on the part of the teacher, or impatience, may lead him to follow it immediately with other questions, or to modify the original, qualify it, re-word it or explain it. Such addenda merely confuse children. Indeed, British research indicates that student and beginning teachers often ask more questions than they receive answers. Brown[12] suggests that their failure to obtain answers is often due to lack of pauses and no variation in the delivery of questions. The efficacy of the teacher sometimes accepting two or three answers before responding should also be noted. A varied pattern of this nature thus encourages volunteering, contributes to group co-operation, and achieves a more realistic social situation which can be further enhanced by allowing other members of the class to respond to a child's answer ('John, was Peter's answer correct?').

Box 57

Possible purposes of questioning in relation to the suggested class lesson plan

Stage	Questioning
Introduction	to establish human contact to assist in establishing set induction devices to discover what the class knows to revise previous work to pose problems which lead to the subject of the lesson
Presentation	to maintain interest and alertness to encourage reasoning and logical thinking to discover if pupils understand what is going on
Application	to focus and clarify to lead the children to make observations and draw inferences for themselves to clear up difficulties, misunderstandings and assist individual pupils
Conclusion	to revise the main points of the lesson to test the results of the lesson, and the extent of the pupils' understanding and assimilation to suggest further problems and related issues

---

The techniques of *prompting* and *probing* are often useful in class questioning sessions. Prompting involves giving hints to help a child. In addition to eliciting appropriate answers, prompts backed up with teacher encouragement help hesitant children reply more confidently.

On receiving an answer, it is sometimes necessary to probe a child for additional information and this may be especially the case after a factual question. Probing in this context may take the form of seeking further information, directing the child to think more deeply about his answer, inviting a critical interpretation, focusing his response on a related issue or encouraging him to express himself more clearly. (Two illustrations of prompting and probing are given in Box 58.) As Brown[12] observes, probing questions with older children tap the highest levels of their thinking.

Sometimes a correct answer needs to be repeated to make sure all have heard it. It is inadvisable to accept unsolicited answers that have been called out as such habits can lead to problems of control. Wrong answers can be of value in clearing up misunderstandings, obscurities and difficulties providing they are treated tactfully and without disrupting the lesson to any great extent (to respond to a wrong answer, for instance, with 'That's nonsense' or 'What rubbish!' is to ensure that the flow of answers from the class will quickly dry up!). Clearly, a sense of humour is an invaluable asset at this stage in a questioning session.

It is very important for children to receive information on the correctness or otherwise of their answers. This is especially the case for low achievers. Feedback from the teacher is the easiest way to maintain interest and is most effective when given after an individual response. In most instances, the feedback does not need to be long; a word or two will suffice to let a child know he's on the right lines – 'That's right, John'. Praise and censure should be used with discrimination. Praise is quickly devalued if used too readily; and undue censure can be discouraging. Excessive criticism directed at weaker pupils can do nothing but harm.

One final point remains to be briefly considered: the children's questions to the teacher. As Davies and Shepherd[6] note, nothing shows more clearly that a teacher and class are on friendly terms than evidence of children sensibly questioning him about difficult points. Desirable as this kind of relationship is, however, it can pose problems for the less experienced teacher. He must, for instance, avoid having too many interruptions and being side-tracked from the main theme of his lesson. One way of dealing with difficulties of this kind is to ensure that he anticipates the class's questions with the ones he puts to them. Another way is to invite questions from the class at appropriate points in the lesson (towards the end of the *presentation stage*, for example). Some questions may not be directly relevant to the lesson in hand, in which case the teacher should inform the class that they will be dealt with in future lessons. If you do not know the answer to a question, don't be afraid to admit it, but say you will find out the answer as soon as you can.

Box 58

Prompting and probing

Prompting

Teacher: Would you say that nationalism in Africa is now greater than it was twenty years ago?
Pupil: Greater.
Teacher: Yes. Why is that?
Pupil: Because there are more nations now.
Teacher: Yes. Mmm. There's more to it than that. Can anyone else give some reasons?
Class: (Silence)
Teacher: Well, basically it's because . . .

This is an example of what frequently happens in the first discussion lessons given by a teacher. The discussion drags and degenerates into an unprepared lecture. This can be avoided by prompting any weak answers given. In the example, the teacher could have said 'Yes. That's right. There are more nations now and there are more nations because African people wanted to be independent of the Europeans. What has happened in the past twenty years which has helped them to become independent?'

Probing

Teacher: Jessica, you went to Paris this year. What did you think of it?
Jessica: Mmm. It was nice.
Teacher: What was nice about it? (Pause)
Jessica: Well, I liked walking down the avenue which had trees. I liked watching the boats on the river. I liked listening to Frenchmen. The metro was exciting and, oh, I liked the French bread and butter.

The simple probe 'What was nice about it?' evoked from this seven-year-old girl a series of impressions which revealed her interest in sights, sounds and food.

Source: Brown[12]

For occasions when an awkward pupil proposes a series of difficult or even silly questions, Davies and Shepherd recommend that if the questions have no direct relationship with the topic under consideration, the teacher is fully justified in making that explanation to the pupils in such a way that he does not prohibit further questions.

The student teacher anxious to acquire command of this most vital skill of questioning a class should make every effort to build short questioning sessions of from five to ten minutes into his lessons. He can then get some idea of his progress by constructing a simple self-evaluation schedule based on the suggestions outlined earlier and checking his performance, say, once a week as part of his routine lesson criticisms. For further guidance in this respect, we refer the reader to Unit VI in Brown,[12] and for additional information on empirical studies in this area, we suggest he consults Turney *et al.*[15] and MacLeod *et al.* (in Chanan and Delamont[16]).

Notes and references

1 Hanson, J. (1975) *Use of Resources*. London: George Allen and Unwin.
2 Edwards, R.P.A. (1973) *Resources in School*. London: Evans.
3 Romiszowski, A.J. (1974) *The Selection and Use of Instructional Media*. London: Kogan Page.
4 Coppen, H. (1969) *Aids to Teaching and Learning*. Oxford: Pergamon.
5 Hearnshaw, T. and Kitching, J.B. (1974) *Audio-visual Aids in Teaching and Learning*. Bradford: Bradford University.
6 Davies, W.T. and Shepherd, T.B. (1949) *Teaching: Begin Here*. London: Epworth Press.
7 Trowbridge, N.E. (1974) *The New Media Challenge*. London: Macmillan.
8 Cable, R. (1972) *Audio-visual Handbook*. London: University of London Press.
9 Oates, S.C. (1971) *Audio-visual equipment: A Self-instruction Manual*. Dubuque, Iowa: Wm C. Brown.
10 Marland, M. (1975) *The Craft of the Classroom*. London: Heinemann Educational.
11 Mills, H.R. (1972) *Teaching and Training: A Handbook for Instructors*. London: Macmillan.
12 Brown, G.A. (1975) *Microteaching*. London: Methuen.
13 Bloom, B.S. (1956) *Taxonomy of Educational Objectives Handbook 1: Cognitive Domain*. Harlow: Longman.
14 Gall, M.D. (1970) The use of questioning in teaching. *Review of Educational Research*, 40, 707–21.
15 Turney, C., Clift, J.C., Dunkin, M.J. and Trail, R.D. (1973) *Microteaching: Research, Theory and Practice*. Sydney: Sydney University Press.
16 Chanan, G. and Delamont, S. (1975) *Frontiers of Classroom Research*. Windsor: NFER.

Index